A RACE FOR REAL SAILORS

THE BLUENOSE AND THE INTERNATIONAL FISHERMEN'S CUP, 1920–1938

KEITH M^CLAREN

A RACE FOR REAL SAILORS

DAVID R. GODINE · PUBLISHER

BOSTON

To the memory of Richard John LeBlanc
January 21, 1945–April 2, 1993
A fine shipmate and friend.

First published in the U.S. by
DAVID R. GODINE, *Publisher*
Post Office Box 450
Jaffrey, New Hampshire 03452
www.godine.com

Published simultaneously in Canada by
Douglas & McIntyre Ltd.
2323 Quebec Street, Suite 201
Vancouver, BC V5T 4S7
www.douglas-mcintyre.com

Library of Congress Cataloging-in-Publication Data
McLaren, R. Keith, 1949–
A race for real sailors : the Bluenose and the International Fishermen's Cup,
1920–1938 / Keith McLaren.— 1st U.S. ed. p. cm.
"Originally published in 2005 by Douglas & McIntyre Ltd., Canada"—T.p. verso
Includes bibliographical references (p.   ) and index.
ISBN 1-56792-313-5
1. International Fishermen's Race—History. 2. Bluenose (Schooner) I. Title.
GV832.M38 2006   797.1´4091631—dc22   2005037876

Editing by Jonathan Dore
Jacket design by Jessica Sullivan
Text design by Peter Cocking and Jessica Sullivan
Front jacket painting: *Racing Schooners, circa 1921,*
by Dusan Kadlec, portrays the *Bluenose* and the *Elsie* racing
off Halifax. Reproduced by kind permission of the artist.
Back jacket photographs (left to right): Leslie Jones, Boston Public Library
(p. 66); Edwin Levick, Mariners' Museum, Newport News, Virginia (p. 182);
Wallace MacAskill, Nova Scotia Archives and Records Management (p. 54)
Printed and bound in China by C&C Offset Printing Co. Ltd.
Printed on acid-free paper

CONTENTS

PREFACE *1*

INTRODUCTION *5*

{1} The Grand Banks *11*

{2} Fishing Under Sail *15*

{3} A Skipping Stone *31*

{4} "A Race for Real Sailors": 1920 *45*

{5} The Lunenburg Flyer: 1921 *67*

{6} Turmoil in Gloucester: 1922 *89*

{7} "I Am Not a Sportsman": 1923 *119*

{8} The Storm Years: 1924–29 *143*

{9} The Lipton Cup: 1930 *163*

{10} The Revival: 1931 *179*

{11} The Last Fishermen's Race: 1938 *189*

{12} In the Wake *215*

APPENDIX: RACE RULES, 1920–38 *222*

GLOSSARY *236*

ACKNOWLEDGEMENTS *240*

SELECTED BIBLIOGRAPHY *242*

INDEX *246*

‹ **FLEET AT ANCHOR**, Lunenburg Harbour, 1898.
Nova Scotia Archives and Records Management

PREFACE

ON A CHILLY DAY in late October 1938, a crowd of thousands gathered on the shores of Nahant Bay, northeast of Boston, arriving from all over the eastern seaboard of the United States and Canada. They were about to witness the concluding chapter in a two-decade-old challenge between the fishing-schooner fleets of Canada and the United States.

The schooner fishery was one of the last all-sail commercial fleets left in the Western world. At its zenith, hundreds of large offshore boats filled the ports from Newfoundland south to Massachusetts. This was the culmination of a traditional way of life that had evolved over two and a quarter centuries. When the International Fishermen's Cup races were first proposed in

1920, the fishing schooner was already on its way out, being rapidly replaced by power-driven trawlers. This transformation occurred much more quickly in the United States than in Canada, which hung on and even actively resisted the introduction of the mechanized trawler to its fishing ports. Americans embraced the new technology, steadily forcing the older, traditional fishermen from the market. Although her time was nearly done, the fishing schooner remained a presence on the banks, an anachronism in the modern era, for far longer than anyone would have predicted. As the number of working sailing vessels decreased, their romantic appeal with the public rose. The fishermen's races became a fond last hurrah for a fast-disappearing way of life.

The timing of the races fitted neatly into that tumultuous period between the two world wars and became for a time the most popular sailing event in North America. Heralded as "a race for real sailors," the series began as a friendly match between the schooner fleets of Lunenburg, Nova Scotia, and Gloucester, Massachusetts, the two largest fishing communities on the east coast. They were originally proposed in response to the perceived timidity demonstrated in the America's Cup races, where the elite sailed beautiful but tender vessels barely capable of withstanding a decent breeze. In contrast, the fishermen's races were to be a working man's event, a tough, no-holds-barred affair, with few rules and fewer regulations; a showcase for a rugged, rigorous way of life that was on its way out.

The series, scheduled for the fall of each year, became instantly popular and initially ran like clockwork. The spectacle greatly appealed to the public and soon eclipsed even the venerable America's Cup as the race of choice to a generation. Unfortunately, the growing attention from the public and media provoked the well-meaning committee members to expand and elaborate the rules, ostensibly to ensure the competition remained true to its mandate. In so doing, a rather simple and straightforward affair became a complicated and confusing business, fraught with interpretations of legalities, much to the dismay and consternation of the competitors. Even though the series continued to draw a huge following, the tone often became rancorous and bitter, with competitors accusing the various committees of everything from favouritism to corruption. The fact that it carried on as long as it did is a testament to the single-mindedness of the competitors and to the passion for sail in the quest for the title "Queen of the North Atlantic Fishery."

While researching this book, I was immediately struck by the tremendous popularity of these races. Reading accounts published in contemporary magazines and newspapers, I was overwhelmed by the incredible amount of coverage given over to them. Although the series was ostensibly a sporting event, the reportage was almost never in the sporting pages. Front-page exposure and banner headlines heralded each new series, with top reporters and photographers from major newspapers in Canada and the United States dispatched to cover every angle, no matter how insignificant. Even in 1938, with the world poised on the brink of war, the races dominated the front page alongside the ominous news from Nazi Germany.

My own interest began in my grandfather's house, where a model of the *Bluenose,* given to him by Captain Angus Walters upon his retirement in 1934, held a place of honour on the mantel above the fireplace. The stories of the schooner from Lunenburg highlighted my youth. Years later, I secured a berth on the replica schooner *Bluenose II* and spent two seasons sailing on her, expanding my knowledge of her predecessor's skipper, Angus Walters, and her illustrious past. There has been much written about the races over the years, especially in Canada, but many writers have tended to oversimplify and exaggerate, too often ignoring the controversies and rancour that frequently plagued the event. I wanted to explore the story as fairly as I could, which meant from both sides of the border, so, to that end, I visited Massachusetts and Nova Scotia to gain insight into their respective points of view. What I found, after much reading and talking, was that the debate and passion about one of the great maritime tales of North America, with a cast of characters whose egos and eccentricities were second to none, is still very much alive. Far from diminishing the power of the story by examining its flesh-and-blood details, I hope this book will help bring to life an amazing chapter in maritime history. Readers unfamiliar with nautical or fishing terms will find a glossary of these on page 236.

My sources in Gloucester and Boston provided me with mountains of material—rivalling anything I found in Canada—and it took months to organize and compile it into a usable form. During my visits to Massachusetts and Nova Scotia, I was given extraordinary help and assistance by many; everyone, it seemed, had a unique story to tell. The debate about which was the fastest schooner lives on in Gloucester and Lunenburg, as if the races had been held only yesterday. National pride and passion, when it comes to the working schooner, run deep.

INTRODUCTION

T**HE REAL QUESTION** is, why would anyone still care?

A century ago, schooners were the workhorses of the east coast. A Cape
Breton neighbour once told me that when he was a boy, a constant stream of
schooners sailed past his boyhood home on the Great Bras d'Or, carrying gypsum
and shingles, coal and potatoes.

"It must have been a beautiful sight to see," I said.

He shrugged.

"Never thought about it," he said. "Do you go ooh and aah over every eighteen-
wheeler that goes down the road?"

If you think of the International Fishermen's Cup races as contests among
eighteen-wheelers, why would we still care about them? What would prompt

a successful twenty-first-century mariner like Keith McLaren to write yet another book about them? And if such a man did write such a book, would he find anything new to say about the ships and the races and the people involved?

Amazingly enough, he would. Captain McLaren is interested in the overall story of the races as seen from both sides. As a result, this is perhaps the most fair and even-handed account of them yet written—fair not only to the competitors and their boats, but to the story itself, in all its mythological splendour, intrigue, glory and outright venality.

› VIEW OF Gloucester Harbour, c. 1900. *Cape Ann Historical Association*

Our culture cherishes a sentimental notion that sporting events encourage sportsmanship and fair play. Perhaps they do—but they equally encourage greed, pride, envy, anger and various other sins both deadly and venial. The international schooner races were no exception. They were loaded with meaning: working fishermen versus the plutocrats' fragile America's Cup racers; Lunenburg versus Gloucester; Canada versus the United States. Because they meant so much, people cared passionately about the races—and when people care that much, they compete right out to the uttermost limits of fair play. And even a bit beyond.

The races were also the defiant valedictory flourish of a fading culture of canvas, wood and handlining against a corporate culture of steel motor vessels that would ultimately destroy the fishery altogether.

In 1920, when the races began, fishing schooners were already obsolescent; in 1938, when they ended, the vessels were completely obsolete. As McLaren notes, even by 1930, when *Bluenose*'s last challenger was launched, the notion that the races were competitions between working fishermen was being tacitly ignored. *Gertrude L. Thebaud* went fishing to qualify, but she was never going to pay for herself as a fishing vessel. She was built to beat the *Bluenose*.

Bluenose herself, of course, had also been built to race. But that was ten years earlier, when a Grand Banks schooner could still pay her own way in the fishery. After 1930, even *Bluenose* had difficulty justifying herself economically. Still, the appeal of the schooners—though they had represented innovative fishing technology in an earlier day—was never entirely economic, and even as they died out, they recalled a more human way of relating to the world.

There is nothing beautiful about a trawler. It is hard to imagine anyone loving one. A trawler is an expensive corporate-owned fish-killing machine and nothing more. But a schooner could be built in any little notch of the coast by a gang of skilled men with access to wood, a building site and sharp hand tools. And the same men could sail their schooner, fish it, trade with it and prosper. The

schooners represented beauty versus force, honed skills versus raw power, human strength versus mechanical energy, art versus engineering.

The Lunenburg shipwright David Stevens, the great heir of that great tradition, liked to say that a ship was more like a living thing than anything else a man could build with his hands. The truth of the observation can be seen throughout Captain McLaren's book. There is something alive and individual, something like a personality, in each of the racing schooners—the quick and sturdy little *Esperanto*, the unlucky and out-of-sync *Haligonian*, the aristocratic and isolated *Mayflower*, the swift and ethereal *Columbia* and the fleet-winged *Puritan*, running through the fog so fast that she killed herself on Sable Island.

And, of course, the powerful, indomitable *Bluenose*.

Was there some extra quality, something akin to a greatness of heart, in the champion schooner from Lunenburg? Angus Walters, her captain, certainly acted as though there were. In moments of stress he would coax her, cajole her, shout at her. And she would always respond.

But maybe the unconquerable greatness of heart was in Angus himself, who knew and loved his vessel as few vessels have ever been known and loved. He was not an amiable or easygoing character, nor was he a particularly gracious winner. As Captain McLaren reminds us, he needled his opponents mercilessly, and, like them, he was not above a little discreet chicanery. But even the marine historian Howard Chapelle, who detested him, admitted that Angus Walters was "a prime sailor."

The races took place at a unique moment in history, a period that produced a great many legends in sports, exploration, the arts and entertainment—Joe Louis and Babe Ruth, Greta Garbo and Clark Gable, Amelia Earhart and Seabiscuit and Duke Ellington. The reasons are complex—the interwar period was a transitional time in many respects—but the 1920s were a period of dizzying change, and the 1930s were a decade of economic catastrophe.

So the public was in need of distraction, and at that very moment, the new technology of mass communication meant spectacular events could be reported to millions of people simultaneously, as they occurred. As McLaren notes, the schooner races were given astonishing play in the newspapers, and they were among the first sporting contests to be broadcast live. In today's multi-channel world, the mass audience has fragmented; only colossal events are reported to everyone. In the 1930s, however, the same newscast reached the whole audience and "fame" meant something it never meant before or since.

The echoes still linger. During his research, McLaren reports, he learned that the debate and passion about the races is still very much alive. Indeed it is; people still do care. When Canadians compete with their larger, more powerful neighbour, they normally lose—but this time they didn't, and since the races can never be held again, that victory is permanent. It has become one of the legends of our national life, and Canadians remember it every time they look at a Canadian dime. No wonder we care about it.

Americans naturally care much less about the story, but those who remember it care for the exact opposite reason. The Marines are supposed to land, the cavalry is supposed to arrive, the Revolution is supposed to succeed, everything is supposed to come out right in the final reel, and this story is a galling exception. It jest ain't fittin'. Americans feel, with some justification, that they *could* have won, perhaps *should* have won, but the prize is now forever out of reach.

Nova Scotians care particularly strongly because the races symbolize both our capacity and our decline. At one point in the nineteenth century, Nova Scotia was the fourth-largest trading nation in the world—or would have been, had it actually been a nation—and it entered Canada as the most prosperous of the founding provinces. That prosperity was based on wooden shipbuilding and resolute seafaring, and by the 1930s it was only a mirage in the communal memory. But *Bluenose* emerged from that history, and her triumphs forever remind Nova Scotians of what they once were, and what they could be again.

And sailors everywhere care because the races were a supreme moment of glory in an art they cherish, hard-fought contests using a style of sailing vessel that was at its peak of development just at the moment it was poised to disappear.

The enduring appeal of the schooners is their beauty and their ordinariness. Fundamentally, these were working boats sailed by working men, not high-tech wonders sailed by scientifically enhanced athletes. There was harmony and balance not only in the way they sailed, but also in the way they lived. They raced for fun and for fame, and then they went fishing.

These sailors were amateurs in the root sense of the word, men who competed for the sheer love of the thing itself, testing their mastery against that of their peers. That's what echoes down through the years—the beauty and danger of a working life under sail, and the pride of the men who did it.

SILVER DONALD CAMERON
D'Escousse, Nova Scotia · www.silverdonaldcameron.ca

1

THE GRAND BANKS

FOR CENTURIES the Grand Banks, situated off the east coast of Canada, were considered one of Earth's most important fishing grounds, feeding much of the Western world. The banks are undersea plateaus that rise from the continental shelf, a relatively shallow part of the North Atlantic that extends just under two hundred miles from the shore before the ocean bottom drops 6,000 feet (1,800 metres). There are over twenty individual banks, ranging from the largest, the Grand Bank of Newfoundland, in the northeast, to Georges Bank off Cape Cod in the south, and they are known collectively as the Grand Banks. The water depth on these plateaus descends from 100 to 600 feet (30 to 180 metres). The icy Labrador Current, flowing south over most of the banks, mixes with

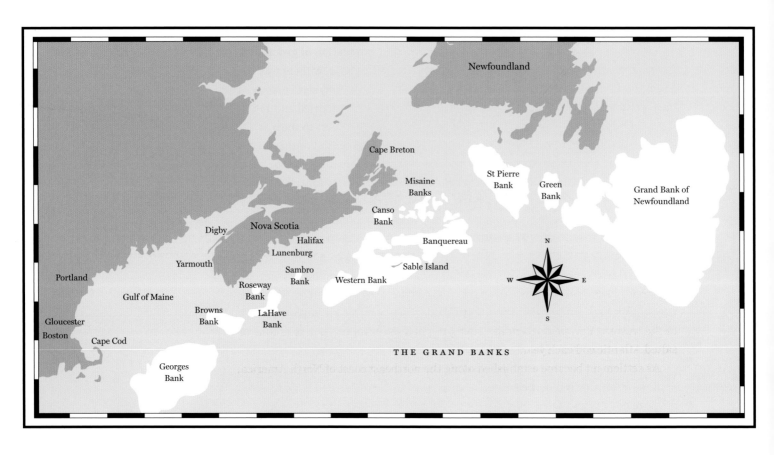

Newfoundland

Cape Breton

Misaine
Banks

St Pierre
Bank

Green
Bank

Grand Bank of
Newfoundland

Canso
Bank

Digby

Nova Scotia

Halifax

Banquereau

N

Lunenburg

Yarmouth

Sambro
Bank

Sable Island

W

E

Portland

Roseway
Bank

Western Bank

S

Gulf of Maine

Browns
Bank

LaHave
Bank

Gloucester

Boston

Cape Cod

THE GRAND BANKS

Georges
Bank

the warm waters of the Gulf Stream sweeping north along the eastern coast, as well as the freshwater currents flowing down from the Gulf of St. Lawrence. The swirling and mixing of the currents over the banks, along with the shallow water depth, creates a nutrient-rich environment that produces a dense growth of phytoplankton, the first link in the marine food chain.

Until recently, this habitat sustained a tremendous population of groundfish (those living near the bottom). The most important species to grow there was the Atlantic cod. This fish alone was primarily responsible for the early settlement and colonization of North America. Cod was easy to catch and, when dried and salted, could be preserved for long periods, allowing for transportation to markets in Europe. Basque fishermen were the first to discover the potential of the fishery, in the fifteenth century, and they kept its location a secret until John Cabot stumbled across it in 1497 on his first voyage of discovery to North America. Cabot reported to his English masters that the waters off Newfoundland were so thick with fish that the progress of his vessel was impeded. Inspired by this vivid description, the powers of Europe rushed to stake their claims on the fertile fishing ground. By the mid-1500s, more than half of the fish eaten in Europe was from that source, and by the time the Pilgrims arrived at Plymouth Rock in 1620, the banks were providing an income to over a thousand vessels from England, France, Portugal and Spain. The fishery had quickly become an important part of the western European economy, supplying markets with thousands of tons of salted Atlantic cod each year.

As settlement became established along the northeast coast of North America, communities such as Gloucester and Lunenburg became homes to large fleets of offshore boats. Until the turn of the twentieth century, fishing methods remained virtually unchanged from the days of the early Basque fishermen. Wind-powered vessels and hook-and-line fishing were the standard methods of the time. Although the banks had been heavily fished for four centuries, the techniques used were relatively sustainable until modern methods were introduced. Over-fishing, combined with the use of the indiscriminate wire mesh trawl, which dragged the bottom and destroyed everything in its path, brought about the demise of the fishery. The seas that had fed the mouths of hungry North Americans and Europeans for hundreds of years are now considered by some to be a marine desert. Unable to support human demands, the Grand Banks fishery is likely to remain in a state of collapse for many years to come.

‹ MAP of the Grand Banks

2

FISHING UNDER SAIL

O**N THE WATERFRONT** in Gloucester, there is a hauntingly beautiful sculpture of a fisherman grasping the wheel of a banks schooner. Wearing traditional oilskins and sou'wester, he appears to be straining every muscle to hold his schooner on course. His face is etched with tension as he gazes intently at the unseen sails aloft. The rough grey-green patina of the bronze casting has been permanently streaked by rain and sea spray. Below, the inscription reads: THEY THAT GO DOWN TO THE SEA IN SHIPS, 1623–1923. The memorial commemorates the many lives lost at sea in Gloucester's first three centuries and is now surrounded by ten tablets listing the names of more than five thousand fishermen. In Lunenburg, near the Fisheries Museum, is another monument—not, like its Gloucester cousin, a figurative representation, but equally powerful and poignant. Eight polished black granite slabs rise up from the earth in a Stonehenge-like cairn, each positioned on the directional points of a compass, with a ninth pillar in the centre. Names of the dead, a seemingly endless list of them, are etched into the surfaces. The two communities share a common bond of loss, a bond further strengthened by the fact that twelve hundred of the names on the Gloucester memorial belong to Nova Scotians who crewed Gloucester vessels.

Back in Gloucester and just up the street from the famous Man at the Wheel is perhaps the most moving monument of all. It was commissioned in August 2001 by the Gloucester Fishermen's Wives' Association to commemorate the families, the women and children, left to mourn those lost at sea. It is a simple statue of a mother and two children facing seaward, searching for a glimpse of the tall masts of the husband's and father's schooner. The sculpture strikes an even deeper chord than do the other two, speaking to the awful grief of the survivors who must somehow find a way to cope with the desolation of loss and carry on. The lives of those who depended on fishing for a living were always hard and too often ended in tragedy.

There was no romance in a working life at sea. The dirty and often brutally exhausting labour took place in uncertain and perilous conditions, where survival depended on constant vigilance and good fortune. Simply slipping from a footrope or being struck by a swinging boom could end a life in an instant. Many were swept overboard, lost in heavy fog or swamped in dories holding too many fish. Sometimes entire vessels and crews would go missing, smashed to pieces on a lee shore, run down by an Atlantic steamer in thick fog or torn apart in a hurricane, leaving no clues as to their passing. However, the promise of better pay than for work ashore, the camaraderie and the pride in doing the job well were viewed as compensation for the constant risk. Fishing was always a gamble, dependent on nature and the market for a reasonable return. Companionable shipmates, a competent skipper, a good cook and reasonable fo'c'sle crew made any hardship tolerable.

Life aboard a fishing schooner was more of a co-operative venture than the rigid hierarchy of the merchant marine. Fishermen worked as shareholders, and so their livelihood depended on the fortunes of their vessel and how hard they worked. They were engaged on a share system, their compensation paid out in proportion to the catch, after the vessel's costs had been deducted: the food, bait, salt, ice and wages for the paid members of the crew (the cook and perhaps one or two deckhands). In addition there could be one or two children on board who were paid a small wage to work as "throaters" or "headers," until they were considered old enough to work the dories. These children were often as young as ten or eleven, sent to sea to help out their families and learn the trade. The largest share went to the boat's owners—for the hire of the vessel—followed by the skipper, who normally took twice that of his crew. The rest was divided among the fishermen in one of two ways. If the crew were known to the skipper as hardworking men, he would generally give them "even shares," regardless of how many fish were caught in each dory. If, on the other hand, he had a crew of strangers whose fishing abilities were unknown to him, the skipper would have the catch divided "by the count." With two men to a boat, dory-mates were credited with the number of marketable fish they caught as a pair, and those catching the most took the highest share. Although there were reasonable arguments to be made for both systems, some skippers insisted on "by the count" on all occasions because they thought it encouraged competition and therefore greater catches. Those that counted highest were ranked "high dory," whereas those who consistently came out "low dory" often lost their jobs. "Even shares" was considered more democratic and fair by some, as the loss of gear and fish was often the result of bad luck rather than incompetence. But a good skipper had to be sure of his crew before he offered "even shares."

The crew of a typical banks schooner consisted of sixteen to twenty-four men. If a schooner was running eight dories, it would require a crew of sixteen. In addition to the crew, there was the skipper, a cook and one or two paid hands, who did not fish but tended to the ship and the needs of the men. These hands were also available to launch and recover dories and work the ship until the crew returned. When not fishing or on passage, the fishermen were required to help stand watches, provide lookouts, steer the vessel and handle sail. Once on the banks, they were either fishing or sleeping—and usually very little of the latter. When handling sail, even for the smallest job the entire crew would be called out, so there would be no accusations of favouritism.

Depending on the distance between port and the fishing ground, it could be hours or days until the men began to fish. Once on the banks, the day usually started at about three or four in the morning when they began putting bait on their trawls and readying their boats. The reason for starting so early was explained to writer Fred Wallace by Captain Harry Ross of the schooner *Dorothy M. Smart*. It was "better," he said, "to begin your fishing early than to fish late. When you swing 'em over at two, or three or four—'specially during broken weather—the men have daylight ahead of them should it breeze or shut down thick. I'd sooner be caught with my dories astray in a fog or a snowstorm at four in the morning than at four in the afternoon. More chances of pickin' 'em up."[1] Once the crew was "baited up," the skipper would sing out to cast off, with his schooner slowly jogging along or hove to under foresail and jumbo sails. The top dory in each nest would be readied with all her thwarts or seats, plugs and gear securely in place, and was then lifted over the side by means of dory tackle descending from the main and fore mastheads. The two-man crew would carefully time their jump into the boat once it was over the rail, illuminated only by lantern and guttering kerosene torches, often with quite a sea running. The dory was then allowed to drift astern and was tied up to the quarter rail. After each was let go, it would be led aft and made fast to the others until there was a long string of boats behind the schooner. With all the boats in the water, the skipper would head off to a favourite fishing spot and let the dories go, one at a time, along a line several miles long. This was known as a flying set. The schooner would then act as a mother hen tending her chicks, jogging up and down the line or heaving to, ready at any time to service the boats. Once a dory crew had set their trawl, they would row back to the schooner and go aboard for a coffee break or mug-up before heading out again to haul in the trawl. The dorymen would signal the schooner when their boat was full of fish, by raising an oar or waving one of the torches, and the schooner would come alongside to pick up the load.

Some skippers preferred another method whereby they anchored their boats and had their dories fan out in all directions, like the spokes of a wheel. The dory crew would row to a likely spot, sometimes a mile from the schooner, to set their trawls. This was a method favoured by salt fishermen, but it had its drawbacks. If the wind and sea picked up, the men left aboard the schooner would be unable to raise the anchor on their own except by cutting the cable, and those dories on the leeward side would have a hard pull upwind to safety. On the other hand, if thick fog were to settle in, the dory crew would have a good idea of the direction and distance in which to find their schooner.

The dory was the workhorse of the Grand Banks fishery. It was a small, flat-bottomed craft with flared sides, a pointed bow and a tombstone stern, cheap to

build and stout enough to withstand the rigours of offshore fishing. It could easily be handled on and off the schooner and, after the thwarts were removed, nested onto another, so taking up little space on deck. An 18-foot (5.5-metre) dory seemed a mere sliver on a distant sea but had the capacity to carry more than two tons of fish without swamping. The banks dory was legendary for its stability when laden, and a crew of skilled fishermen could keep it afloat in very rough seas. The dory was not only a workhorse but also the lifeline of the fishermen, who depended on its famous durability and stability to keep them safe in almost any weather. A pair of oars, a small mast and sail, pen boards to contain the fish, a bailer, a water jar, a bait knife, a compass, a small wooden winch called a hurdy gurdy, a fish gaff, and the tubs, trawls, floats and anchors used to set gear was all that was required to equip it.

In the early days of fishing on the banks, fishermen worked from the deck of a schooner, standing along the rails and handlining for groundfish from the relative safety of a stable platform. Each man would tend several weighted lines to jig fish from the bottom, not much different from the method employed by the sports fisherman of today. It was a slow and labour-intensive method that did not produce a large catch. The introduction and adaptation of dory trawling in the late 1800s made the industry far more efficient, but at the cost of considerably increasing the risk to the fishermen. Hundreds of hooks could be laid out at a time, but the men handling them were no longer comfortably ensconced aboard a mother vessel. They were alone in a small boat, often miles away.

After a dory was dropped from the schooner, one man would ship the oars and row his boat as directed by the skipper, while his dory-mate attached the end of the first tub of line to a small anchor and tossed it over the side; standing in the stern, he would flick the baited hooks and line into the sea with a short wooden stick. Three, sometimes four tubs of line were attached together and laid out across the ocean floor. At the other end another anchor would be set to keep the trawl in place. Often a mile of line with thousands of baited hooks was laid out, marked at the ends with only a small flag or black ball. After setting the trawl and enjoying a mug-up aboard the schooner, the men would return to tend the gear. The man at the bow would now haul the line out of the water over a small wooden roller. The fish caught on the line were twisted off the hooks with a deft flick of the wrist and chucked into the bottom of the boat, and the line would either be coiled back into the tubs or "under-run"—rebaited and returned to the water for another set. The man at the oars would also be keeping a wary eye on the sea, ready to twist the boat into any oncoming waves to prevent a swamping. Once a ton or two of fish had been caught, they would either row or sail back to the schooner or signal it to come and off-load the catch. After a day of fishing, the night would be spent gutting, splitting and cleaning. Only when all the fish had been salted or iced in the hold could heads be put down for an hour or two of sleep.

A typical day on the banks was described in an article in a Lunenburg newspaper in 1911 as follows:

> All get up at three o'clock, cut bait, and row to their trawls before getting any breakfast; if the trawls have not been parted during the night, either by sharks or chafing against rocks, they haul them up, take off the fish, rebait, and return to the vessel at half after five, and have breakfast. They stay on board until nine thirty when they revisit their trawls, and repeat the same work mentioned above. Those who have been unfortunate enough to have had their trawls parted are not able to return until eleven thirty. In the meantime the other dories have landed two loads. The usual dinner hour is about twelve thirty, and after which meals they return to the trawls, and get back in time for tea served at half after three. Four o'clock sees them on their fourth trip, which is usually the last except when the fish are plentiful and the weather is fine they make five or six. In the night after the fourth meal all help to dress the fish, that is, cut off the heads, split them open, clean them and sprinkle them thoroughly with salt. They are then piled away in the hold of the vessel.[2]

It was cold, wet, back-breaking work, with the constant threat of being swamped in a squall or "going astray" in heavy fog. Fog was the worst enemy of a doryman. A day that started out fine and clear could quickly change and disappear under a thick blanket of heavy mist. The warm, moist air of the Gulf Stream drifting over the cold Labrador Current could produce some of the heaviest and most persistent fogs in the world, especially in summertime. Jimmy Connolly, writing in the 1920s, witnessed the conditions first-hand:

> Clear weather or thick, those men put out from the vessel. They put out one night at two o'clock in what fishermen call black vapour—heavy black fog. Each dory left with a lighted flambeaux, a great torch with a two-inch wick. The flambeaux

were for the dories to show, to keep track of each other in the black night. The vapour so thick that even the flare of the big torches could not be seen from one dory to another. The men then had to halloo from dory to dory so as not to go astray. *Hi-oh! Hi-oh-h! Hi-oh-h-h!* To be standing on the vessel's deck and hearing them call to each other and not be able to see them—it was as if a lot of dead men had come to life and were calling to each other in some graveyard.[3]

Masters were always wary of changing conditions, but they often walked a fine line when it came to stopping fishing and calling back the men. Keeping track of boats spread out over the ocean was a demanding and tricky business in thick weather. Some skippers had an uncanny ability to locate their men in any conditions, but for many it was more luck than skill, and fishermen disappeared. Fortunate were those who were picked up by other schooners or passing steamers; most had to fend for themselves, waiting out the weather or rowing to safety, sometimes a hundred miles away.[4] Too many perished, drowned in a swamped dory, froze to death or simply died of dehydration, but there were also many incredible stories of survival. As Connolly wrote, "Men that go in for this life are not worrying overmuch about being lost. They may not enjoy the prospect of it, but the thought never overburdens them. If they feared death overmuch they would hardly be trying to make a living at banks fishing."[5]

One of the greatest survival stories was that of Howard Blackburn, a young Nova Scotian who joined the crew of the Gloucester boat *Grace L. Fears* in January 1883. He and Tom Welch, his dory-mate, lost their schooner in a blinding snowstorm on Burgeo Bank, off Newfoundland's south shore. In desperation, they headed for shore, more than sixty miles away, fighting mountainous seas and freezing rain. After Blackburn lost his mittens overboard on the first day, he froze his hands around the oars so that he could continue rowing. He and Welch had to constantly pound the ice forming on the dory and bail to stave off capsizing. Blackburn's hands became battered wrecks and Welch froze to death, succumbing to the bitter cold on the second night of their ordeal. With his dead partner in the stern, Blackburn continued to pull for shore, bail the water that sometimes rose to his knees and pound off the ice, all the while trying to stay on course for land. After five days with no rest, food or water, and in constant fear of capsizing, he finally made it to a desolate south shore settlement. The astonished inhabitants nursed him back to health and, although he lost all of his fingers and half of each thumb as well as a number of toes, he survived, eventually making his way back to Gloucester. His fellow citizens were so taken with his heroic journey that they raised enough money to buy him a saloon on the Gloucester waterfront. He was also paid his share from the halibut trip of the *Grace L. Fears,* $86. This legendary figure in the Cape Ann community further enhanced his reputation by twice crossing the Atlantic single-handed in later years.

The relationship of a banks skipper with his men was not defined by the shipping acts and articles of agreement, which gave masters in the merchant marine a great deal of authority. On a fishing schooner, life was much more informal. The skipper was in charge only by common consent, and the men were not bound to the schooner in any manner. There was no rank, and there were few rules regarding behaviour and none regarding dress. Men shared the same food and slept wherever a bunk was available, often in the master's aft cabin. The skipper's authority was based largely on his personal reputation and the confidence he inspired in his crew. Ultimately, the success of any trip depended on his abilities as a navigator, sailor and fisherman, and as a manager of men. Reporting to the United States Fish Commission, Captain Joseph Collins wrote in 1887 that a fishing skipper

> must be a natural leader, and generally gifted with superior intellect and tact, in order to get along with the crew, there being no special laws like those of the merchant service, which give him authority over his men. In cases of insubordination he must have recourse to his physical strength. If he cannot sustain himself in this manner, his influence over his crew is gone.[6]

Once ashore, skippers could easily get rid of troublemakers or unproductive crews, a threat that kept most crew members on their toes.

Fishing skippers began their careers young, learning the trade from the bottom up as ordinary fishermen, gutting and cleaning fish. By the time they were grown, they knew everything that was to be known about men and boats, fish, weather and markets. It was not an overly crowded profession, as most fishermen preferred to follow rather than lead. There were no formal qualifications, and training depended on finding a skipper willing to teach. Because authority had to be earned, a skipper had to prove himself before he could become successful. It is little wonder that many became larger-than-life personalities with reputations that took on almost mythic proportions. A skipper who was known to be a "sail

dragger and fish killer" would have no trouble attracting a top-notch crew, no matter how hard he worked them at sea. When a schooner came upon a productive area, the men were expected to fish until they literally dropped, sometimes working for days on end without sleep. Some skippers were ruthless when it came to crew safety, launching dories under terrible conditions. Any reluctant crew member would be landed ashore at the first opportunity and branded a coward. All too often a returning schooner came home with a flag at half-mast, marking the loss of life that resulted from the actions of an overzealous skipper. One disillusioned fisherman explained the indifference to the men's safety as follows:

> The skipper'd send you out as long as you could get out—long as you could get the dories off an' get out. Some of 'em was pretty rusty characters... hardly ever stop you from goin' off. He'd care only about the fish... and he's sleepin' while you was out haulin'. The one Cap'n I was with—he kept a dog aboard, see. There was many a night... blowin' a gale an' stormin'... why he'd call that dog in an' leave the men out. The men were out an' they'd stay out... on deck or in the dories. Made no difference to him. He must o' lost seven or eight men when I was with him... more or less.[7]

The promise of income made men endure the hardships inflicted on them by these ambitious and merciless souls. On the other hand, if a skipper could not find fish and fared poorly on the banks, he would have a hard time finding a boat, let alone a crew.

The master of a fishing schooner had to have the confidence and skill to be able to sail miles from shore in variable sea conditions, tidal currents and poor visibility. A crew's livelihood and safety depended on his being able to pinpoint a prime fishing spot, sometimes hundreds of miles from the home port, and make landfall safely after the trip was finished. There were no radars, radios or electronic navigation aids of any kind. A few skippers could use a sextant to perform celestial sights, but most were content with the basic navigational tools: a compass, a chart, a lead line and the confidence that comes from years of experience and local knowledge. As Fred Wallace explained in his excellent book, *The Roving Fisherman:*

> [The skipper's] sense of location, of tidal and current sets, of wind, is guided by compass indications. Coupled with this continual mental plotting of courses and fixing of positions, is his intimate knowledge of what is underneath the ocean

< **TWO FISHERMEN** of the Gloucester schooner *Killarney* haul on the forward dory tackle, as a third steadies it for launching. Another dory can be seen in the distance, already pulling away from the schooner. After being hauled out of her nest, the dory would be loaded with thwarts, oars, sail, trawl tubs and a variety of other items needed for a day's fishing before being sent on its way. *Al Barnes Collection, Mariners' Museum, Newport News, Virginia*

surface in depth of water and character of bottom. Give him but one or two casts of the sounding lead, and the whole layout of the fishing ground he is working upon spreads out before his mind's eye... The average fishing skipper of the old days was superior to most deepwater merchantship masters in keeping "a grip on the bottom" and knowing where they were at any time.[8]

Wallace supplied proof of the skipper's knowledge after a trip with Captain John Apt of Yarmouth in 1912. While Wallace found the ship's position by using a sextant and making calculations from the appropriate tables—a skill he had learned from his father—Apt, after scribbling a few notations on a stovepipe with a nail, came up with the same location in half the time. There were even stories of masters whose knowledge of the coast was so detailed they could navigate by identifying the bark of a dog ashore. At the very least this would tell a skipper he was close to land!

A bad cook could doom a trip to the banks before it started. A good one played a major role in the maintenance of crew morale, especially on long trips. The cook was expected to have good grub available at all times of the day and night, three square meals as well as numerous "mug-ups." A "quick lunch locker" was to be kept well stocked and a pot of coffee always available on the stove. Some cooks were legendary for the extraordinary meals they could produce and their seemingly unlimited capacity to keep a crew satisfied.

Along with cooking duties, cooks kept an inventory of provisions, especially water, to ensure there was enough for the trip home. They usually tried to have water available for the men to clean up when heading in, but this was not always possible. Keeping track of stores was a prodigious job, especially on a salt banker, which could be at sea for months at a time. Provisions were a considerable investment for the owners, who hoped to more than recoup the expense at the end of the trip. The following list was from the Atlantic Supply Company for their schooner *Columbia* in April 1923:

> 16 barrels of flour, 1,100 pounds of sugar, 60 pounds of tea, 40 pounds of coffee, 7 bushels of beans, 75 pounds raisins, 100 cans of evaporated apples, 120 gallons of kerosene, 16 cases of milk, 15 gallons of molasses, 1 bushel of dry beans, 50 pounds of rice, 60 bushels of potatoes, 150 pounds of onions, 5 bushels of turnips, 11 barrels of beef, 1 barrel of corned shoulders, 300 pounds of salt spare ribs,

1 barrel of salt pork, 200 pounds of smoked ham, four cases of eggs, 300 cans of beets, squash, blueberries, string beans, clams, corn, peas, peaches, and tomatoes, 40 pounds of crackers, 40 pounds of baking powder, 15 cans of cream of tartar, 15 pounds of saleratus, from two to four pounds each of nutmeg, pepper, allspice, clove, ginger, cassia, mustard, etc., 20 packages of corn starch, 30 boxes of salt, 60 pounds of jam, 30 pounds of lemon pie filling, 20 pounds of mince meat, 24 boxes of lemon extract, 24 bottles of vanilla extract, 25 pounds of prunes, 48 packages of pudding, 24 bottles of ketchup, 12 mugs of prepared mustard, 25 packages of currants, 15 pounds of barley, 25 pounds of evaporated peaches, 100 pounds of fresh meat, 24 pounds of cheese and 100 pounds of slack salted polluck, also 40 bars of soap, 25 packages of washing powder, 24 packages of soap powder, 24 gross matches. In addition to the supplies for the men are included six tons of coal, four feet of wood, 450 hogsheads of salt, three gross of wax candles, 20 yards of towelling, 25 yards of torch wicking, one dozen torches, four coils buoy line, 30 dozen seven-pound lines, 10 dozen twenty-two-pound lines, 700 pounds of lead to be melted and used for jigger hooks, 24 dory gaffs, 18 fish forks, 20 pairs of oars, 32 two-pound anchors, 20 gallons of gasoline, 36 pairs of rubber boots, 20 dozen pairs of cotton gloves, five dozen pairs cotton mitts, 150 yards cotton cloth for dory sails, four dozen suits of oil skins, one dozen oiled petticoats, 24 bail buckets, 28 mattresses, 24 water jugs, besides the dishes, silverware, crockery, cooking utensils, tools, dory tackle and painters, etc.[9]

Cooks were also required to be on deck to tend to the vessel when the men were away fishing, and they would often supplement their wages by jigging for fish from the deck of the schooner while the dories were gone.

The forecastle, or fo'c'sle, was the heart of a schooner. This was where the crew ate, slept and relaxed. It was also the liveliest part of the boat, up in the bow, under the foremast. Men could feel the hull slicing and crashing through rough seas and hear the timbers creak and groan. Rows of bunks were set into the sloping bulkheads of the hull, and a large, wedge-shaped table on which food was served and cards were played thrust out between the rows. A large cast-iron cook's stove, sitting at the after end, would be kept well stoked throughout a trip to warm the men and dry their constantly sodden clothes. The galley and larder, also located near the stove, were home to the cook in his endless preparation of meals. The fo'c'sle was a tight but comfortable space. Wet clothing was hung everywhere; only the outer layers—woollen socks, sweaters and oilskins—were laid out to dry. The inner layers stayed on for the night, in case the men were called out to fish or tend sail. The smells of the stove, sodden wool clothing and as many as twenty working men—blending with the aromas of tobacco, fish, cooked food and the pungent bouquet of fishy brine from an unpumped bilge—made life in the forecastle an experience for the senses.

Schooners were seldom still, except on those rare days of perfect calm. All too often they pitched and rolled, making life on board, especially when hove to in a gale, far from easy. Every movement on board would become an effort, a simple walk across the deck a frantic dash from one post to another. Muscles were strained and sore from attempts to stay upright. Fishing would usually cease once it became impossible to launch the dories, and everyone would lie low, only standing watches, until the gale was over. The constant rolling and plunging, not to mention the danger of being thrown out of your bunk, made a good night's sleep impossible. However, a seasoned crew would weather it out and relax as best they could, knowing the seas would eventually settle and they would soon be back fishing.

For the men that went down to the sea in ships it was a hard, tough life for little return. Unless they were with a particularly good highline skipper, they would always be just dollars away from the poorhouse. There was always the promise of the large haul but, averaged over the year, they were not going to get rich. It was little wonder that men from the Maritimes migrated south in large numbers, since the work back home was usually seasonal and paid less. The New England fishery, by contrast, was year-round, to satisfy the large American market. Winter fishing paid more, but the perils were greater. It is hardly surprising that few landlubbers were attracted to the life, but, with all its drawbacks, for the men who worked the seas there was little alternative. The job of their grandfathers, fathers, brothers, neighbours and sons was all they knew, or wanted to do.

NOTES

In the notes following each chapter, citation by surname indicates an entry in the Selected Bibliography.

1 Wallace, *The Roving Fisherman*, p. 43
2 *Lunenburg Progress Enterprise*, n.d., 1911
3 Connolly, *The Book of the Gloucester Fishermen*, p. 37
4 All references to miles in this book are as used by mariners—*nautical* miles. A nautical mile is defined as one minute of arc of a great circle (such as the equator), or one-sixtieth of one degree. In practice this equals 1,854 metres, or 1.15 statute miles. Speed over water is expressed in knots, which is a measure of nautical miles per hour.
5 Connolly, *The Book of the Gloucester Fishermen*, p. 21
6 Goode, *The Fisheries and Fishery Industries of the United States*
7 Barss, *Images of Lunenburg County*, p. 41
8 Wallace, *The Roving Fisherman*, p. 54.
9 *Gloucester Daily Times*, April 25, 1923

3

A SKIPPING STONE

THE SCHOONERS of the east coast fishing fleet at the beginning of the twentieth century were the product of more than two hundred years of evolution. By the second decade of the century, the schooner had reached its peak in design but ironically was teetering on the verge of extinction. The introduction of reliable marine engines into the fishing industry had made sail obsolete. The use of sail—one of the oldest forms of propulsion, dating back to the beginnings of human history—could not compete with the superior power and reliability of the marine engine, and the schooner found itself quickly replaced by the dull but dependable trawler. Even so, it would take several decades before the working schooner made its final departure from the banks.

For the last half century of its existence, the schooner was greatly admired and often described as the finest fishing vessel in the world. Its powerful hull, seaworthiness and versatile sail plan made it perfectly suited to the harsh, demanding job of offshore fishing. The hull was staunchly built and rugged enough to withstand the most relentless of seas, and the configuration of sails was so flexible that the amount of canvas carried could be adapted to any weather, from light airs to hurricane-force winds. Schooners were fast, stable and could work their way to windward, a huge advantage in the variable wind conditions of the east coast. They also required fewer men to work them than other fishing vessels, something that appealed to both owners and fishermen. It is no wonder that the schooner could be found fishing and trading from Labrador to South America and Europe. The last all-sail schooners built in the 1920s were breathtakingly beautiful, with long, graceful hulls, upswept spoon bows and overhanging transoms. Their masts, over one hundred feet (thirty metres) tall, soared skyward, often carrying more than 10,000 square feet (930 square metres) of canvas. A design that combined aesthetic beauty and practical perfection would become a source of pride to owners, skippers and fishermen alike.

The schooner first appeared in North America on the shores of Cape Ann in Massachusetts in the early years of the eighteenth century. The precise origins are hard to place, as there are no plans, documents or models that have survived from the period. There is evidence in early Dutch engravings that the schooner rig was used in Europe in the mid-1700s, but the unique American version seems to have evolved independently earlier in the century. The local lore in Gloucester has it that a Captain Andrew Robinson invented the schooner in 1713 while building a new fishboat on the eastern shore of the harbour. According to legend, a spectator watching the passage of the unusual vessel was heard to remark, "Oh, how she scoons!" (A possible derivation of "scoon" is a Scots verb meaning to skip over the water like a flat stone.) The delighted builder is reputed to have replied, "A scooner let her be!"[1] The term "schooner" applied more to the rig than the hull, and with a relatively simple repositioning of the masts it became easily adaptable to existing colonial craft. The schooner rig was so practical that even fishermen, who were notoriously resistant to change, could immediately see the benefits of the innovation. The schooner was faster, easier to handle, and could carry more canvas than any existing craft.

Prior to the development of the schooner, the colonial ports in both Canada and the United States were populated by sailing craft that had been either brought over from Great Britain or built locally to a familiar design. The shallop was a small, open boat, propelled by an oar or sail, carrying a large for-and-aft main sprit-sail or rigged two-masted with square sails. These were suitable only for the inshore fishery that was then accessible to the developing colonies, as there were plenty of fish to be caught in the nearby fishing grounds.

The more likely forerunner to the schooner, however, was the ketch, which carried two masts, one larger mainmast forward and a smaller mizzen mast aft. It was generally larger and more seaworthy than the shallop, having a covered, flush deck. Both types were popular throughout the colonies, on each side of the border, but both were generally unsuitable for the harsh, variable wind and sea conditions, especially in winter. It does not take much to imagine Captain Andrew Robinson, or a kindred spirit, experimenting with the ketch and coming up with the more efficient schooner rig. All that was needed was to move the smaller mizzen mast from its aft position to forward of the mainmast, rig it with both fore and aft sails, and the schooner was born.

These colonial vessels were replaced by a specialized fishing vessel called the Marblehead schooner, which was a far cry from the elegant fishing schooners of the early twentieth century but met the needs of the coastal fishery. The design originated in the town of Marblehead, Massachusetts, the state's largest fishing port until the rise of Gloucester in the mid-nineteenth century, and spread rapidly around the New England coast and into Canada. There were many variations, but most had finer lines and were faster sailers than the earlier forms. They had a bluff bow, high stern and were bulky enough to carry a substantial cargo of fish. There were no bulwarks forward of the quarterdeck, since it was then regarded as unsafe to prevent the unobstructed sweep of water across the main deck. As a result, except on very calm days, fishing was done from the relative safety of the higher, drier quarterdeck. Schooners gradually grew in length, some up to sixty feet (eighteen metres), making them better suited to offshore fishing, and some were used to trade cargo as far south as the West Indies. There is little record of the earlier models, but later depictions show a high, proud stern, which made them look like an upturned shoe—hence the nickname "heeltapper." Their reputation for speed was noted during the American Revolution, Napoleonic Wars

and the War of 1812, when schooners were appropriated by the fledgling U.S. Navy and by the British and French for use as privateers. Sailing to windward, schooners were easily able to outdistance the heavier, more cumbersome square-rigged vessels in pursuit.[2]

Immediately after the American Revolution, the depletion of fishing boats virtually crippled the industry in New England. Two distinctly new schooner designs appeared as cheap alternatives to the Marblehead: the Chebacco boat and the Pinky. The Chebacco was very popular and was built in huge numbers on the Cape Ann peninsula. It was a smallish craft and carried two masts, schooner-fashion, with the foremast up in the bow. As there was no bowsprit, the sail arrangement had no jibs, foresails nor, for that matter, topsails. Some such schooners were double-enders and others, called "dogsbodies," were built with square ends. Because of their size, they were usually restricted to the inshore fishery.

The evolution of the other schooner design, the Pinky, paralleled that of the Chebacco boat and became equally accepted off the New England coast. The Pinky was a fast sailer with a double-ended hull but, unlike the Chebacco, had a bowsprit, allowing for fore- and topsails. These schooners were seldom longer than fifty feet (fifteen metres) and had a distinctive stern that swept gracefully upwards into a narrow tombstone transom. The hulls were so symmetrical from front to back that they would constantly pitch like a rocking horse in any seaway. However, the Pinky's superior ability to sail to windward was a quality much sought-after in the prevailing wind conditions off the east coast ports. After the War of 1812, a more refined version was developed that was suitable for working farther from home. Squabbles over fishing treaties between the United States and Great Britain ended with the imposition of a three-mile limit around the shoreline of Britain's North American territories and the barring of Americans from fishing in those waters. Bays and harbours that were previously open to Yankee fishermen were now closed; as fishermen always followed the fish rather than the law, the ban led to wide-scale poaching. Their illegal activities made "clipper Pinkies," a larger, faster version of the boat, well known in the Maritime provinces, where they were adopted in turn by the Canadian fishery. They remained in common use up to the 1830s, when they were gradually replaced by the broad-hulled, low-quarterdecked schooner that began to dominate the industry. The Pinky's popularity may have waned, but the design continued to be favoured by many well into the twentieth century.

< THE WRITER Fred Wallace was able to take this dramatic photograph of the *Effie M. Morrissey* by climbing out on the bowsprit with her captain, Harry Ross. Shortly after this was taken, the helmsman let her "come-to" a little, burying the whole lee side and thoroughly soaking the pair forward. *F.W. Wallace Collection, Maritime Museum of the Atlantic*

The development of larger, more substantial schooners called "market fishermen" or "bankers," which could range farther out to sea and carry far greater loads of fish, was a response to the pressures of the rapidly growing American domestic market. Most of these larger vessels could sail great distances from port, going to anchor on a likely spot and fishing until full before returning with a cargo of gutted, split and salted fish. The new boats were met with suspicion by many fishermen, their natural aversion to change reinforced by news of the loss of many of these boats and their crews in winter gales. Critics called them unsafe. Writing in the *Gloucester Advertiser,* Captain Joseph Collins made "invidious comments" on the new boats, stating that "these schooners were very slow sailers—more suited to drifting than sailing—and not weatherly. In addition, their lack of depth and, in fact, their general form, made them liable to being knocked down and swamped in a gale."[3] As Howard Chapelle has observed, supplying the market and making a profit came first:

> While all these were practical objections to the type, none of them were really valid reason for disregarding the old model, for the safety of fishermen and vessel property were not always prime considerations in the improvement of vessels, the brutal facts being that the men lost cost the shipowner nothing, and insurance could take care of the loss of vessel property.[4]

Unfortunately, this sentiment prevailed among shipowners, not only in the fishing industry but also in the commercial shipping trade.

The next changes in schooner design were a radical departure from the older, fuller-hulled vessels of the past and were a response to the need for speed to meet the demand for fresh fish in the American market. In the 1840s, the introduction of crushed ice as a means of preserving fish changed the industry almost overnight. Fishing took on a far more competitive tone. It was now a race to the grounds and a race to be the first back to port with a fresh cargo. Shipowners had a compelling financial incentive to underwrite changes to schooner design, and designers competed with each other to come up with the best new vessel. Faster boats meant higher profits, since the first boat to the pier with a load of prime, iced cod or halibut earned the best price from dealers ashore. These early "sharpshooters," as they were called, had long, straight keels with almost flat bottoms, shallow-drafted to suit the shoal water in Gloucester Harbour. The biggest departure was the long, pointed, "sharp" bow, a feature that added to the racy character of the boat. Again, the local fishermen had grave doubts about the seaworthiness of the new designs. They were felt to be too dangerous without a full, bluff bow, as many thought that if the vessels dived into a head sea they would never recover.

This period of intense rivalry among both shipowners and designers became a frenetic pursuit of speed. As the demand for fresh seafood grew, the tendency was to build longer, shallower, extremely sharp vessels with a minimum of ballast. Huge piles of sail were crowded on, to the extent that the vessels became dangerous; their flat bottoms meant stability depended almost entirely upon the width of their beam. In fair weather, these boats could carry as much sail as possible, but in a blow they often met with disaster. If a vessel heeled over too far, the centre of gravity was not sufficiently low to right her, often resulting in capsizing and the loss of the crew. The madness continued throughout the seventies and eighties: in the ten years from 1874 to 1883, the town of Gloucester lost eighty-two schooners and 895 men. It was obvious to anyone with a rudimentary knowledge of ship design that the answer lay in increasing the vessel's draft and lowering the centre of gravity.

One man with a desire to put things right was Captain Joseph W. Collins, a highly respected, self-educated fishing master who had spent most of his life at sea. He began a personal crusade to reform the industry and make it a safer business. He was horrified by the tremendous losses he saw around him and began writing articles critical of current fishing practices and vessel design. As a member of the United States Fish Commission, he was able to persuade the government to build an experimental schooner that would incorporate all the practical innovations he and designer Dennison J. Lawlor had been advocating. The schooner, *Grampus*, represented a huge leap ahead of common practice. She was narrower of beam, had a deeper draft, a plumb stem, and an altered sail plan resulting from changes to the masts and rigging. Special attention was given to the vessel's stability; the ballast and cargo were properly secured to prevent shifting, and limits were put on the weight aloft. At the same time, it was essential to preserve qualities that would ensure the vessel could be competitive. Although keenly aware of the objections to the adoption of a deep hull because of the shallowness of Gloucester Harbour, Collins and Lawlor insisted that safety should be paramount. "Safety of life and property should supersede all other considerations and will."[5]

The *Grampus* and other similarly designed schooners were great improvements on the older, "sharp" vessels. They proved to be fast as well as safe. With deeper holds and a lower centre of gravity, they could not only stow more fish but also could carry sail without fear of capsizing. The "sharp," hollow lines of the earlier boats were replaced with the long, easy curves that typify the modern schooner. The graceful stern was narrowed considerably, ending in a long, over-hanging transom, and the elegant clipper bow was fuller on the waterline. The model proved fast and seaworthy and quickly became a favourite of fishermen and owners alike. This style of schooner went through further evolutions in the coming years, but the basic template became the norm for the industry until the end of the all-sail era. Hulls became larger, especially in Canada where the salt-fish trade continued, and that meant longer, deeper keels that could carry great amounts of sail aloft. The round, spoon bow that marked the next generation would make these beauties even more impressive. The final incarnations of the type, which were built to race in the international competitions of the 1920s, were the ultimate in the refinement of commercial schooner design, their almost yacht-like appearance belying their blue-collar purpose.

If this narrative seems heavily American in its description of the evolution of schooner design, it is because New England, with its far greater population base than the Maritimes' and consequently huge market demands, provided the most fertile ground for schooner development in North America. Their geographical proximity meant that the Maritimes naturally benefited from innovations from the south, and they were quick to adapt new designs for their own use. Canada had many fine designers and master builders, but, with a few exceptions, adaptation, not innovation, was the rule. The Tancook whaler, for instance, was a distinctly Nova Scotian variant. It was a double-ended schooner, similar to the Pinky but with a finer entry, more rake in the ends and a clipper bow. Generally, however, when Nova Scotians saw a new vessel from the United States they took what they could from its design and applied it to their own. David Stevens, a master builder from Second Peninsula in Nova Scotia, related a story of his grandfather building the first spoon-bowed schooner in the province.

> He was fishing on the Grand Banks…and saw what he thought was a very strange vessel coming down close by. He couldn't take his eyes off her…About two weeks later he was in port and here was that vessel laying alongside at the wharf, so he took a piece of paper and a pencil and got off on the side and he drew a profile of

the shape. It was a spoon bow schooner out of Gloucester with a transom stern…
He brought the drawing home to his father and his father immediately made a
half model and began to build what is known as the Tancook Schooner.[6]

It was always a matter of pride for schooner masters to carry a lot of sail and
carry it well. Reputations were built on how hard a vessel could be pushed and
how much speed could be squeezed out of her hull. A "highliner" was a master
who could not only catch fish but also could drive his vessel to market in record
time. It is no wonder that when vessels met at sea there were often spontaneous
hookups and unspoken challenges, when all thoughts of fish and markets were
put aside for the joy of a race. Egged on by their crews, masters threw caution to
the wind, sometimes losing dories and gear over the side. Howard Chapelle felt
compelled to comment on this practice in his superb book *The American Fishing
Schooners:*

> In the late 1800s and early 1900s carrying a heavy press of sail on all occasions
> was common practice among fishing skippers. One of these hard-driving skip-
> pers lost five sets of spars during his career, with even greater damage to rigging
> and sails. This characteristic of many fishing skippers was the result of the work
> of a great short-story writer, James B. Connolly, whose tales of the Gloucester
> fishermen attracted widespread attention during this period. Connolly glorified
> and publicized hard-driving skippers, so a reputation for being a sail carrier
> became much sought after, though the result was sometimes an exhibition of
> recklessness.[7]

Americans generally hold that the first fishermen's race occurred in Boston
in the mid-1880s. However, an earlier contest was held in Halifax, Nova Scotia,
at the Great Aquatic Festival in 1871. Although the four-day festival was primarily a rowing regatta, bringing together the best rowers in the world, it was also a
showcase for Nova Scotia fishermen, and one of the event's features was a fishing-
schooner race. There were several races, each designed for a different class of boat,
including two categories of schooners, wherries, gigs and whalers. The star of the
series was a small forty-ton schooner called *Flash*, which was entered in the second class of schooners (fifty tons and under). Although her race started half an

hour after that of the first class (fifty tons or over), the *Flash* not only won but crossed the finish a mere two minutes behind the leader of the larger group, a sixty-six-ton vessel called the *Ida E.* The *Flash*'s spectacular performance astonished the race watchers.[8] Twenty schooners had entered the competition, and although this was a fairly modest affair, it was likely the first time fishermen had had the opportunity to show off their racing skills to a hometown crowd.

Fishing-schooner racing on a formal basis proved to be a popular though rather sporadic sport over the next half century or so. Fishermen were understandably more interested in earning a living than in playing games and could ill afford to take time off to race. Thomas McManus, a naval architect and the self-professed "Father of the Fishermen's Races," organized a competition in Boston in May 1886 when a strike by fish handlers ashore was forcing the schooners to lie idle. The young designer could not bear to see the fleet inactive, so he arranged for a no-handicaps "boat for boat" contest. Vessels were allowed to be hauled out and cleaned, but nothing else. It was a fairly dull and listless event with little wind, but it pleased the spectators just the same and McManus's own boat, the *John H. McManus*, designed by himself and named for his father, won the race.

There were no more than eight official fishermen's races from 1871 until the start of the International Fishermen's Cup series in 1920. Several, sponsored by the international sportsman Sir Thomas Lipton, were held off Boston and Gloucester. The Brittain Cup series, named for the owner of a fish plant, was held in Digby, Nova Scotia, at the end of the first decade of the new century and inspired the young writer Frederick Wallace to chronicle the fishing industry in North America. But it was the race off Gloucester in 1892 that attained a legendary stature that made it the yardstick by which future races were measured. James Connolly did not witness the race, but he coined the phrase "the race it blew" when he wrote about it years later and modelled many fictional characters in his later books after the real-life participants in this race.

In the summer of 1892, the town of Gloucester was marking the 250th anniversary of its incorporation with a six-day celebration, capped off with a fishing-schooner race on August 26. Ten vessels entered to race the long, forty-one-mile triangular course that would take them around Massachusetts Bay. A southwest leg to Nahant Bay followed the start at Gloucester. From there, the route went south to Minot's Ledge and then returned to Gloucester along a seventeen-mile leg. There were two categories of vessels; the class of eighty-five feet (twenty-six metres) and over drew seven entries, and three competed in the eighty-five-foot-and-under. Most of the boats had arrived early to prepare, but one schooner, the *Harry L. Belden,* did not arrive in town until the evening before the race. Maurice Whalen, her skipper, had been out fishing for mackerel but was hit by light airs that delayed his arrival back home. Whalen had no time to off-load his cargo, let alone paint or trim his vessel.

On the morning of the race the weather appeared ominous, with a grey, scudding sky, slashing rain and, in answer to the prayers of many, plenty of wind. Governor William Russell of Massachusetts was to have been a guest on board one of the competing vessels, the *James S. Steele,* but after observing the conditions prudently declined the invitation. Off Eastern Point, the racing committee was tossed about in the heavy sea and could barely see the contestants for the wind and spray. As they waited for the start, none of the competitors saw fit to shorten sail in the growing breeze.

Then the race was on. It is said that the wind picked up to fifty knots halfway to Nahant Bay and the sea was getting wilder by the minute, with mountainous, white-capped waves washing over each vessel as she staggered along. The lead boat, the *Ethel B. Jacobs,* broke her main gaff while jibing around the first mark and was forced to take in her mainsail and retire from the course. Two others, the *Grayling* and the *James S. Steele,* also found conditions too trying and stood off with the spectators. The rest of the fleet managed to hang on as they headed towards Minot's Ledge with a howling gale just forward of the beam. Arthur Millet of the *Gloucester Daily Times* wrote:

> With every sheet hauled flat and every sail drawing, they pounded and staggered into the heavy seas, burying their bowsprits and washing decks at every jump. Lee rails were buried and the water was up to the hatches as the schooners laid over before the strength of the fierce northeaster. Sea after sea they shipped and sometimes dove into them to the foremasts.[9]

The madness continued as the remaining boats in the fleet pressed for home on a windward beat. Captain Tommie Bohlin, the skipper of the *Nannie C. Bohlin,* must have regretted shedding a few tons of ballast, since his vessel had difficulty staying upright in the storm-force winds. Nonetheless, he was hot on the tail of the *Belden,* which had taken over the lead from the *Ethel B. Jacobs.* Dr. William Hale, a guest on the *James S. Steele,* described the drama.

> During the long thrash to windward, every vessel sailed on her lee rail, with deck buried to the hatches. Huge seas broke continually over the staunch flyers and swept the decks. The brave, laboring craft would roll under surging seas to the second and third ratlines; then would follow awful moments of suspense, as the unflinching crew, with teeth set and hands clenched, watched to see if their craft would stagger up again, or go down under her grievous load. Desperate as the chances were, not a vessel luffed or reefed, as to be the first to reef would make her the laughing stock of the town, and there was not a skipper in the fleet who would not carry away both sticks rather than be branded as a coward.[10]

The *Belden,* with her eighty thousand pounds of mackerel on board, "stood up like a church" in the heavy weather as she made for the finish, but even as Whalen tacked one final time, his jib tore away and flogged to pieces as he passed the finish in the lead. Although it bordered on insanity to be racing in such conditions, it did prove one major point: In their ability to withstand such adverse conditions, the schooners had shown they were far superior to and much safer than the earlier designs, and schooner skippers would not miss a chance to prove it.

Sadly, by the second decade of the twentieth century the schooner fleet and the days of sail were coming to an end. There were good, rational and practical reasons to move into the power-driven era, and few would regret the old ways. The uncertainty and danger that went along with sailing was soon replaced by the predictability, safety and almost monotonous regularity of engine power. The industry could now be run with far less loss of life and property than in the past, but the dull, graceless hull of a dragger, powering along under a pall of smoke, could never replace the splendour of a schooner under full sail with a gut-load of fish, racing to market. Those who had sailed them loved them and mourned their passing.

NOTES

1 Garland, *Down to the Sea*, p. 5; Dear and Kemp, *Pocket Oxford Guide to Sailing Terms*, p. 159
2 Greenhill, *Schooners*
3 Chapelle, *American Fishing Schooners*, p. 64
4 Ibid., p. 64
5 Ibid., p. 136
6 Gordon McGowan, "Two Tall Ships," CBC interview, n.d.
7 Chapelle, *American Fishing Schooners*, p. 210
8 *Morning Chronicle*, August 18, 1871
9 *Gloucester Daily Times*, August 27, 1892
10 Hale, *Memorial of the Celebration*

‹ A BOISTEROUS SEA and a stiff wind were common fare to east coast schooner fishermen who spent their lives battling the elements to earn a living. The sturdy banks schooner was the workhorse of the North Atlantic. *Nova Scotia Archives and Records Management*

4

"A RACE FOR
REAL SAILORS": 1920

O N JULY 24, 1920, two slender-hulled sailboats jockeyed about in the turbulent waters off Sandy Hook, New York, awaiting a decision from the committee boat nearby. Both the British *Shamrock IV* and the American *Resolute* were rigged for weather, their mains reefed and storm sails forward. The masters of these two thoroughbreds watched for the sign that the race was on.

Begun in 1851 by the Royal Yacht Squadron in Cowes, England, the America's Cup series was the world's premier yachting event. The Yankee schooner *America*, sponsored by the New York Yacht Club, had sailed to Britain for the first race and won it, and American boats had held onto the cup ever since. The silver trophy, donated to the New York club in 1857 by the *America* syndicate, had been given the name "America's Cup" for the first winning boat. The 1920 series was the thirteenth since the inception of the race, and the Irish tea baron Sir Thomas Lipton was making his fourth attempt to return the coveted trophy to Britain. Sir Thomas had entered a succession of boats in the 1899, 1901 and 1903 series. In 1914 he had sailed the *Shamrock IV* across the Atlantic to compete, but the outbreak of World War I forced the cancellation of the race. The series had remained in limbo until the summer of 1920. Both the British and the American vessels matched to race before the war now had another chance. Spectator enthusiasm was ripe for such a contest in the post-war years, and the series proved to be an exciting match.

The first race was beset by thunderstorms, rain squalls and shifting winds. The *Resolute* led throughout, but as she came up to the last mark, the peak halyard on her main gaff parted and dropped, cutting off a good portion of the mainsail. The crew's effort to lower the rest of the sail and carry on with only a jib proved inadequate, forcing them to give up and retire from the course. Charles Adams, the *Resolute*'s skipper, was heavily criticized for not using more seamanship to at least finish the race.

The second contest brought light and fluky winds. The *Shamrock*'s start was spoiled when her large balloon jib became tangled and would not fill. William Burton, her master, ordered the crew to clear the sail, but it tore in the process and had to be removed. Meanwhile, the *Resolute* flew along with a fully filled ballooner, steadily inching away from her competitor. Burton jury-rigged a flying jib, which set well, and the *Shamrock* slowly gained on the sleek white hull of her competitor. She not only had to beat the *Resolute* but also to make up a seven-minute handicap assigned to compensate for the difference in hull length. When she crossed the finish line first, she did so to a roar from twenty-five thousand cheering spectators, winning the second race by two and a half minutes on corrected time in the best-of-five race series. With two wins to her credit, all the *Shamrock* needed was one more to take the cup home.

The next day, the public anticipated a spectacular contest and was not disappointed. The beat to windward was a long haul for the *Shamrock*, unable to point nearly as high as could the *Resolute*. She tacked almost twenty times to keep pace with the American boat. Downwind, it was another story. She flew along, steadily gaining on her rival, to cross the finish line in the lead, but not by enough to make up the handicap.

During the fourth race, the boats appeared evenly matched and both were superbly handled. Nathaneal Herreshoff, the aged designer of the *Resolute,* had appeared on the scene to oversee adjustments to her rigging and sail plan. The buoyed crew of the American boat worked her like clockwork and the *Resolute* took her second win by a full ten minutes.

The stage was now set for a nail-biter of a fifth race. With the series tied at two apiece, the public was in a frenzy of anticipation. The morning of Saturday, July 24, brought the first real wind of the series. The *Resolute* and the *Shamrock,* both with shortened sail, ventured out from the shelter of Sandy Hook into a boisterous seaway. The *Boston Globe* reporter wrote that "short work was made by both vessels on the run out to the light vessel, the 20-knot southwester carrying them along at express train speed... It was the kind of day that one reads that real sailormen like to weigh anchor in and head seaward with their craft carrying every sail."[1] Sails snapped loudly and nerves were pulled as tight as the halyards as the winds whipped through, while both crews watched for the start signal from the committee boat.

A *Toronto Telegram* sportswriter commented: "The race committee was in a quandary... it was rough, very rough. The committee possibly had some 'inside' information to that effect. And in this rough weather either vessel might break down. *Resolute* might break down. And that meant the loss of the cup... the committee made a seasick signal: 'Do you consent to the race being called off for the day?'"[2] Both skippers agreed. The regatta committee justified its ruling by stating that, with heavy seas sweeping the decks, great damage to the boats, and possibly loss of life among the crew, was a strong possibility.

The decision to call off the race was received by many with disappointment and disbelief. What should have been an exciting finish to a close series was, in the opinion of the spectators, ruined by the timidity of the racers. The *Toronto Telegram* reporter noted that "it was blowing only a wholesale breeze Saturday. Highest estimates of the wind velocity were 28 miles per hour. That is only 'half a gale' and the registering instruments were at a great level. On the lower level it is questionable if the wind was blowing harder than 20 knots."[3] The weather had not prevented local fishermen from being out in their small skiffs; nor had the fleet of spectators stayed away. It was reported that even a forty-foot (thirteen-metre) Long Island Sound schooner had carried full sail, and carried it well.[4] The cancellation and the ensuing hue and cry made the last race, when it was finally held on the following Monday, and won by the *Resolute*, into a mere footnote. The cup returned to its home at the New York Yacht Club, but the debate raged on.

The yachting pages in the North American papers were awash with discussion of what had become of the America's Cup series. The fact that these boats were too delicate to sail in anything but light winds troubled most devotees of the sport. The *Boston Globe* said that "neither *Resolute* nor *Shamrock* are like the cup boats of 25 years ago. They are of lighter construction and rigging and in addition have extremely tall rigs for boats of their length. Therefore they are not at all suitable for racing in strong breezes."[5] The correspondent for the *Toronto Telegram* was more critical when he wrote that Burton, as master of the *Shamrock*, could have done more to emphasize the absurd rules and conditions by insisting on a race. "It would have been worthwhile if he had split *Shamrock* from stem to stern doing so."[6] But it was the *New York Globe* that was most scathing when it referred to the contenders as "paper napkin" boats and suggested the race would have been far more exciting had it been held in a bathtub.[7] The public clearly wanted more from their heroes than mere competitiveness. They wanted a spectacle, a show of courage, steadfastness, resolve and mastery of the elements.

All this was not lost on the commercial fishing community, which was still dominated by the banks schooner. The fishermen's interest in the races was more professional. As men who worked under sail, they felt they had the credentials to assess the contest with a true sailor's eye. The cancellation became a popular topic of conversation in sail lofts, taverns and smoke-filled fo'c'sles in ports up and down the eastern seaboard. The series was discussed, chewed over and spat out in disgust by fishermen from Massachusetts to Newfoundland. To men who made their living at sea, it seemed ridiculous that sportsmen in their highly refined racing machines were cowed by a little bit of breeze. Twenty knots of wind would barely press the wrinkles out of the sails of a banks schooner. The timidity of the America's Cup yachtsmen was too much for the fishermen of the North Atlantic, and they began to talk about a real test, a contest between the men who worked the schooners that sailed the great offshore banks. Now that *would* be a race.

It was Colin McKay, the great-grandson of the famous clipper-ship designer Donald McKay, who brought the subject forward to the public when he wrote an editorial for both the *Halifax Herald* and the *Montreal Daily Star* on August 11, 1920, asking simply: "Why not a fishermen's race between Canada and United States?"[8] He suggested that such a race would be a fitting way of inaugurating a fishing treaty the two nations were expected to sign shortly, and he said the only conditions needed for such a race would be that the vessels have the same water-line length and sail plan as when they entered the fishery. This aroused a great deal of interest, and the idea was taken up immediately by magazines and newspapers all across the Maritime provinces. In the opinion of many, such a regatta would enhance the image of the fishery, stimulate improved vessel design and raise the profile of the North Atlantic fishing industry, inspiring more people to eat fish! Whatever the side benefits, the primary goal was expressed by the Sydney correspondent of the *Halifax Herald:* "Old salts and fishermen, he says, want to see a real race—not a lady-like saunter of fair weather freaks."[9]

William Dennis, the owner of both the *Halifax Herald* and Halifax's *Evening Mail*, had also reacted with derision when he read about the America's Cup fiasco. He agreed that the series had become far too refined and, focussing on the local fishery, proposed a true sailors' contest for the fishermen of Nova Scotia, a real ocean race, not of the "pink tea" variety that had recently been witnessed off New York.[10] The race could be a "sort of a preliminary canter to an International Sailing Race," to be held the following year between American and Canadian schooners, to be run off Halifax in the first week of October.[11] Only working, bona fide fishermen and true banks boats that had completed at least one full season offshore could participate. Dennis put up a cup with the cumbersome name "The Halifax Herald and Evening Mail Nova Scotia Fishing Vessel Championship Trophy" and promised to raise a suitable purse by public subscription. The course would be a large triangle, beginning in Halifax Harbour and running well out to the open ocean, beyond Chebucto Head, a true test of a vessel's sailing capabilities. Nine schooners, "the pride of the Lunenburg fleet," immediately signed up for the event.[12]

Public interest grew daily, and subscriptions for prize money came pouring in. It was believed by many that the event would put Halifax on the international stage. The excitement was tangible in every editorial and article on the subject. "Never in this generation has Nova Scotia attempted the like—It must be made a success." "They are making elaborate preparations to make the race the greatest event ever held in North American waters."[13] The organizers planned everything to the last detail: waterfront merchants and ship owners were requested to decorate their premises and boats; factories and ships were asked to blast their whistles; fire bells were to ring and cannons to fire from the Halifax Citadel when the boats neared the finish. Four forty-mile courses were mapped out, giving the race organ-izers alternative choices depending on the wind directions on the day of the race.[14]

Halifax was in the mood for celebration, as it was only just recovering from a devastating event in 1917. The city had been the North American staging point for convoys carrying troops, munitions and relief supplies to the battlefields in Europe. On the morning of December 6, 1917, the Belgian-relief ship *Imo* was departing Halifax Harbour when she collided with the incoming French muni-tions vessel *Mont Blanc*, carrying 2,500 tons of TNT, benzol, picric acid and gun cotton. Twenty minutes after the collision, when large crowds of citizens had gath-ered on the foreshore to watch the burning ships, the *Mont Blanc* erupted, causing the biggest man-made explosion of the pre-nuclear age. In a single moment, Hali-fax was transformed from a bustling wartime port into a shattered relic. The blast, which broke windows fifty miles away, immediately killed more than 1,600 people and injured 9,000 others. The whole north end of the city was levelled, and its people were crippled beyond belief. Relief poured in from the Canadian and Brit-ish governments and from as far away as New Zealand and China. Haligonians were most grateful for the quick response of a volunteer relief committee from the state of Massachusetts, which was among the first to deliver funds and goods to the stricken citizens. The rebuilding of the city was nearing completion by 1920, and its citizens were ready, willing and able to put the past behind them and to take on the joyful task of hosting such an important event.

In the United States, there was only passing interest in the proposed schooner race in Halifax, as most of the Massachusetts boats were then at sea. The fishermen of both nations used the same fishing grounds and caught the same catch, cod and halibut, but they processed the fish differently. The Nova Scotian crews worked a "salt fishery" that was seasonal, from early May until mid-September. Their boats would stay out for extended periods and, since their catch was split and salted down, there was no need for refrigeration. Fishermen came into port only when their holds were full or when they were in need of supplies such as salt or bait.

The Americans, on the other hand, had developed a fresh-fish industry. Boats went out for shorter periods and the catch was gutted, iced and delivered to port while it was still fresh. As theirs was a year-round occupation, when Nova Sco-tians started talking about schooner racing Americans were paying little attention. While the entire fleet was in port in Lunenburg, there were few boats alongside or at anchor in Boston and Gloucester. The first indication of any American interest

in the race up north was a small article in the *Gloucester Daily Times* on October 1, 1920, but aside from the writer, nobody seems to have taken much notice.

On October 11, nine boats—the *Delawana,* the *Gilbert B. Walters,* the *Alcala,* the *Mona Marie,* the *Bernice Zink,* the *Freda L. Himmelman,* the *Democracy,* the *Ruby Pentz* and the *Independence*—headed out into Halifax Harbour under a clear blue October sky. The local correspondent for the *Evening Mail* wrote:

> To the landlubber who awakened early this morning, the swishing curtains at the bedroom window bespoke a wind, and a wind meant a race… No tugs were needed to get the vessels from their berths today. Under part sail, they majestically rode from the docks. Out they came, one at a time, and each as trim and pretty as the other.[15]

With the wind blowing at about fifteen knots, whitecaps spread across the harbour and the sails of the great schooners flapped loudly as they waited for the start. Thousands of the citizenry crowded vantage points along the docks and out along the shore at Point Pleasant Park. The *Mail* reporter continued:

> It was a glorious day for such a grand event. The sky was never bluer, the sun was never brighter, the breeze was never more favourable and the weather man in general, never was in better humor than he was this morning, when the great sea classic for which thousands have awaited news for days, was started.[16]

It was nervous work as the nine schooners jockeyed about at the start in the fresh nor'westerly breeze. A signal indicating course number 1 was hoisted on the flag halyard at the breakwater and, at the gun, they were off.[17] The *Gilbert B. Walters,* with Captain Angus Walters at the helm, was first across the starting line. Forty-five seconds later, Captain Tommy Himmelman of the *Delawana* was hot on his heels. The breeze blew straight down the harbour and all the boats carried every stitch of canvas aloft. The schooners made a glorious sight as they headed out on the course, most of them running down to the Inner Automatic Buoy with their sails wing and wing. The romance of the occasion was not lost on reporters. "It was a sight for angels and men the way those boats made the buoy, their great sails bellying in the wind and giving a spread of white over the blue waters wonderfully fine."[18]

The fleet was now making a steady nine and a half knots out of the harbour. Even the venerable old committee boat, *Tyrian*, failed to keep up and steadily lost ground to the schooners. The *Walters* passed the first mark leading, with the *Delawana* close on her tail, followed by a progression of boats tight on her stern. Himmelman was pushing Walters hard, but lost ground passing the second mark, the Outer Automatic Buoy. On a beam reach to the Sambro Lightship Buoy, the boats increased speed to more than ten knots. Six of the fleet passed the third mark within seven minutes of each other. "The craft had all sail set and looked like great white and black birds in an elongated flock of life and action," stated the evening paper.[19]

But it was the *Delawana* and the *Walters,* "with spray flying in splendid sheen from the bows of each of the swiftly moving craft," that provided the real race.[20] Himmelman steadily gained on his rival, cutting the lead to one minute, forty seconds by the third mark. They now faced a windward beat down the harbour and headed towards the fourth mark with a wind blowing at twenty knots. It was hard to tell from the committee boat which was in the lead, but the *Walters* had the windward advantage. She was barely holding her own, however, as both vessels matched tack for tack up the harbour on the six-mile run to the finish. Eight minutes after passing the final buoy, the fore-topmast on the *Walters* snapped and came crashing down. Confusion on deck, as the crew sorted out the mess, meant even more time was lost. After over four hours of hard sailing, Tommy Himmelman passed his rival at Marr's Rock and proceeded to gain on every tack, crossing the finish line four minutes, twenty-seven seconds ahead. Whether the *Walters* would have beaten the *Delawana* with her fore-topmast undamaged is open to speculation, but Captain Walters showed nothing but high regard for the winning skipper and offered his hearty congratulations.

When the fleet returned to the harbour, the noise of the crowd, whistles, horns and sirens was deafening. The city went wild with delight and jubilation. The event had lived up to its promise, and Haligonians had every reason to be proud. A large banquet held at the Carleton Hotel in honour of the participants was attended by the lieutenant-governor, the city's mayor and many other local dignitaries. The idea of an international race was raised again and received with much enthusiasm, but with a winning schooner and crew ready to compete, a race committee already in place and the courses laid out, the obvious question was: why wait a year? William Dennis proposed holding the international series immediately and sent off a

challenge to the fishing fleet of Gloucester, offering as prize the "Halifax Herald North Atlantic Fishermen's International Trophy."

A sad end to the festivities occurred when the youngest skipper in the racing fleet drowned as his boat, the *Ruby Pentz,* left harbour the next day. Captain Calvin Lohnes was knocked overboard by the main boom and died before he could be rescued.

The good citizens of Gloucester, Massachusetts, opened their newspapers on October 13, 1920, to find a challenge from the Nova Scotia Ocean Racing Committee awaiting them:

> Committee in charge of ocean race met tonight and carefully considered all details of proposed race between a Nova Scotia fishing vessel and an American vessel. It was decided to hold the race over 40 mile course off Halifax not later than three weeks hence for a suitable silver trophy and a prize of $5,000, $4,000 to the winner and $1,000 to the loser, under the following conditions:

> 1. Vessel must be bonafide fisherman with at least one year's experience on the banks.
> 2. Vessels to carry inside ballast only.
> 3. Sails used in race to be made of commercial duck and be of no greater area than those in ordinary use on banks and to be limited to mainsail, foresail, jumbo, jib, jib topsail, and fore and main working gaff topsails and fisherman staysails.
> 4. Crew to be limited to 25 men.
> 5. Skipper to be bonafide fisherman captain with at least one year's experience on the banks.
> 6. Vessels to be not more than 150 feet overall.
> 7. Notification of acceptance of this challenge must be received within one week from receipt of these conditions.
> 8. Race to be sailed boat for boat without time allowances.
> 9. The decisions of the sailing committee on which you will have representation to be regarded as final in the interpretation of the above conditions.

> Please let us have definite answer by wire if you mean business and representatives of our committee will leave for Gloucester at once to arrange final details.[21]

‹ THE AMERICANS were caught unprepared by the challenge to participate in the proposed International Fishermen's Cup race, to be held in Halifax in the fall of 1920. They had few boats in port from which to choose and no time for an elimination race as most of their fishing fleet was still at sea. The schooner *Esperanto* was hurriedly made ready for the race and the legendary Gloucester skipper Marty Welsh was chosen to command her. *Wallace MacAskill, Nova Scotia Archives and Records Management*

This news was met with delight by the fishermen of the port of Gloucester, followed by lively debate as skippers and crews argued over which boats were the most likely candidates to represent their town. Even before the proposal was brought officially to the Board of Trade for discussion, a consensus among fishermen had it that schooners such as the *Stiletto*, the *Joffre*, the *Catherine Burke*, the *Esperanto* or the *Marechal Foche* could easily win against anything that Lunenburg could produce.[22] The Gloucester skippers wanted all the particulars so that the details could be worked out quickly. National pride was at stake! No red-blooded Yankee could turn down such a challenge. Nova Scotia and Massachusetts had long shared fishing grounds, mingling and jostling on the banks like jealous brothers at sea. Ironically, countless captains and crews of the American boats were former Maritimers or their relations who had headed south across the border in search of better pay or the exciting city life found in Boston and New York.

However, the challenge also represented for Gloucester a problem that lay in the nature of the year-round fishery. Most of the boats the town had in mind were either at sea or otherwise unavailable, and captains and crews were too occupied in making a living to take time out for racing. As they had not kept abreast of events in Canada, they were unprepared for the challenge. Although there were a few possible contenders available, there was too little time to organize an elimination race. With only days to spare, the fishing firm Gorton-Pew offered as challenger its schooner *Esperanto*, which had just arrived back in port. For captain they recruited the highly respected veteran Marty Welsh. The *Gloucester Daily Times* wired the *Halifax Herald* that the challenge had been accepted, and the *Herald* immediately answered that representatives were on their way to work out the details.

"A RACE FOR REAL SAILORS," declared the Halifax press. "Nova Scotia's Great Epic of the Sea."[23] This series promised the excitement and drama that the America's Cup race lacked; it would be a true ocean classic. No careful measurement of hulls or exhaustive comparisons with tape and rule. This would be a real race with no frills, no handicaps and no nonsense, a straight boat-for-boat affair with no favours given. It would be a true working man's race, sailed in the rough waters off Chebucto Head. The International Fishermen's Cup race, it was hoped, would easily eclipse the America's Cup in popularity. Gloucester's only addition to the rules was that instead of a single race, there should be a best-of-three series in order that the American crew, who were not as familiar with the waters off Halifax, should not be at a disadvantage.

Some Gloucestermen figured the odds were against them already, since the Nova Scotian boat was chosen, tested and in racing trim. Most, however, were decidedly optimistic about the odds and figured that, with any significant wind at all, their boat would be a runaway winner. When the *Esperanto* was hauled out of the water to have her propeller and shaft removed, she was soon beleaguered by a mob of curious Gloucester townsfolk, eager to inspect the challenger. A large gang of riggers, painters, caulkers, carpenters and sailmakers descended upon her to work late into the night, bringing her up to fighting trim in the short time left. It is doubtful whether any vessel in the port, before or since, has been given as exhaustive and thorough an overhaul in such a short time as was the *Esperanto*.

Although he had never before stepped aboard this schooner, the choice of Marty Welsh as skipper was met with universal approval along the waterfront. He was highly regarded as a fisherman and sail carrier who had worked in the industry since boyhood. There was no lack of talent from which to pick his crew. Eager captains and experienced fishermen all lined up to sign on in anticipation of a chance for glory. Comparing the experience and knowledge of the crews from both sides, the *Gloucester Daily Times* concluded that, though the Gloucestermen had a reputation along the coast for taking greater chances, "if the skipper of the Nova Scotian is the same Himmelman about whom they used to tell the story of knocking off the revenue cutter's figurehead with his main boom, the race is likely to be a lively one."[24]

The *Esperanto* came off the ways after her refit looking like a new boat. "Her spars and rigging and new paint glistened like a pot of gold in the early morning sun... One could hardly realize that she was the same *Esperanto* which came in less than two weeks ago after a long summer's hand lining trip to the Grand Banks."[25] On October 25, she slipped her moorings and headed out of the harbour to the roar of the thousands who had lined the docks. She was off to Halifax to win—or blow her sticks out in the attempt!

In Halifax, one would have been hard pressed to find anyone who did not have some opinion on the upcoming race. The newspapers were full of the progress of the Gloucester challenger, with articles covering everything from the refitting of the vessel to vignettes of the captain and crew. Journalists from all the over the east coast arrived to cover the race, and tourists packed the hotels. The *Boston*

Post alone sent one photographer and three reporters in an attempt to get as much coverage as possible. The young George Holland would write from the deck of the *Delawana;* James Brendan Connolly, the famous American writer of sea stories, was to be aboard the *Esperanto,* and James T. Kinsella, who was one of the best "waterfront" men in Boston, would follow the race from the committee boat. Frank Palmer Sibley, star reporter from the *Boston Globe,* arrived during the week to add his perspective, also from the deck of the American boat.

The *Delawana* departed from Lunenburg on Thursday with great fanfare, escorted by the *Gilbert B. Walters.* Like the *Esperanto,* the *Delawana* had had no end of willing hands to sand, paint and tidy her up. Even a prominent local clergyman was noticed wielding a paintbrush.[26] The small army of outfitters that boarded the vessel left nothing to chance. Everything that could be overhauled was stripped down and reassembled. A new topmast was stepped into place, the sails carefully mended, the topsides painted with a fresh coat of black and the underbody with a rich green, a broad three-inch white stripe indicating the waterline. Thus transformed from a traditional black-and-red fisherman to a snappy-looking racer, she sailed off to Halifax on Thursday morning anxious to meet her rival.[27]

When a grey dawn broke on the following Saturday, October 30, 1920, heavy cloud was hanging over the harbour. The wind that had raged all night had exhausted itself into a mere breath, and the *Delawana* and *Esperanto* lay quietly side by side at the Mitchell and Campbell wharves. The Union Jack and Old Glory hanging from their masts fluttered lazily in the zephyrs that floated down from the citadel. By seven, the boats were alive with activity as their crews readied them for the day. By the time the *Esperanto* was towed out into the stream, the first puffs of wind were ruffling the surface. The large crowd of Lunenburgers took this as a cue to begin chanting *"Delawana! Delawana!"* The two contenders, now out in the harbour, quickly hoisted sail in the growing wind and gracefully dipped their hulls into the swells.[28] The dozens of spectators who were dockside in the early hours had steadily grown in number, and the crowd now covered the breakwater and Point Pleasant Park so thickly that its presence actually changed the dark silhouette of the shoreline.

As the nine o'clock start approached, the light southwesterly breeze began to freshen, and the race committee raised the signal for course number 4.[29] The *Delawana* was leading slightly and leaning well over in the breeze, her captain working for the favourable windward berth. Marty Welsh calmly sucked on his pipe, watching the Lunenburger tacking and filling across the harbour, carefully observing local conditions before making his move. At the gun, the sun broke through the clouds and the sails of the two schooners glowed a brilliant white against the blue wavelets sparkling across the water. Forty seconds later, the *Delawana* surged across the line with *Esperanto* twenty-five seconds behind. As the boats shrank into the distance towards the first mark, the American was gaining.

Marty Welsh wrapped himself around the wheel of the *Esperanto* and did not relinquish it for a moment during the entire race. With his crew lying low along the windward rail and the lee scuppers awash, he caught the *Delawana* off the first mark. The men on the Canadian boat saw a fleeting glimpse of the gilt lettering on the stern of their rival when they rounded the Inner Automatic Buoy. Heading for the second mark, the Yankee was well away and sailing faster. " 'Don't let her beat us, Captain Tommy,' pleaded one of his men, appeal in heart and eyes."[30] The Nova Scotian crew was still hopeful they would catch her on the windward leg but began to fear the worst as the distance between the two vessels increased. If the lads on the *Esperanto,* tucked under the rail and hugging the deck, were feeling pleased with themselves, they did not show it—they still had a long way to go.

By the time the boats reached the open sea and the Outer Automatic Buoy, the wind had picked up to twenty knots. It was a long way short of the gale everyone hoped for, but at least it had some snap to it. On board the *Esperanto,* steadily gaining on the run down to the third mark off Shut In Island, "the white stuff was whish-shing past our quarter and more white stuff coming in fine waterfalls over our lee bow."[31] Although the crew of the *Delawana* admitted they might have met their match in the *Esperanto* in the off-wind work, they still had hopes that their boat would prove her worth during the windward leg.

Optimism returned to the crew of the Lunenburger as they watched the American boat falter around the third buoy. The wind shifted briefly while they were settling into the windward work. The *Delawana*'s gains on her run for the buoy were short-lived, for the *Esperanto* shook off her sluggishness and began to work to windward again. During that long, close-hauled leg, the Yankee did the most damage to the Nova Scotian boat, masterfully riding through the white-topped swells on her way to the last mark while the *Delawana* appeared to slam heavily and hesitate. "When Captain Himmelman went below for chow at noon he predicted the race's finish. She's way to windward. We'll not be coming on her no more today."[32]

Just after three o'clock, the *Esperanto* crossed the finish line to a huge roar from the crowd along the shoreline. It seemed all work in the city had ceased that day and the whole population had turned out to witness the spectacle. Throughout the race, the crew had been holding its collective breath until the last inshore buoy was cleared. At last the men were able to rise up and give the boat and skipper a fine cheer. She had beaten her rival on every point of sail.[33] The *Delawana* crossed the finish eighteen minutes later. As they came into the harbour there were filled eyes among the disappointed crew when they, too, received the cheers of thousands. "Passing the first dock Mate Roger Conrad leapt atop of a dory yelling, all together boys, three cheers for the *Esperanto* and remember Monday's another day!"[34]

After being beaten so decisively in Saturday's race, Himmelman decided to lighten the *Delawana* and replace the stone ballast with iron. As Sunday was a legal day of rest in Nova Scotia and no work was allowed, this had to be done surreptitiously. The captain had the boat towed out beyond Georges Island, where he and the crew discreetly set about the arduous task of removing the weight from inside her hull. One hundred and thirty tons of good Lunenburg stone was heaved, a bucket at a time, over the side. At four in the morning, the *Delawana* was hauled up to the dockyard, where sixty tons of chain was manhandled into her. On her return to Mitchell's wharf, her trim was further refined by adding more iron and bags of salt, bringing her slightly down at the head. The work finished just in time to hoist sail and make ready for the race. A decidedly lighter, better-trimmed *Delawana*—with an exhausted crew—was now ready to take on her rival.

The morning was foggy and grey, with a light westerly breeze. Despite the poor visibility, spectators were filling the vantage points along the shore. However, the lack of wind quickly raised doubt as to whether there would be a race at all. As the schooners slowly made their way to the start, the crew of the *Esperanto* commented on the increase in the green-painted underbody showing on the *Delawana*'s hull. "Sixty tons they say they have taken out her? Seems more like a hundred," Marty Welsh was heard to say. "Let this wind stay light and she'll worry us," reported writer Jimmy Connolly.[35] The wind was just tickling the surface of the harbour, barely creating a ripple, but blowing enough to give the craft headway as they closed in on the start. When the gun fired, Welsh got the jump on the Lunenburger, but only by a little over a minute.

Neither boat was making much headway, but the *Delawana* was footing faster. Eager to avenge her loss, the Canadian boat slowly and relentlessly closed on the

Yankee's quarter as they headed off on the same course as in the previous race. In a mere three minutes, the *Delawana* had overlapped her opponent, and in five she was well past and making better headway. There was no doubt that removing the ballast had improved her performance. When they came out from under the land and into a fresher breeze, both boats picked up the pace. As Himmelman rounded the first mark, his lead had improved by almost five minutes and, at the second mark, on a flat sea and in steady rain, she was one mile ahead. Desperate for wind and in true fisherman fashion, the men on the *Esperanto* appealed to the wind god by whistling loudly and tossing out coins.[36] Nerves were on edge as they watched their opponent increasing her lead.

On the third leg, the *Delawana* lost ground. Heavy mist had obscured the turning buoy off Shut In Island and, even with a lookout posted aloft in the spreaders, she overshot her mark by a good two miles, astonishing both the crew of the *Esperanto* and those on the committee boat. The *Esperanto*'s sailors could not believe their luck. By the time the Canadian finally found her bearings and made for the buoy, the American had gained and was closing on the leader. After rounding the mark, both skippers held well away to leeward of the next mark, fearing that the wind would come up from the west again and head them up. Well off the course, the vessels sailed towards the north shore. Three times the *Esperanto* attempted to come up the *Delawana*'s windward side, but Himmelman luffed and held her off. Since he did not have the speed to cross her bow, Welsh tried a different tactic and attempted to sail through her lee.

Coming up fast was a rocky shoal sticking out from Devil's Island. The *Esperanto*, on the *Delawana*'s lee, was pinched between her opponent—who was still playing the luffing game—and the breaking surf. Welsh could call for the right-of-way, as vessels cannot be forced ashore, but he chose to say nothing and hold his course. Presently his vessel was only two boat lengths off the beach, close enough to make the lightkeepers on the island light their lens to warn him off.[37] The *Delawana*'s continuing effort to crowd the *Esperanto* made the Halifax pilot aboard her nervous enough to warn Captain Welsh of the danger. Welsh nodded to signify he had heard the warning but continued on his course. He was now in so close that falling off would mean fetching up on the beach. Drawing a foot less than her opponent, the *Delawana* kept pushing her towards the shoaling water. "Captain, you have now less than a foot of water under your keel," said the pilot, and from aloft, Mikey Hall, the masthead man, yelled down that he could see the kelp on the bottom. Welsh looked at Russell Smith, whose father was part owner of Gorton-Pew, and said, "You represent the owners, Russell." To which Smith's response was blunt: "To hell with the owners." Welsh stuck to his course.[38]

Himmelman was also in a bind. If he held on too long, both ships were in danger of running aground, but if he came about, he would lose the coveted weather berth and possibly the race to his rival. Ultimately, he had no choice but to swing his vessel to port, allowing his opponent sea room. Both ships turned so tightly that the main boom on the *Esperanto* hung over the stern quarter of her rival.

With wind freshening, both vessels sheeted hard, running side by side for the next three miles to the last mark. When they rounded the Inner Automatic Buoy, they were so close that while the peak of the leader's gaff was flying the American flag, the bowsprit of the Canadian was over the stern of *Esperanto*. Both crews seemed to work in tandem, trimming sheets and beating it, tack for tack, in the driving rain up the harbour, but the *Esperanto* held the advantage in the windward work, and in six short miles she had gained so much on her rival that she finished seven minutes ahead. Whereas the first race had been a rather easy victory, this race had had it all: drama, brinkmanship, a crucial error and excellent seamanship. It was as fine a race as anyone could ask for and a fitting end to the series.

The following day a luncheon held at the Halifax Hotel to present the cup and to honour the contestants was attended by dignitaries such as the mayor of Halifax, the lieutenant-governor, the premier of Nova Scotia and a representative of the governor of Massachusetts. Grand speeches were made extolling the fine nature of the contest and the sportsmanship shown by both sides. Lavish praise was heaped on the winning skipper, Captain Marty Welsh, who sat through the occasion with his face flushed, embarrassed by all the attention. The general manager of Gorton-Pew Fisheries, Mr. Carroll, who accepted the cup on behalf of the owners of the *Esperanto*, spoke enthusiastically of her captain: "No better man ever sailed out of any harbour in the world. No better man ever walked the deck of a vessel or the streets of a city." Welsh was then called upon to respond. The highly skilled mariner, able to face any manner of danger at sea, was clearly out of his element. "He gurgled in his throat in the effort to speak, but couldn't make it. So he just bobbed his head a couple of times, grinned amiably and sat down again and the guests nearly took the roof off at his eloquence."[39]

A giant siren that had been set up outside the *Times* office in Gloucester was cranked up at the news of the triumph. Soon every bell and whistle in the town was pealing out in "the greatest conglomeration of noise since the armistice was signed."[40] Schoolchildren just dismissed from classes were dancing in the street, and staid old fishermen were shouting and laughing with delight.[41] When the *Esperanto* arrived back several days later, a victory broom tied to her masthead, she was greeted like a conquering hero. A huge banquet was held in the drill hall of the State Armoury where, once again, the reluctant man of the hour, Marty Welsh, blushed brilliantly with every compliment bestowed upon him. The American vice-president-elect, Calvin Coolidge, saw the bravery and courage of the crew as a "Triumph of Americanism… Your wonderful victory shows to all the world what Massachusetts stands for and what America is bound to accomplish."[42] The victory was hailed by every newspaper across the United States. The *New York Tribune,* at the end of a long editorial, nominated the win as "the supreme sporting event of 1920."[43] In Nova Scotia, however, the mood was quite the opposite. Devastated by the unexpected defeat, plans were already underway to make certain America would not keep the cup for long.

NOTES

1 *Boston Sunday Globe*, July 25, 1920

2 *Toronto Telegram*, July 25, 1920

3 Ibid.

4 Ibid.

5 *Boston Globe*, July 25, 1920

6 *Toronto Telegram*, July 25, 1920

7 *New York Globe*, July 25, 1920

8 *Montreal Daily Star*, August 11, 1920; *Halifax Herald*, August 11, 1920

9 *Canadian Fisherman*, September 1920, p. 195

10 *Toronto Telegram*, October 2, 1920

11 *Canadian Fisherman*, September 1920, p. 190

12 *Evening Mail*, October 5, 1920

13 Ibid.

14 See course maps, pp. 230–31

15 *Evening Mail*, October 11, 1920

16 Ibid.

17 See course maps, pp. 230–31

18 *Evening Mail*, October 12, 1920

19 Ibid.

20 Ibid.

21 *Gloucester Daily Times*, October 13, 1920

22 *Gloucester Daily Times*, October 14, 1920

23 *Evening Mail*, October 19, 1920

24 *Gloucester Daily Times*, October 19, 1920

25 *Gloucester Daily Times*, October 23, 1920

26 *Halifax Herald*, October 26, 1920

27 *Evening Mail*, October 26, 1920

28 *Evening Mail*, October 30, 1920

29 See course maps, pp. 230–31

30 George Holland, *Boston Post*, November 1, 1920

31 James B. Connolly, *Boston Post, Evening Mail*, November 1, 1920

32 Holland, *Boston Post, Evening Mail*, November 1, 1920

33 Connolly, *Boston Post, Evening Mail*, November 1, 1920

34 Holland, *Boston Post, Evening Mail*, November 1, 1920

35 Connolly, *Boston Post, Evening Mail*, November 2, 1920

36 Frank P. Sibley, *Boston Globe*, November 2, 1920

37 Ibid.

38 Connolly, *Boston Post*, November 2, 1920

39 Sibley, *Boston Globe*, November 3, 1920

40 *Gloucester Daily Times*, November 1, 1920

41 *Gloucester Daily Times*, November 2, 1920

42 *Gloucester Daily Times*, November 9, 1920

43 *Canadian Fisherman*, November 1920

5

THE LUNENBURG FLYER: 1921

NOVA SCOTIANS were left shocked and humbled by the defeat of their beloved *Delawana*. To have their boat so soundly beaten, and the new trophy whisked out of their arms with such apparent ease, had been unthinkable. Race enthusiasts did not take long to figure out that the boats in the large Lunenburg fleet were too heavily modelled to be real competition for the Americans. Nova Scotian craft were designed for packing large quantities of cargo rather than for fast sailing. In summer these boats were out for months at a time salt fishing, and in the winter they carried dried fish or lumber south to the West Indies and South America, bringing salt back to Canada on the return trip. A schooner that could pay its way with large cargoes usually had only moderate sailing

qualities. The type of craft preferred in Gloucester, by contrast, was generally smaller and quicker than the Nova Scotians', with less cargo capacity and an ability to engage in the quick turnaround of the fresh-fish industry, so vital to the economy of the eastern U.S. fishery. Speed was essential to the Americans, and the Nova Scotians realized they needed a finer hull design to compete.

It is said that within ten minutes of the *Esperanto* crossing the finishing line, funds were committed to the building of a worthy contender for the next series.[1] A group of like-minded Nova Scotians, drawing on the affectionate nickname for the people of their province, formed the Bluenose Schooner Company to fund the building of the new boat and invited Captain Angus Walters, the feisty Lunenburg skipper of the *Gilbert B. Walters,* to sign on as her master. A young naval architect named William Roué was approached and asked to design a schooner that would outsail any fisherman afloat. Roué was familiar with the races, as he had sat on the sailing committee of the first series, but he was more of a hobbyist than a full-fledged designer, his primary income coming from his family's soft-drink business. Despite his lack of experience as a naval architect, he had successfully designed a small number of yachts and working boats; he realized that taking on something as large as a banks schooner would be an opportunity to make his name, so he threw himself into it heart and soul. By December 1920 he had presented his plans to Walters and the company and won their approval—scarcely dreaming of the impact his schooner design would have on the outcome of the races of the coming years, nor of the resulting fame that would come his way.

The conclusion of the 1920 races had brought about several changes to the organization of the event. The first series had been thrown together quickly with little thought to the future interpretation of the dozen or so rules that dictated how the races would be run.[2] With the huge success of the event, and its continuation apparently assured, William Dennis and his committee set about drafting a proper deed of gift for the disposition of the trophy.[3] A testament to the importance of the International Fishermen's Cup is the list of trustees set down in the deed; they include the premier of Nova Scotia, the mayor of Halifax and the governor of Massachusetts.[4] The rules regarding the qualification of vessels were tightened, with the intention of keeping the competition fair, limiting the races to "bona fide" fishermen and keeping out "freak" vessel designs that could threaten the character of the series. Several of the changes had a significant impact on future races: the overall length of vessels was reduced from 150 to 145 feet (45.73

< **THOUSANDS** crowded the Lunenburg shore around the Smith and Rhuland shipyard in March 1921 to witness the launching of the schooner *Bluenose*. Built to beat the Americans in the Fishermen's Cup races, she proved to be not only fast under her wily skipper, Angus Walters, but also one of the highline fishermen on the coast. *Wallace MacAskill, Nova Scotia Archives and Records Management*

to 44.20 metres), the all-important maximum waterline length was set at 112 feet (34.15 metres) and the vessel draft limited to 16 feet (4.88 metres). The most technical change came with the measurement of the total sail area, which was to be no bigger than 80 per cent of the square of the waterline length as expressed in feet. Although this rule did not apply to vessels built prior to 1920, it affected all vessels built after that date and later led to a major disruption in the series.

In December the keel of the new Nova Scotian vessel was laid at the Smith and Rhuland shipyard in Lunenburg, and on the nineteenth of the month the governor general of Canada, the Duke of Devonshire, arrived from Ottawa to drive in the ceremonial spike. The solemnity of the occasion was somewhat diminished by the actions of some His Excellency's friends, who had absconded with him prior to the event and plied him with drink. When he was called upon to perform the deed, he found that his spirit was willing but his eyesight was not—he missed the spike with the first swing of the maul, much to the dismay and disapproving looks of the staid spectators in the crowd. After several more equally errant and dismal attempts, a kind soul rescued the heavy maul from his grasp and drove the spike home.[5]

Angus Walters fussed over his new boat through all stages of construction, like a worried mother over a newborn child. When the ribs of the 143-foot (43.6-metre) schooner began to take shape, Walters insisted on one controversial change: he required the freeboard in the bow to be raised by eighteen inches (forty-five centimetres) to provide more headroom in the fo'c'sle for the crew. This fuelled speculation later that the change greatly enhanced the boat's windward capabilities. However, it is unlikely that this modification significantly improved her sailing performance, though it did make the boat drier forward and the fo'c'sle more comfortable. On March 26, 1921, Audrey Smith, Walters's niece and the daughter of the shipbuilder, Richard Smith, christened the glistening black hull of the *Bluenose*. The people of Nova Scotia were known on the east coast as "Bluenosers," perhaps referring to the blue mittens worn at sea—often used to wipe runny noses—or perhaps to noses made blue by the frigid temperatures. In front of hundreds of onlookers, the vessel slid down the ways and into the placid waters of Lunenburg Harbour.

Angus Walters was not the only Nova Scotian captain caught up in racing fever. Captain Joe Conrad, a popular skipper from LaHave, postponed his retirement and engaged the seventy-one-year-old designer and builder Amos Pentz to draw up plans for another contender. On April 6, the powerful-looking, 138-foot (42-metre) hull of the *Canadia* slid down the ways of the old McGill shipyard in Shelburne. Admirers found her hull a little finer and a trifle racier than anything previously turned out by Pentz, and on her shakedown cruise she made a very fast run from LaHave to Halifax, proving she was a more than capable sailer. Word also came in from Newfoundland that at least one vessel would be ready from that colony for the elimination races in October. No matter where one went in fishing circles, the chief topic of conversation was fast fishing schooners.

In the United States, excitement was brewing over a new vessel under construction in the J.F. James and Son yard in Essex, Massachusetts. Work on this schooner, the *Mayflower*, had not begun until February 4, allowing little time for completion considering the necessity of putting in a full season of fishing to qualify for the races. She was backed by a group of disgruntled Boston businessmen who had felt more than a little put out that the 1920 series had been offered exclusively to the Gloucester fleet. "It seems that the Gloucester people have felt right all along that the international races were intended solely for Gloucester and Nova Scotia fishing vessels," said an editorial in the *Atlantic Fisherman*.[6] Fred Pigeon, who headed Schooner Mayflower Associates, hired the distinguished yacht designer Starling Burgess to draw up plans for a fast fishing schooner that was to be built with Boston money and crewed and captained by Boston men. Only modern methods were to be employed in her construction; she was to be engineered with mathematical precision instead of the rule-of-thumb shipyard techniques that were then the norm. Due to the tight time frame, a gang of Boston shipwrights was brought up to Essex to rush construction along, something that did not sit well with the local shipyard workers.

Grumbling about the Boston boat began from the outset, the main bone of contention being that the *Mayflower* was too "yacht-like." In fact, all the new vessels—the *Bluenose* and the *Canadia* included—were coming under fire for being "racers" and not true "banks" schooners, but it was the *Mayflower* that looked the most radical and bore the brunt of the criticism. The Cape Ann fishermen were the most vocal in their condemnation, due perhaps in part to what they perceived as the superior attitude of the Bostonians. The Gloucester fishermen had yet to decide which boat was to represent them in the upcoming races. A Boston magazine patronizingly admonished the old fishing community for not coming up with an entry. "Too bad Gloucester is not represented by a vessel of her own. Somehow the prospect of a fishermen's race without a Gloucester entry loses much of its charm."[7] That must have ratcheted up regional resentment by a few notches!

In lengthy editorials, the Boston papers attempted to deflect any criticism of what they considered their boat, but this proved to be an uphill battle. Much was made of the *Mayflower*'s "radical design," referring to her shorter, stubby transom, intended to reduce pounding in a seaway. A dolphin striker and upswept laminated spreaders added to her yacht-like appearance. In an attempt to silence opposition, the owners invited delegations of race trustees to visit Essex to view the launching. The Canadian delegation, arriving on a boat from Yarmouth on April 11, was met at the dock by Wilmot Reed, the secretary of the Gloucester committee. The *Mayflower* representatives arrived shortly afterwards, and the heated discussion between them and Reed ended with Reed left alone on the steamship wharf and the embarrassed Canadians, in the company of the Boston men, departing for their hotel.[8] Among the Canadian group was William Roué, the designer of the *Bluenose,* and he, along with the others, had ample time to examine the hull on the slipway before the launch. Eight thousand spectators were on hand the following day to watch the *Mayflower* be christened by the designer's daughter, Starling Burgess, and slide gracefully into the Essex River.[9] Unfortunately, the long-winded speeches had thrown off the schedule, and the falling tide had lowered the water level in the river enough for the vessel to become stuck on a mudbank half a mile away from the shipyard. As Dana Story, whose father owned the shipyard next door, suggested years later, "perhaps it was an omen of things to come."[10]

After inspecting the *Mayflower,* the Canadian delegation declared themselves satisfied that there was no material difference in the construction of this boat and that of any other American fishing schooner. They kept well clear of the conflict between Boston and Gloucester by saying her eligibility for the coming international race was up to the Americans, and thus in the hands of the race committee in Gloucester. The *Mayflower* was towed to the famous T-wharf in Boston, where a swarm of riggers worked furiously to step new masts and rig her for sea. The vessel had less than a month to be on her way to the banks to put in a full season fishing. A constant crowd of admirers looked on as work progressed, and the general opinion was that the fine, smooth hull looked every inch a match for anything on the sea. At 143 feet (43.6 metres), she equalled the new Canadian schooners, *Bluenose* and *Canadia,* in almost every respect, including sail area.

> ▸ **THE SCHOONER** *Mayflower* was built to take on the Canadians in 1921 but was barred from racing for being too yacht-like. Gloucester fishermen refused to sail against the Boston-owned boat in an elimination series to choose a defender and the Canadian trustees denied her bid to participate in the series. She carried a dolphin striker forward, laminated spreaders and a truncated stern that was not in keeping with the traditional design of the fishing schooner. *Edwin Levick, Mariners' Museum, Newport News, Virginia*

On April 28, two days before the deadline, her master, Henry Larkin, took his vessel out to sea, heading first to Shelburne, Nova Scotia, to pick up two crew members. Shortly after leaving Gloucester Harbour, he came across Felix Hogan, an old friend, in command of another recently built Essex schooner, the *L.A. Dunton*. Hogan suggested a race to Shelburne, and Larkin was more than eager to oblige. The two vessels set off in thick weather and lumpy seas but did not stay together for long. The *Mayflower* soon showed her heels to the *Dunton*, making her way alone in the heavy headwinds and lying snug in Shelburne Harbour a full seven hours before the *Dunton* arrived. The following day both vessels headed out together again, this time to Canso to take on ice. The Boston boat once more proved herself handy in a breeze and beat the *Dunton* by nine hours. Canso in Nova Scotia was the end of the race; the boats parted ways and the *Mayflower* went on to the Magdalen Islands for bait before sailing to the Grand Banks.[11]

Despite her time as a working boat, the controversy around the *Mayflower* would not go away. She was still thought to be a "schooner-yacht" and her efforts at the fishery were met with suspicion; she was accused of heading to the Grand Banks only to lounge around and catch a token amount of fish in order to comply with the rules. However, as the Canadian delegation had given her the thumbs-up, the American committee had little choice but to allow the schooner to participate in the upcoming elimination race to choose the official defender. Local resentment persisted, and the Gloucester masters and crews demonstrated their anger by vowing not to race the *Mayflower*. In their opinion, she was little more than a camouflaged yacht, and the competition between her and a bona fide schooner would not be fair. With no competitors, the race was cancelled and the *Mayflower* was declared the defender by default.

The trustees of the international trophy in Halifax had been happy to let Boston and Gloucester fight it out over the eligibility of the *Mayflower,* no doubt expecting that the Boston boat would eventually be disqualified. Now that she had been declared the defender, they were forced to face their own concerns about the vessel. Even though their delegation had given the *Mayflower* a clean bill of health, members of the fishing fraternity of Nova Scotia became more and more sceptical about her right to call herself a genuine schooner. As early as May, editorials in the *Halifax Herald* began to voice an opinion on the matter and questioned whether, by permitting the *Mayflower* to race, the series would deviate from its mandate as a venue for honest-to-goodness fishermen. In an attempt to shake off the growing criticism that his schooner was unable to withstand the rigours of winter fishing, Captain Larkin of the *Mayflower* threw out an open challenge to all other fishermen for an open-sea contest to be held at any time of the year. He specifically targeted Angus Walters, as his vessel was the biggest of the new Canadian schooners. Walters apparently agreed, but suggested a race "with a cargo of salt fish from Newfoundland to Brazil, thence to Turk's Island for a lading of salt to be carried to a port in Nova Scotia."[12] Neither skipper followed up on the other's offer. By mid-September, the decision had been made by the trustees to refuse the American entry on the grounds that her design was too yacht-like and extreme for a fisherman and her inclusion would violate the spirit of the deed of gift. Besides, they decided, she had taken too long to get to the banks to start fishing. Representatives of the *Mayflower* were dispatched to Halifax to plead her case, but to no avail. The American race committee, heavily weighted in Gloucester's favour, had plenty of chances to protest the Canadian decision but was only too happy to accept the judgement. It moved quickly to strip the *Mayflower* of her title of cup defender.

The Americans reorganized an elimination contest off Gloucester for mid-October. Five local schooners entered: the *Arthur James*, the *Elsie*, the *Philip P. Manta*, the *Elsie G. Silva* and the *Ralph Brown*. There was certainly no question that all of these schooners were "bona fide" fishermen; not one was less than five years old, and the oldest, the *Philip P. Manta* from Provincetown, had been built in 1902. Her good-natured captain, Ben Pine, had never skippered a fishing schooner before and had borrowed her for the races. He knew the elderly little schooner would not be a match for the others, but he was eager to participate. The clear favourite now was the little *Elsie,* whose masterful skipper, Marty Welsh, had commanded the *Esperanto* to victory the year before. Sadly, the *Esperanto* herself was missing from the contest. On May 30 she had hit a submerged wreck off Sable Island in heavy fog and sunk shortly after; the crew escaped in dories just before she went down. Ironically, the vessel that rescued them was none other than the *Elsie.* On October 12 and 14, she handily won both races in the elimination contest, fairly romping around the course and leaving her adversaries in her wake. The eleven-year-old veteran of the banks was formally declared the cup defender.

Enthusiasm for the international race may have dimmed somewhat in Boston with the exclusion of its vessel, but the people of Gloucester were over the moon about their entry. Boston papers initially groused about the unfairness of it all but

were soon caught up in the spirit and gave over the front page for coverage. Racing fever was definitely in the air. The only question remaining was which Canadian boat the *Elsie* would be facing. Eight schooners had entered to race in the elimination Nova Scotia Fishing Schooner Regatta: the *Uda R. Corkum*, the *Bluenose*, the *J. Duffy*, the *Donald J. Cook*, the *Independence*, the *Canadia*, the *Alcala* and the old favourite, the *Delawana*. All the boats were handy and fast, but the two new ones, *Bluenose* and *Canadia*, were considered the ones to watch. The *Canadia*, with her bottle-green hull, looked smart and capable, her clean, true lines inspiring as much confidence as did her master, Captain Conrad, the venerable old salt who had nearly six decades of schooner fishing behind him. The *Bluenose*, the other favourite, was sparred and rigged to a queen's taste. Everything about her was perfect, from the truck to the keel—"fit to be put on a mantle [sic]," as one wag declared.[13] She was not yet ready for Captain Walters, who, determined not to be defeated for a second time, took the vessel through a trimming spin and adjusted her ballast. Another vessel worth watching was Captain Albert Himmelman's *Independence*, sporting a new bowsprit that would definitely improve her windward work from the previous year's. Her informal sorties with the *Bluenose* outside the harbour had caused much excitement. And, of course, the *Delawana* was not to be discounted. Since 1920's races, she had acquired a much larger mainsail and a new thirty-foot (nine-metre) keel shoe that would help her keep a greater grip on the wind. As news broke from Gloucester of the *Elsie*'s win, anticipation intensified at the thought of another contest against Marty Welsh.

In the first race of the Canadian eliminations the *Bluenose* demonstrated her superiority, winning by four minutes ahead of her nearest rival, the *Canadia*. The second race was decidedly different. The *Delawana* put up a game fight and took an early lead, holding onto it during the runs and reaches. It must have given the backers of the new boats pause to see their vessels upstaged by the old-timer. Not until the windward thrash did the *Bluenose* wake up and take off like a scared dog to the finish, crossing the line fifteen minutes ahead of the fleet after four and a half hours of sailing. Her nose for weather showed her to be a true sea hound. Unfortunately, the *Canadia* made a poor showing. Her ballast had been badly distributed and she proved exceedingly tender in the choppy seas, disappointing both captain and crew. She followed her rival across the finish line forty-five minutes later. It was obvious that the design of the *Bluenose* gave her a distinct advantage over the others in the Lunenburg fleet. She seemed to come alive in the

‹ IF CARRYING SAIL alone could win a race, the *Elsie* would have prevailed in the 1921 series, but she needed more hull in the water, not more sail aloft. In a fruitless attempt to overhaul the *Bluenose*, her skipper had crowded on more sail than was prudent and, over-canvassed, she lost her fore-topmast in the heavy wind. Her bow plunging deeply, Welsh continues with the race as his crew fights to drag in the headsails. *Wallace MacAskill Collection, Nova Scotia Archives and Records Management*

windward work, especially in rough water and choppy seas. Gloucestermen had long held the view that, compared with their own sleeker, faster craft, the Nova Scotian boats were comfortable and stable sea-going arks: "Great vessels to pack a cargo of fish, ye know, but not much for travelling."[14] News of the *Bluenose* win made them sit up and take notice.

As the *Elsie* and her crew made their way up the coast to Halifax, grumbling began to surface from the New York papers about the differences between the two vessels. The complaints that had been made about the *Mayflower* now found their way to another target; the familiar charge was that the *Bluenose* had been specifically designed to win the race and the *Elsie* was built solely as a deep-sea fisherman. The *Bluenose* was much larger than the Gloucester boat, with a longer waterline and much more sail, and then there was the issue of the eleven-year age difference between the two. "It is a simple matter to argue from this that the *Bluenose* should be faster than the *Elsie*," said the *New York Herald*.[15]

Critics agreed that the real test would occur when the skills of Marty Welsh were pitted against those of Angus Walters. Welsh had a reputation as a remarkable sail handler in rough weather. In Halifax, speculation about the two vessels grew every day and, by the time the *Elsie* arrived on October 20, superlatives used to describe the features of the ship and the character of her captain were causing a good deal of nervousness in the Canadian camp. Rumour had it that the *Elsie* had topped the unlikely speed of seventeen knots during her voyage north. Reports of Welsh's crew's extraordinary ability to handle sail must have given the jitters to Walters. He recruited Commander Beard, the captain of the Canadian naval destroyer *Patriot*, to drill his crew in sail handling and tacking. Hours were spent in Bedford Basin in the early mornings before the race with Beard running the *Bluenose* crew through its paces.[16]

Walters had a formidable reputation himself. He had been only thirteen in 1895 when he had first gone fishing and was still in his early twenties when he became master of his first ship. He was known as a "driver," a no-nonsense, hardnosed skipper with a flinty character and a caustic edge to his tongue. He was blessed with a remarkable ability to carry sail and a sixth sense when it came to fishing; his vessel was always amongst the top boats when the biggest catches of the season were reckoned.

The *Elsie*, designed by Thomas McManus, was built in Essex, Massachusetts, in 1910. She was a smart-looking vessel, lean and low in the sides, with black topsides, a red underbody and a broad green strip along her waterline. Her white hawse pipes made a distinctive feature at the forward end. In contrast, the *Bluenose* had longer overhangs, higher sides and a lengthier hull. Her black body carried a yellow moulding stripe with a white boot-top and a copper-brown underbelly. Once Welsh caught sight of the *Bluenose*, the size of the schooner, nearly twenty feet (six metres) longer than his own, must have given him pause for thought. However, the dimensions of the *Bluenose* were not unusual. Nova Scotian boats were generally larger than the Americans', and nearly a fifth of the Lunenburg fleet was of similar size. The two boats may not have been evenly matched as far as size went, but the Gloucester vessel had exceedingly sweet lines, and her sails fit like a glove. Neither captain nor crew of the *Elsie* voiced any objection to the *Bluenose*.

Saturday, October 22, 1921, was crisp and frosty, with a fresh breeze. It was the perfect day for a race, the northwest wind rising from twenty to thirty knots as the race progressed over the forty-mile course off Halifax. Everything that could float was on the water: Government steamers, cable ships, fishing boats, yachts, tugs and ferries—all loaded heavily with spectators—wallowed near the start. At the five-minute gun, both schooners swung into position, the *Elsie* easing her sheets and running the line towards McNab's Island, while all on board hoped for the seconds to pass quickly. The signal cannon from the breakwater sounded the start and Welsh cranked over the helm, shooting over the line ten seconds later. With the Stars and Stripes snapping at the main peak and a twenty-knot nor'westerly snorting over her starboard quarter, the *Elsie* flew down the course as if she had an engine in her. She was several boat lengths ahead of the *Bluenose* at the outset. Observers aboard the steamer *Lady Laurier* felt the Nova Scotian had been caught napping and began to experience that unpleasant "all gone" sensation.[17]

However, it was not long before the *Bluenose* perked up and fairly smoked after the *Elsie*. A luffing match on the broad reach for the first mark ended when the *Elsie* crossed over her opponent's bow and took the weather berth. Walters attempted to pass on her weather side, but Welsh sheeted in and stood up towards the unyielding granite rocks of the western shore, two miles to windward of the course. Walters put his wheel hard up and swung across the *Elsie*'s wake, making for the Inner Automatic Buoy. The *Elsie* followed suit and covered her rival. The two fairly flew across the water, all sails filled in the stiff quartering breeze and hulls rolling heavily in the deep chop. "The end of *Bluenose*'s 80-ft. boom was now in the water, now half way up to the masthead as she gained on her rival. The

Elsie rolled still harder and three times brought her main boom across the *Blue-nose's* deck, between the fore and main rigging."[18] It was a constant battle for the weather berth, with members of both crews either handling lines or working aloft or hugging the windward rails. Anyone daring to raise his head above the weather rail on the *Bluenose* caught the edge of Walters's caustic tongue. The skippers strained at the wheels of their vessels, see-sawing back and forth in increasingly heavy seas. Walters finally gave up the fight for the windward berth and managed to shoot past the *Elsie* by coming up under her lee. By this time, both vessels were logging twelve to thirteen knots, the *Elsie* a mere minute and a half astern of the *Bluenose* as she rounded the Inner Automatic Buoy.

As they turned the mark, the wind piped up to twenty-five knots. It was a good fisherman's sea, with plenty of "lop" to it. The competitors eased off on their sheets for the run to the Outer Buoy, just over six miles away. Every kite was flying, booms were off to port and lee rails buried in the boisterous sea. The spray smoked off the crests at each plunge. It must have been a wild ride for the masthead men, whipped around the sky in that cool October wind. The *Elsie* stuck to the stern of her rival and hung on during the run to the second mark. At times, the *Bluenose* would haul ahead and then the *Elsie* would come up on her weather side, her main boom dipping over the stern of her rival. Back and forth they went. As they neared the mark, both doused their staysails and clewed up the fore-topsails, preparing to jibe around the buoy. The big Lunenburger rounded first, followed a mere thirty seconds later by the tough little Gloucesterman. "The great booms swung across the decks and fetched up on the patent gybers with staggering shocks as the crews roused the sheets in for the reach to Shut In Island bell buoy."[19] It was during this leg that the *Bluenose* began to run away from the defender, and she made the nine-mile reach in just forty-two minutes, taking the buoy two minutes ahead of her opponent.

Now began the real test: the thrash to windward. The ability to drag herself off a lee shore in a gale and claw her way to safety proves the real worth of any vessel. When the *Bluenose* rounded the mark and sheeted in hard on a starboard tack for the upwind trial, the wind was cresting at thirty knots. Her staysail and fore-topsail doused, and a roaring "bone in her teeth," the *Bluenose* began plunging into the heavy sea, burying her lee rail. The *Lady Laurier* observers could see her entire deck as she heeled to an angle of forty degrees. The boat appeared to revel in it, her long body punching through the heavy sea and her crew stuffed up under

the windward rail "like bats to a barn rafter," with Walters and his mate at the lee and weather sides of the wheel.[20]

As he passed the mark, Welsh threw his helm over and quickly hoisted his ballooner. The old *Elsie* rolled over onto the starboard tack with every sail aloft. Welsh could not have enjoyed seeing the big Lunenburger flying away from him and desperately raced after her. If carrying more sail alone could win a race, it would have been the *Elsie*'s.

In his article for *Yachting* magazine, F.W. Wallace wrote:

> Now there is this difference between a fisherman and a skilled yachtsman. The latter knows something about the science of spreading canvas and will forebear to drive his craft under a press of sail when she will make better sailing without too much muslin hung. Not so with the average fishing skipper. He is out to carry the whole patch and nothing gladdens his heart so much as to see his hooker lugging the whole load with her lee rail under and everything bar-taut and trembling under the strain. A roaring bow wave, a boiling wake, and an acre of white water to loo'ard looks good to him, and he often imagines this to be a sign that his vessel is smoking through it at a rate of knots.[21]

Perhaps these skippers lacked the refinement of the yachtsman, but they had far more experience and skill in handling their boats under these rugged conditions. The America's Cup contenders would most certainly have been hunkered down under the lee of Sandy Hook waiting for the weather to settle. This was not the environment for those fined-tuned yachts, but a real fishermen's race that James Connolly later called "the greatest race ever sailed over a measured course."[22]

The combination of wind and too much sail proved to be more than the *Elsie* could bear. First to go was her jib topsail halyard. As a crewman scampered out onto her bowsprit to re-reeve the halyard, the bow plunged deeply into the sea, burying the bowsprit to the third hank of her jib. Moments later, the foremast snapped off at the cap and both jib topsail and staysail came down in a mess of wire stays and rigging. Without missing a beat, the crew set about clearing up the wreckage. The mate and a couple of fishermen headed out on the bowsprit to cut away the jib topsail that was now dragging under the forefoot. "Down into the jumping sea went the bowsprit and the three sailors were plunged under five feet of water. They cut away the sail and brought it in with the crew behind them hauling it inboard thru the green-white smother."[23] Those aloft worked frantically to secure the topmast, assorted wires, blocks and halyards.

Within six minutes the *Elsie,* under forcefully shortened sail, appeared to be making better time than she had before. Angus Walters reacted in the spirit of sportsmanship by immediately dousing his own jib topsail and clewing up his main topsail. Marty Welsh stood inshore on a port tack and raised his main gaff topsail and, by so doing, could have risked losing his main topmast. Once again he was carrying more sail than his rival in the thirty-knot breeze. However, what he needed was more hull in the water, not more sail aloft. *Bluenose* streaked for home "like a kerosened cat through Hades," with her lee rail buried so deep that, according to the press on board the *Lady Laurier,* "we reckoned you could drown a man in her lee scuppers."[24]

After four and a half hours of hard sailing over a distance of about fifty miles, the *Bluenose* ploughed a furrow of white water across the finish. Walters and his crew became instant heroes, arriving home to a chorus of steam whistles and sirens. The valiant *Elsie* followed twelve and a half minutes later. The Gloucester crew was beaten but not defeated, and their captain remained steadfastly optimistic about their chances, saying, "The best boat won in the weather of the day, but there's another race and maybe two, acoming."[25] Russell Smith, the Gloucester observer on board the *Bluenose,* stated that "Captain Angus Walters sailed one of the finest races it has ever been my privilege to witness," but he added, "There are two handles on that old trophy—and you fellows have hold of one of them. It is not a case of perhaps there will be three races; there WILL be three races."[26] Captain Walters, when asked about the race, commented that "the man and boat that are out to beat Marty Welsh and the *Elsie* have no small job on their hands; they have a fine boat and a real racing skipper to go up against."[27] The city of Halifax was delirious with excitement.

The second race, on October 24, appeared to be more to the Americans' liking, with lighter winds over a smoother sea. The little *Elsie,* sporting new topmasts, streaked across the start at nine knots, a full minute and a half ahead of her challenger. *Bluenose* had loafed too far back and, as she moved lethargically to the start, one wag was heard to comment that "Angie must have stayed up late last night."[28] Observers became even less charitable when the Yankee banker began to widen the gap. Walters later rebuffed his critics: "It ain't who crosses the starting line first that counts. If we can cross the finish line first—that's the main thing."[29]

It was a grand, crisp, clear day for sailing, the ruffled blue water flecked with snappy white crests. The experts predicted the *Elsie* would show her stern to the Lunenburger in such weather and, at the start, it looked as if they were right. Both vessels' sails filled beautifully with eased sheets and booms over their port quarters, an absolute delight to the eye in the brilliance of the morning sun. The *Bluenose* finally found her stride and began, slowly, to foot on her rival, passing the Inner Automatic Buoy only forty seconds behind as they hauled up west-south-west and headed seaward to the Sambro Lightship Buoy, more than eleven miles away. Both vessels moved closer inshore under Chebucto Head, where the wind picked up under the land. The *Bluenose* appeared to surge ahead in the puffs until she was slapping the *Elsie*'s wake.

At this point, a familiar boat appeared from seaward. The *Mayflower,* under four lowers and in winter rig with no topmasts, was paralleling the course of the two racers. Bound for the banks with twenty dories nested on her deck and loaded down with ice and fishing gear, the Bostonian was in no trim to race but had come over to have a look at the contest. Her appearance caused a commotion among the journalists, who immediately began pumping out wild commentaries over the wireless. The Boston schooner kept to leeward of the racers and was really too far out to do any true pacing, but she did run with the committee boat for a time. She appeared to move quickly under her short rig, but was very wet forward. Most observers agreed she would have been a marvel in light winds and that the *Elsie* and the *Bluenose* were likely far better in rough seas.

Both racers jibed around the Sambro Buoy, where the wind was now blowing twenty knots, the *Bluenose* twenty-six seconds behind the *Elsie.* Walters kept tight onto Welsh's weather quarter, looking for a break on the nine-and-a-half-mile leg to the Outer Buoy. For twenty-seven miles the little Gloucester schooner had led the way and it was beginning to look as if she might come home the winner. The undaunted supporters of the Lunenburger, however, were waiting for the windward work to begin. When the vessels closed in on the Outer Automatic Buoy, Walters performed a masterful bit of helmsmanship and capitalized on the small opening between the *Elsie* and the buoy. He came up on her inside, leaving only a foot between his boat and the buoy, a feat that inspired a *Toronto Telegram* reporter to write that "the buoy (was shaved) so closely that, while it was properly cleared, it must have felt like shrieking for witch-hazel and talcum powder."[30]

< **HER CREW** clinging to the windward rail "like bats to a barn rafter," the *Bluenose* streaks to the finish and victory in the 1921 series. Her big, powerful hull, enormous sail area and tenacious skipper, Captain Angus Walters, proved too much for the little American schooner *Elsie* and her determined master, the defending cup-holder Captain Marty Welsh. *Wallace MacAskill, Nova Scotia Archives and Records Management*

The *Elsie*'s slim lead at the buoy gave her no chance to tack and cover her rival. Both vessels sheeted hard and boiled along, but it was the *Bluenose* that could point higher. "They were showing twelve knots and the big white bone which the *Bluenose* carried in her teeth suggested the old comparison of a big growling mastiff and a little fighting terrier."[31] Despite a valiant effort, it was all over for the *Elsie*. She could not sail as close to the wind, and there was no overcoming her rival's powerful hull. The *Bluenose* had the windward legs and walked away from her opponent. Bunting and flags flying from scupper to truck, the great Lunenburger entered the harbour a champion. "When they tied up to the dock, Angus Walters was, as someone graphically remarked, like a piece of chewed string after almost five and a half hours of constant strain and anxiety."[32] The International Fishermen's Cup race was over and the trophy was back in Canadian hands.

The 1921 series brought all the excitement and thrills expected of a working fishermen's race. In spite of the ensuing argument over the difference in size of the vessels, the public on both sides of the border thought they had received their money's worth. Although the series had been taken in only two races, there had been no shortage of anxiety and high drama, largely due to Welsh's superb seamanship. He had proved to be a tenacious sailor and a splendid tactician, who had pushed his boat to her limits. Had his vessel been on more even terms, the outcome might have been different. Walters was every bit his equal, and had more than demonstrated his ability to drive his boat hard, and his willingness to take chances when necessary. Perhaps the result was simply proof of the old adage: a good big boat will always beat a good small boat. The one certainty was that *Bluenose* would not remain unchallenged for long, and next year's contest was going to be in American waters.

NOTES

1 *Atlantic Fisherman,* May 1921, p. 15
2 See Appendix, (1), (2)
3 See Appendix, (1), (3)
4 The Halifax Herald North Atlantic Fishermen's International Trophy was also known as the Fisherman's Cup, Herald Cup, Denis Cup and the International Fishermen's Cup. I have chosen to limit the names to the International Fishermen's Cup and Herald cup or trophy to avoid confusion.
5 Backman, *Bluenose,* p. 36
6 *Atlantic Fisherman,* February 1921, p. 7
7 *Atlantic Fisherman,* April 1921, p. 3
8 Story, *Hail Columbia!,* p. 35
9 Miss Burgess was named Starling after her father, but would later assume the name Tasha Tudor and become famous as a writer and illustrator.
10 Ibid.
11 *Atlantic Fisherman,* May 1921, p. 2
12 *Canadian Fisherman,* June 1921, p. 130
13 *Evening Mail,* October 14, 1921

14 *Canadian Fisherman,* November 1921, p. 252
15 *New York Herald,* October 20, 1921
16 *Canadian Fisherman,* November 1921, p. 257
17 Ibid., p. 253
18 Snider, *Rudder,* December 1921, p. 4
19 *Canadian Fisherman,* November 1921, p. 253
20 Wallace, *Yachting,* November 1921, p. 215
21 Ibid.
22 James Connolly, *Evening Mail,* October 24, 1921
23 Ibid.
24 *Canadian Fisherman,* November 1921, p. 254
25 Wallace, *Yachting,* November 1921, p. 215
26 *Evening Mail,* October 24, 1921
27 Ibid.
28 *Canadian Fisherman,* November 1921, p. 254
29 Wallace, *Yachting,* November 1921, p. 255
30 Snider, *Rudder,* December 1921, p. 44
31 Connolly, *Evening Mail,* October 25, 1921
32 *Canadian Fisherman,* November 1921, p. 256

6

TURMOIL IN GLOUCESTER: 1922

HE 1921 SERIES and the triumph of the *Bluenose* left the Americans with the realization that this was no longer an event for "off the shelf" boats. The *Bluenose* had been built well within the specifications of the deed of gift, but her design was not that of the "comfortable sea-going ark" that Gloucester fishermen associated with the Nova Scotian fleet. Her size was a problem for the Americans, not because she was a "freak," since the Lunenburg boats were generally larger than those of the Americans, but she was faster than the general run of Lunenburg vessels and so a much more challenging competitor. There was no question that she could fish and carry "highliner" loads of over 225 tons of salt cod, but her hull was finer than the average boat and everyone knew she had been built to beat the Yankee challenge.

As the defeat of the *Delawana* had spurred the Nova Scotians to develop the *Bluenose,* so the *Elsie*'s loss gave the Americans reason to do the same. If they were going to be able to compete effectively, they were going to have to build a fast schooner of comparable size. Shortly after the end of the 1921 series, a group of Gloucestermen met over dinner at the Halifax Hotel to discuss the situation. There was much more than just civic pride at stake; winning the race had become an issue of international honour. Captain Jeff Thomas, his brother Bill, Ben Pine and several others from the Gloucester business community agreed they would build their own boat to be ready for competition the following year. Pine, who was still soaking in the exhilaration of crewing on the *Elsie* under Marty Welsh, was especially eager to take part. A critical look at the fleet in Gloucester had left the group convinced they had nothing that could come close to challenging the black-hulled beauty from Lunenburg. The organization called itself the Manta Club after the little schooner Pine had skippered the previous year. No one could question the pedigree of the backers of the new boat, all of whom were closely associated with the fishing industry and with Gloucester.

Only three days after the *Elsie*'s defeat, the club announced that a new challenger, to be named the *Puritan,* would be built in Essex.[1] Curiously, the club hired Starling Burgess, who had designed the *Mayflower,* to draw up a hull. His new design proved to be quite similar to that of the Boston boat but smaller, with a longer, traditional, overhanging transom and none of the *Mayflower*'s "yachty" features.

Great efforts were made from the outset to assure all parties that the vessel was to be a fisherman first, putting to rest any fears that she might be too refined. Apart from the need to abide by the deed of gift, the vessel had to be a money-maker, as none of the investors had cash to throw away. As further proof of their intentions, the Manta Club announced that her size would be smaller than that of the *Bluenose,* 137 feet (41.8 metres) in length and 105 feet (32 metres) on the waterline, since a larger boat would not be profitable in the fresh-fish trade. "If she shows us anything," said Captain Thomas, in his characteristically blunt style, "you will hear from us in the races next Fall; If she doesn't, well, you won't."[2]

Another Cape Ann skipper caught up in racing fever was Clayton Morrissey, known locally as Captain Clayte. He was a tall, lean, quiet-spoken family man with a solid reputation as a sail dragger and fisherman, and his schooner, the *Arethusa,* was one of the largest, fastest knockabouts in the fleet. George Hudson

‹ **SHORTLY AFTER** launching in 1922, the *Henry Ford* fell victim to a series of unfortunate incidents. First she became stuck in marsh weed after she slid down the way and then, as she was being towed from Essex to Gloucester for fitting out, she came up hard on a bar at the mouth of the Essex River. Unbelievably, she was left unattended until morning by the tug crew and, during the night, floated off on a tide, fetching up on Coffin's Beach, perilously close to some rocky outcroppings. Fortunately, she suffered only minor damage and was floated off four days later. *Peabody Essex Museum*

of the *Boston Herald* remarked on Morrissey's skillful handling of sail: "He hangs the duds aloft until it pipes and pipes, but lowers away and furls in the nick of time and fools the gale. Morrissey is quite clever that way."[3] However, the *Arethusa* was getting on in years, and Morrissey found himself itching for a newer, faster boat that might be able to meet the *Bluenose* challenge. His quiet ways and habitual stammer disguised a forceful, determined and short-tempered personality. He sold the *Arethusa* to Captain Bill McCoy, who changed her name to the *Tomaka* and put her to use "bottle fishing," the term given to rum-running in the early days of Prohibition. Morrissey and his wife, Bessie, joined forces with three of Gloucester's exclusive Eastern Point residents, Jonathan Raymond, F. Wilder Pollard and Frank C. Pearce, along with the boat builder Arthur D. Story, who often took a financial interest in the vessels he was constructing when he found a skipper to his liking. Morrissey then hired the venerable old boat designer Thomas McManus to draw up plans. McManus had been the obvious choice for Morrissey because, apart from being the grand old man of fishing-schooner design, he had also been the designer of the *Arethusa*. At sixty-six, he had produced more than four hundred often-copied designs, and he was already working on a plan when Morrissey called. The defeat of the *Elsie,* which had been one of his personal favourites, plus a detailed description of the *Bluenose* from Marty Welsh, had driven him to the drafting table. He quickly turned out plan number 419 for Morrissey's approval.[4]

By April, two new challengers sat on the ways in Essex—the *Henry Ford* at the A.D. Story yard and the *Puritan* at the J.F. James and Son yard. There was so much interest and speculation about both vessels that the town of Essex became a favourite destination for touring "automobilists" and sightseers. Both hulls had very similar dimensions, though Morrissey's boat was a little fuller and longer on the waterline.

The *Puritan* was launched first, on March 15, before a crowd of two thousand, and christened with champagne by Ray Adams, a young female friend of Ben Pine's. A month later, after being rigged and fitted for sea, the *Puritan* was turned over to her captain, Jeff Thomas. She left Gloucester under the tow of a converted submarine chaser—accompanied by cheers, whistles and cannon fire—on her maiden trip "halibutting" to the banks. Her sails began to feel the press of wind as she left the outer harbour and she quickly overhauled her tow, which was going a steady eleven knots. It was an auspicious beginning to a sea-going career and left the residents of Gloucester with little doubt that she could be counted on to recover the honour they believed to be theirs.

On her return in early May, loaded with halibut, Captain Thomas fairly bubbled over with enthusiasm for his new vessel, calling her "fast on every point without playing any tricks."[5] By all accounts she was the fastest vessel yet to come off the ways at Essex, a reputation enhanced by an impromptu matchup with the *Mayflower*, which she met off Cape Cod on her maiden voyage. She left the Boston boat trailing in her wake. By June 17, Thomas had made two successful fishing trips, and he headed out on a third, to Sable Bank. After stopping at Booth Bay to pick up ice and bait, he took the *Puritan* east on a fateful trip to Sable Island, the notorious mistress of sunken ships, with her treacherous coastline of shifting sands. Thick fog and strong southerly winds accompanied them as they worked their way through the heavy swells for the banks at the north end of the island. The boat was going at twelve knots and carrying a full kit of sail when she hit a bar. She had been making such good speed that she had overrun her dead-reckoning position by a good twenty miles. The impact was so hard that it broke her back and ripped free a lengthy section of keel. Sea water quickly poured in and breakers crashed over the bulwarks as the crew worked frantically to launch the dories. The first dory off capsized, and the three men aboard were tossed into the sea. Two were dragged back, but the third, Christopher Johnson, was lost. Seven men pulled for shore in the pounding surf, while the other fifteen rowed offshore, where they were eventually picked up by a passing schooner.[6] Nine days after the trip had begun, and barely three months after her launching, a short telegram arrived in Gloucester announcing the loss of the *Puritan*: "Struck Northwest Bar, Sable Island, about 7:30 p.m., 23rd."[7] Although all but one member of the crew were still alive, the hopes of the *Puritan*'s backers were not.

Hit hard by the disaster, Ben Pine and his associates nonetheless hardly skipped a beat. So keen was their interest in participating in the international races, they immediately looked for an alternative vessel. Pine went into partnership with Marion Cooney, a sail maker, and chartered the 138-foot (43-metre) knockabout schooner the *Elizabeth Howard*, another fast McManus boat belonging to William Howard of New York. She was quickly fitted out and sailed to the banks in order to qualify for the fall elimination races. The Howard had reputedly made sixteen knots under sail and had even been offered up to the *Mayflower* owners as a trial horse to race against their boat the previous year.[8]

The public was still keenly interested in the new designs and, after the loss of the *Puritan*, pinned its hopes on the *Henry Ford*, launched a month later on April 11. As they had for her rival, people turned out in droves to see the launching of the *Ford*. With a gold stripe along her black hull, carvings on her stem and transom and new bunting fluttering in the northeast breeze, she was christened by Clayton Morrissey's fourteen-year-old daughter, Winnie. The schooner had been named by Morrissey's wife, who held the automobile maker Henry Ford in such high regard that she insisted on naming the vessel in his honour. Once off her blocks, the *Ford* slid into the Essex River so quickly that she had to be hauled off the marsh weeds on the opposite side. This was not the only setback that day. After two tugs had taken her in tow for the trip downriver, she went aground for a second time on the bar at the river mouth. Unbelievably, the tugs failed to stand by their charge and abandoned her until the following morning. At midnight, the *Ford* came off the bar with the tide and floated onto the sandy shore, coming precariously close to the rocky ledges at Coffin's Beach, where she was in imminent danger of breaking up. It took four days of continuous work, with pontoons and tugs, to get her off the beach. Fortunately, fears that the damage would leave her severely warped or hogged proved unfounded. Apart from a strained rudder stock, several broken planks and chunks missing from her shoe, she seemed to have suffered little from the grounding. The repairs and fitting-out caused unavoidable delays and, as the race rules stipulated the vessel must be on her way to the banks by April 30, a dispensation was requested by Morrissey from the trustees. Luckily, they agreed. It took until June 2 to ready her for sea.

With the *Puritan* gone, the *Ford* might have been considered the only contender now in the running. However, the backers of the *Mayflower* renewed their efforts for recognition, certain their schooner could not be barred from competition a second time. She had put in another full season on the banks, carrying respectable loads to market and as well proving herself capable of surviving extreme weather conditions, riding out gales on the banks when others were dismasted or damaged. As far as the *Mayflower* group was concerned, she had paid her dues and demonstrated beyond a shadow of a doubt that she was, in fact, a bona fide fisherman. They applied to the American race committee for qualification and, in August, the *Mayflower* and the *Henry Ford*, the *Elizabeth Howard* and two Boston boats, the *L.A. Dunton* and the *Yankee*, were accepted

for the elimination races that were due to begin on October 12. The inclusion of the *Mayflower* set off another storm of protest concerning her eligibility, but she now had many supporters, as well as detractors, both in the United States and in Canada. Ultimately, it was up to the trustees in Halifax to determine her fate, and although they initially appeared unimpressed by arguments in her favour, they chose to forestall making a decision until September.

Newspapers editorials on each side of the border argued for and against. In contrast to the previous year, in Gloucester a "no *Mayflower*—no race" sentiment was beginning to take hold. The *Mayflower* group, supported by the American race committee, sent representatives, including the boat's designer, Starling Burgess, to plead their case with the trustees in Halifax, but they could see no reason to alter their decision, as there had been no structural changes made to the boat. The decision made the previous year had been based on the argument that the *Mayflower* was too radical and yacht-like in design and the capacity of her hold far too small for her size. As far as they were concerned, therefore, the fact that she had put in a full season on the banks was irrelevant, and there was no basis upon which to alter her status. Angus Walters was disappointed with the decision and put it down to a lack of courage on the part of the trustees, later commenting that "the Committee was scared of us racing the *Mayflower*, though I would have been happy to do so. I had a good look at her on the marine railway once, and I knew then she'd be no trouble. I told them so, but they stuck to their guns."[9]

The American race committee was split on whether to abide by the decision or stand as one to continue the pressure to have it reversed. In a special meeting held at the Gloucester Chamber of Commerce, impassioned debate raged on for five hours. The argument was so intense that at times it could clearly be heard through the closed doors of the committee room by those awaiting the outcome in the hallway outside. After all argument had been exhausted, a compromise that would have allowed the *Mayflower* to race was reached, and a telegram was sent off to Halifax voicing opposition to the trustees' decision and suggesting instead "that the race for the Halifax Herald Cup be suspended for this year, pending a revision and amplication [sic] of the deed of gift, and that in its place, a free-for-all race be held, for a suitable cup and purse between the fastest vessels in the Canadian and American fishing fleets."[10] Knowing that feelings for a fishermen's race ran deep in Gloucester, the American committee was unwilling to give up the series entirely. When the trustees turned down this request, the committee felt it had no choice but to relent. The *Mayflower* group withdrew its entry, but issued a challenge to the winner of the Herald trophy for a separate and entirely independent event.

In Nova Scotia, four vessels entered elimination races, which began on October 7. The odds-on favourite, the *Bluenose,* had put in another successful season on the banks and, by all reports, was sailing better than ever now that Walters had become even more familiar with his charge. The *Canadia,* skippered by Captain Conrad, was also entered and expected to do much better this year as well. She had greatly improved her trim and had had her mainsail recut. Conrad welcomed a second chance at taking on Walters and the *Bluenose.* Two "dark horses" were also in the mix, the *Mahaska* and the *Margaret K. Smith.* There had been considerable interest in the *Mahaska.* Under her skipper, Captain Mack, she had proved herself to be a fast boat during the season, and some expected her to give the others a run for their money. Little was known about the *Smith*; as she had been launched only in August, she would in any case be ineligible for the international series should she win the trials.

The first race on Saturday was a near disaster for the champion. As it was later said, the *Bluenose* won in spite of those on board. Walters was left flat-footed at the start as the *Smith* grabbed the windward berth, shooting across the line ten seconds after the gun, followed closely by the *Canadia* and *Mahaska* less than a minute behind. Sitting off to leeward, Walters found himself caught in irons and could not bring his boat around. When her sails finally filled, she crossed the starting line a full five minutes late. The anxious crew of the defender were busy whistling for wind and making offerings over the side. "Save your wind for the sails," cut in Walters. "Out pipes and overboard with cigars and cigarettes, boys, till the race is over. Keep your heads down and hands ready."[11] The *Bluenose* finally came alive when the breeze freshened on the first leg, and she began to move up on her rivals. Twenty minutes after crossing the start, she was in second place, chasing the *Smith*'s tail. With winds picking up to eighteen knots, the *Bluenose* flew past the *Smith* and made for the Inner Automatic Buoy. She thundered by the mark, leaving it on her starboard side, with the *Smith* close in on her wake.

Jerry Snider, the reporter for the *Toronto Telegram,* was on board to cover the event; he had been reading the race program when they passed the buoy, and "what struck [his] eye like a blast of cinders" was that they had taken the buoy on the wrong side.[12] He broke the news to Walters, who, as he had seen Captain Whynacht on the *Smith* do the same, took some convincing. But the print was plain. Although

the sailing committee had clearly indicated course number 2, nobody on the two leading boats had taken the time at the start to read the program properly and both were headed off in the wrong direction. When Walters realized his mistake, he wasted no time in roaring out orders to come about, lubricating the commands with seasoned curses and sending "thirty oil-skinned figures jump[ing] like scalded cats to various stations."[13] The *Smith* countered quickly and came about for the right side of the buoy before the *Bluenose*. The *Canadia* was now in the lead with *Mahaska* in her wake and, once again, it was a stern chase for the *Bluenose*. "Spit on your hands and never say die, boys," called out an undeterred Walters. "It was my mistake; I got us into this hole, but maybe the *Bluenose* will get us out."[14] Although the *Canadia* was a mile ahead, the *Bluenose*'s persistent forging up to weather paid off. "By speed superiority alone she ate and ate and ate down the long gap that separated her from the LaHave vessel," as Snider described it. Those on board the committee boat could see that when the two leaders reached the Sambro Buoy, the *Bluenose* was going to take it.

Conrad's *Canadia* fought a good race but in the end was no match for the Lunenburg flyer. The fact that the *Bluenose* could recover from not one but two blunders—at the start and at the buoy—and still make up so much time was a testament to the Roué hull and the skills of the skipper. *Bluenose* was declared the defender after the two follow-up events were abandoned due to insufficient winds. She headed for Gloucester on October 12.

"Damn a light sail! Give me four lowers and wind enough to bury her rail—and that's what I call a racing combination," was all Captain Morrissey could say of the light winds in Gloucester's first elimination race on Thursday, October 12. Even so, the light sail was too much for Ben Pine on the *Elizabeth Howard*. He surprised the fleet and crossed first at the gun, but ten minutes later lost his topmast when the crosstree cracked at his main top. Always game, he continued for an hour, but the unfortunate *Howard* was clearly out of the contest. In spite of a listless race and a bad start, the day belonged to Morrissey and the *Henry Ford*. With the neck of his blue sweater rolled up under his chin and a cigar stub clamped firmly in the corner of his mouth, Morrissey drove his vessel around the course, taking the race by nearly eighteen minutes. Before the race he had expressed some apprehension about the *Yankee* from Boston, but she and the *Dunton* finished well behind. Ed Millet, the *Halifax Herald* correspondent aboard the *Ford*, enthusiastically described the vessel to his readers: "The wake is barely perceptible. She

< TAKEN FROM the main cabin roof, this photograph shows the *Bluenose* punching through a heavy sea as she shoulders a comber on her port rail. The *Bluenose* stood up better to the weather than the *Henry Ford* in the 1922 series and barely wet her decks. *Author's collection*

leaves no dead water behind her, and throws but little on her decks. She is very quick in stays and her best point is heading into it."[15] Her captain was far less impressed by the *Ford*'s performance, finding her sluggish and unresponsive during the contest. He spent the next day with Tom McManus correcting her ballast, while Pine repaired his masthead trestle. On Saturday, the *Ford* seemed to sail much better and proved her superiority on just about every point of sail. Pine on the *Howard* gave Morrissey a race but came in second by over five minutes, with the *Yankee* following ten minutes later and the *Dunton* a further half hour behind. The *Henry Ford* had clearly won the honour of challenging the *Bluenose*.

While the citizens of Gloucester slept, the *Bluenose* stole into the harbour unannounced in the early hours of Saturday morning, October 14, 1922. She had left Halifax under the tow of the HMCS *Patriot*, travelling through rough and foggy weather. Their tether soon parted in the boisterous seas and both vessels went their separate ways. News of the *Bluenose*'s arrival in Gloucester spread quickly, when dawn revealed her anchored near Ten Pound Island. As she made her way from her anchorage to the Gloucester Gas Company wharf, she was soon surrounded by a small flotilla of sailing craft. Alerted by the shrieking of sirens and whistles from the boats and factories, crowds began to stream towards the waterfront for a glimpse of the now-famous schooner and, by Sunday, Gloucester had taken on a decidedly holiday spirit. "All that was lacking was the street peddler with his balloons and popcorn to make the carnival scene complete," said the reporter for the *Herald*.[16] American dignitaries such as Governor Channing Cox of Massachusetts, Secretary of State Frederic W. Cook, Senator Henry Cabot Lodge and Secretary of the Navy Edwin Denby were scheduled to arrive, along with an official delegation from Canada, including Lieutenant-Governor MacCallum Grant of Nova Scotia and the province's premier, G.H. Murray. Hotel accommodation became a scarce commodity in the old fishing port. A grand Fishermen's Ball, set for Friday night, drew over fifteen hundred people.

On the day of his arrival, Walters and some Gloucester friends took the opportunity to view the final elimination race from a high knoll on the Magnolia shore. As he was standing there, taking in every detail, a surprise delegation from the *Mayflower* group, headed by Fred Pigeon and Captain Henry Larkin, descended on Walters and attempted to negotiate a race with the *Bluenose*, in the event of her winning the Herald cup. Unwilling to make any commitment, the always cagey Walters suggested they take up the matter with the American race committee. As a result of this discussion, a meeting held later that night between members of the committee and representatives of both vessels resulted in an agreement with Walters that he would race the *Mayflower*, provided the same offer be made to the *Henry Ford*. The date set for the race was two days after the international race was completed.

The following days were filled with last-minute fittings-out and trial spins around the course. One of the first orders of business was the official measuring of both vessels. George Owens, professor of marine technology at the Massachusetts Institute of Technology, had been invited to be the official measurer, but, as he was unable to attend, Evers Burtner, his young assistant, took his place. Burtner was the official measurer for the Yacht Racing Union of Massachusetts and had plenty of experience with yachts, though none with fishing schooners. He was instructed to measure each vessel's waterline and calculate the allowable sail area stipulated by the Eighty Per Cent Rule in the 1921 deed of gift. On Thursday the *Bluenose* went under the tape and was found to be in compliance, as she carried 228 square feet (21.2 square metres) of sail under her allowable limit. The following day the thunderbolt struck when Burtner, in the company of the race officials, measured the *Ford* and found that her sail area exceeded the limit by 490 square feet (45.5 square metres). Burtner proceeded to mark the boom where the excess sail needed to be cut.[17] Morrissey was astounded. His suit of sails had served him well on the banks and he could see no reason to change them now. Tom McManus, the designer, was livid. He had not been allowed to view the measuring and insisted she was in compliance. However, the officials were not to be argued with and at 7 PM that evening, less than twenty-four hours before the first race, Morrissey was forced to cut his sail. "They may cut us all to pieces," he defiantly declared, "but we'll race her anyhow, under bare poles if necessary."[18] Throughout the night, a gang worked on the sails in the United Sail Loft under Morrissey's supervision, liberally assisted by bootlegged refreshment. Two twenty-inch (fifty-centimetre) cloths were removed from the leech of the mainsail and a similar amount from the fore gaff topsail. They finished the job at 8 AM, leaving the crew with barely enough time to bend on the mainsail for the ten o'clock start. Tempers aboard the American boat had begun to smoulder.

In light airs, on October 21, the two competitors were ready to face off near the start of the race at the entrance to Gloucester Harbour. The sailing committee aboard the USS *Paulding* decided the winds were inadequate and postponed the race, hauling up the appropriate signals. The two skippers, however, felt differently. Angus hailed his rival, "What say Clayte, Let's have a race. I'm going to race if I have to sail alone."[19] That was all the challenge it took and, as with any impromptu hookup at sea, the two skippers were off. The sailing committee's attempts to recall the vessels met with failure. After more signalling, a motor launch was sent to stop them, but by the time it caught up, the racers had covered a mile and a half. As no race officials were on board the launch, and both skippers were more interested in racing than in following yachting rules, the recall was ignored. The committee finally gave up trying to stop them, hauled anchor and gave chase in order to mark the times at the turns, giving every indication that the race was now sanctioned. The committee was privately hoping the winds would peter out completely, leaving the competitors unable to finish. To the thousands ashore and in the spectator fleet, it certainly looked as if the race was on. The *Ford* favoured light winds and gained an early and commanding lead, holding onto it for the duration. She crossed the finish a mile and half ahead of the *Bluenose*. All the anger over the sail slashing vanished with the victory, and the town of Gloucester went wild with jubilation.

That night, the sailing committee dropped a bombshell just after the schooners had tied up, declaring "no official race on account of both of the contestants having made false starts," as it was reported by Leonard Fowle.[20] To make matters worse, the official measurer, Evers Burtner, unaware of the uproar his actions would cause and the criticism that would follow him for the rest of his days, dropped another bomb by stating the cutting of the *Ford*'s mainsail had not been done correctly, and she was still not in compliance: another 53 square feet (4.9 square metres) would have to come off. It was obvious to the incensed fishermen that yachting attitudes were beginning to dominate what had been a working man's affair. There was little reaction from the skippers, and what they did say was short and to the point: from Morrissey, "I'm going fishing Monday," and from Walters, "It was a race and the best boat won."[21] He told the race committee to "tally one up for Clayte, he won it—give it to him."[22] Morrissey appealed and the committee went into closed session to review the ruling. His was a difficult position; he was loath to recut his mainsail, his crew was on the point of revolt, but he also wanted to be ready to race again. Feeling there was no recourse open to him, he sent off the sail to be recut.

Speculation ran rampant through the town, and a crowd gathered round the chamber offices all through Sunday while the committee members discussed the issue of the validity of the race. At 1:30 AM on Monday the decision was announced: the ruling would stand. The race on Saturday was unofficial and would therefore not count.

Morrissey's crew's response was out-and-out mutiny. They marched through the streets, shouting that they were through with racing and race committees. They were "good and mad" at having their sails slashed, and they were not going to have any more of it. They were not going to race—and Captain Morrissey was not forcing them. As far as they and many Gloucestermen were concerned, the series had been taken over by yachtsmen, who were instituting yachting rules and regulations. But at eight in the morning, when they headed to the *Ford* to clear out their gear, they were met by Mrs. Jack Raymond (the wife of one of the owners) and Edwin Denby, the secretary of the navy. The feisty lady sailor begged, cajoled and pleaded with the crew to stay the course, "for the glory of Gloucester and in the spirit of sportsmanship." Her pleas fell on deaf ears. The boys would have none of it, so Denby stepped in and appealed to their patriotism, giving them a rousing speech about how the *Ford* represented the United States and it was their duty to man her for the race. Knowing most of the crew originally hailed from Nova Scotia, he pleaded, "Never let it be said the men of Clark's Harbour, the Pubnico's [sic] and Barrington, helped trail Old Glory in the dust."[23] The crew remained unmoved until finally swayed by Morrissey's deep, gruff voice: "Come on boys, let's pick up the sail and bend her on."[24] If Captain Clayte was willing, then they were, too. All but four jumped to it and went aboard. The dissenters were quickly replaced by eager fishermen from the crowd of bystanders that had been watching events unfold. Half an hour later, the *Ford* slipped into the stream and headed out to race.

The first "official" race began in light winds, once again to the *Ford*'s liking. It was an electrifying start as the *Ford* shot across the *Bluenose*'s wake and the two boats crossed the line as one. The *Ford* nosed up alongside her rival, squeaking between her and the committee boat, the USS *Paulding,* and almost scraping the destroyer's stern. Cheers broke out on the deck of the *Paulding* as the *Ford* took the *Bluenose*'s wind and shot into the lead. At the first mark, the *Ford* led by forty seconds, and she continued to gain steadily, proving once more her superiority in lighter winds. By the fourth mark, she had a lead of over four minutes. Then the wind picked up to almost fifteen knots and both close-hauled boats began to smash through the seas, boiling down to the line with their lee rails buried for the first time that day. The Lunenburger finally began to stretch her legs on her best point of sail and moved up on the *Ford,* but it proved to be too late. After forty miles and five hours of sailing, the best Walters could do was close the gap and cross the finish two and a half minutes after his rival.

The *Bluenose* had sailed the race under protest, as she had a splintered keel. During the night, she had settled on a rock at low tide while alongside the gas company's wharf, and when the crew had swept the hull with a rope in the morning they had come up with a four-foot (1.3-metre) splinter of wood. Whether or not this affected the schooner's performance is open to speculation, but in Walters's mind, it had. He complained that his boat had felt sluggish. "When the wind was light today," he told the *Telegram* reporter, "she went so dead that she disgusted me…she sailed worse on the starboard tack than on the port one."[25] The protest flag had flown from her port rigging from the start, but, by that time, the committee was so fed up with complaints it had told Walters to go on with the race and disallowed the protest.

The American boat again headed into Gloucester victorious, but Morrissey had had enough. As far as he was concerned, he had won two races, the first of which even his adversary had conceded was his, and he was not prepared to compete again the following day. He began to ready the *Ford* to go fishing, loading ten tons of ballast rock on board. At this point, it seemed the whole event was beginning to unravel. Tempers began to boil over on the streets of Gloucester, and the banquet held that night at the armoury to honour the crews was boycotted by many. Dignitaries tried their best to reignite the patriotic fervour of the *Ford*'s crew, but Morrissey's men stood firm. They would not race again. Ben Pine was approached to see if he would skipper the *Elizabeth Howard* in the event the *Ford*'s crew remained intransigent. Angus Walters was nonplussed by the attitude of his opponent and expressed his intention to be there, waiting at the start and ready to sail the course—alone if need be.

In a secret session held in the basement of the armoury, the race committee debated whether or not the Herald cup could be awarded to the *Ford* on the strength of her two wins. One member on the American side forcefully declared that "we would be yellow curs if we, as a majority, voted to take the cup. We want to win it fairly and squarely. Let's race for it as we should."[26] In the end it was decided that rules must be obeyed and the first race disallowed. All the debate and acrimony drove the correspondent for the Halifax papers to write:

Since arrival here we have been given few thrills on the water, but ashore all has been impossibility and chaos. The flock of rumours has been bewildering. Somehow or other, this has not struck me as sport. During the past couple of days I have begun to feel more like a war correspondent than a peaceful newspaperman of a peaceful country.[27]

Alarmed by the turn of events and the possibility of the situation developing into an international incident, Jack Raymond, one of the owners of the *Ford*, took matters into his own hands. He invited Captain Morrissey and his crew for a quiet dinner at the Ramparts, his summer home on Eastern Point. As requested, two dozen fishermen arrived at his doorstep to partake of a rather hastily prepared meal cooked by Raymond's mother and sister (the staff had all been dismissed in preparation for shutting the house up for the winter). After the dinner—and a liberal libation of Prohibition whiskey—Raymond took the crew into his drawing room for a fireside chat. What was said there was never fully revealed, but in essence, the crew was told that far more was at stake than they could realize. There had been a great deal of money bet on the races, upwards of $100,000— and, unpatriotically, not all of it wagered on the hometown boat. Whatever the case, Raymond won them over, and the crew voted to continue with the series. All they would afterwards admit about the evening was that "everything had been explained to us at dinner. Now we're going out to fight and win!"[28]

On Tuesday, the ships sat idle while a thirty-five-knot gale howled outside the harbour. Captain Morrissey fell ill and the committee granted the *Ford* a postponement, leaving the *Bluenose* crew grumbling and chafing for a race. This was the kind of weather they had been looking for, and the idea of sitting it out was frustrating and disappointing. Walters's attempt to take advantage of the postponement by having the hull checked was also thwarted, as another schooner was occupying the marine railway all day. Now it was the Canadian's turn to lose patience and he lashed out at the opposition, saying, "I knew it would blow hard today. I told you so last night. How did I know? My barometer told me. Clayte has a barometer too," implying that the Gloucester fisherman was afraid to race in such weather.[29] Nothing could have been farther from the truth. Not only was Morrissey laid up with a painful hernia, but his son was dying. He had been implored by his grief-stricken wife not to continue with the series. Morrissey had lost his appetite to race and desperately wanted to have done with it.

‹ "**ATA BOY**, Henry, go it old socks, she's a hound, I tell you, she's a hound," the ecstatic crewmen of the *Henry Ford* reportedly cried as they casually leaned against the windward rail during the 1922 series. With her lee rail buried so deep that half her main deck was submerged, the schooner laboured heavily under a tremendous press of wind. The strain and drag proved too much, and shortly after this photograph was taken, the fore-topmast let go. *Rosenfeld Collection, Mystic Seaport Museum Inc.*

Early Wednesday morning, with a wind piping up outside the harbour, the *Ford*'s men were back on board removing the stone ballast to bring her back to racing trim. When they raised the foresail, they found the bolt rope on the leech of the sail slashed in three places, in what appeared to be a deliberate attempt at sabotage. Morrissey made light of it and had the damage quickly repaired. His wife, Bessie, and her sister boarded the vessel and, in the most dramatic scene yet, pleaded with him to give up the whole affair and come home. "Come ashore, Clayton; let some one [else] sail her. You're sick, I'm sick and my boy is sick to the point of death; let's get rid of this miserable business."[30] She cried out to the crew:

> "Boys, I appeal to you as sons and husbands, don't go out. Think of my boy dying at death's door… Think of your own mothers and your own wives. Why should you go out at the point of your lives for the pleasure and profit of a lot of miserable millionaires who have money up on this race? You've won two races already. Why should you risk your lives to win a third? Angus Walters says he is willing to call both races you won yours and let the contest go at that."[31]

As she was a principal shareholder in the vessel, Morrissey told his crew, it was only fair to listen to her, and he offered to go over and talk to Walters himself. He arrived at the *Bluenose* to find the Nova Scotians all smiles at the prospect of a heavy-weather sail. The crew poured down into the cabin to hear what was being said, but Walters ordered them back on deck. Initially, Angus seemed to be willing to oblige Clayton: "We're good friends, Clayte," said Captain Walters, "but there's a lot around here trying to make us bad friends. If you lay to the wharf I'm willing to lay to the wharf and if you go out I'll go out," reported Jerry Snider, who witnessed the meeting.[32] After five more minutes of talking, they decided to "cut the knot by racing." Morrissey arrived back at his boat and, speaking to his anxious wife, told her, "Be a good girl and go home now. I must go, they've got me." With tears in his eyes, he ordered his crew to cast off.[33]

The HMCS *Patriot*, having taken over the role of committee boat, stood by with its four-inch gun at the ready to start the race. The twenty-five-knot wind that had been raging all morning had diminished to half that by the time the two competitors moved into position. In a start very similar to that of Monday's race, both vessels hit the line almost simultaneously, but this time with the *Bluenose* in a slight lead. She had outmanoeuvred the *Ford* by coming up to windward at the last moment and blanketing the American. So close did they come together that a crew member could have leapt from one vessel to the other, but no foul was declared. Tension on board the competing boats rose sharply as caustic slurs began to erupt from both sides. "There was a tremendous broadside of language from both ships and it must be confessed that while the Nova Scotians vocabulary is extensive, Gloucester plumbs the depths and scales the heights of expression which Canada cannot attempt," wrote Jerry Snider on board the *Henry Ford*.[34] The *Bluenose* sailed easily to a boat length ahead, while Morrissey held off for a time to escape the blanket. After the great main boom of his rival cleared, he swung down hard on his wheel, crossing the Lunenburger's wake and coming up to windward like an express train. The first leg was a back-and-forth affair, with each boat taking a turn at the lead. When the first serious dips into the ocean swell began, it looked as though both vessels were in danger of losing their main tops. Neither crew had remembered to set backstays, and the slender spruce topmasts curled forward like whips against the sky. "So close were the schooners that the shouts of the men working on the backstay wires of the two seemed to come from one quarterdeck,"[35] wrote Snider.

Bluenose rounded the first mark in the lead by half a minute, and the race continued with both vessels in tandem, tack for tack. The second leg was a real luffing match, with Morrissey fighting for the weather berth and Walters trying to hold onto it. The vessels worked themselves far up to windward as they bore down on the second mark, when the *Ford* finally had a chance to move ahead, gaining her only advantage in the race. The *Bluenose* soon outfooted her and resumed the lead after passing the mark. On the fourth leg it was a close reach, with the wind blowing at over twenty-five knots. Both boats flew along at thirteen knots, the *Bluenose* appearing to stand up stiffer to the weather, and aside from the occasional spurt of water coming up through her scuppers, remaining dry. Captain Albert Himmelman, who was working as a crewman on the *Bluenose*, reputedly walked the deck all day without bothering with seaboots. Snider described how the *Ford*, on the other hand, staggered under the press of wind

> until the blue brine poured in solid torrents over her waist and quarter bulwarks and were heaved up in great deep swibs to the lee comings of her hatches nine feet inboard. The sheer poles of the *Ford* were nearly ten feet above the level of the deck and at times the lee ones were almost buried.

The crew of the *Ford* was ecstatic, crying out, "Ata boy, Henry, go it old socks, she's a hound, I tell you, she's a hound."[36]

The last five-mile leg was dead to wind, a "real muzzler," as the boats hauled almost due west. Both vessels sheeted hard and made for weather. Approaching the last turn, Albert Himmelman rushed to the stern and shouted back to the *Ford*, "If you gentlemen got anything further to say, say it now. From now on it'll cost you… postage."[37] Even Morrissey was struck by the *Bluenose*'s windward work. "She spins like a top and her crew do know how to handle her canvas. I don't mind saying that in a breeze of wind she is too much for us going to windward."[38]

It was an exciting thrash home against the darkening evening sky, with one last bit of high drama to cap it off. When the crew lowered the *Bluenose*'s fisherman's staysail for the next tack, one of the halyards caught crewman Ernie Hiltz around the ankle, snatching him from the deck and shooting him aloft. "While the sail thundered and flailed and threatened to beat him to bits, his shipmates swarmed up the rigging to cut him adrift. Others rushed to the waist ready to catch him should he be hurled clear."[39] After a five-minute battle to cut him free of the halyard, they got him into the crosstrees but in the process loosened the quadrilateral sail, which flogged and flailed itself into a dozen pieces before flying off to leeward. Hiltz survived the ordeal with a badly fractured leg.

Even this mishap failed to slow the *Bluenose* significantly, and she gained three minutes over her rival on the final leg. She crossed the finish seven minutes, twenty-three seconds ahead of the *Ford*, once again proving her mastery of heavy weather. With the series officially tied at a race apiece, the Lunenburg boat was still in the game.

The following morning, both captains had divers down to inspect their hulls before the next race. The atmosphere around the two boats had been poisoned with antipathy, rumour and paranoia. A member of the *Ford* crew had noticed an unfamiliar diver hanging around the wharf the day before, and someone else had reported that on the *Henry Ford* a plank had been fastened across the keel, the rudder damaged and the sails slashed. These stories proved to be groundless; all Morrissey discovered were some small pieces adrift on his keel, and he had a diver remove them. The problems with the steering gear needed only minor mechanical adjustment. The diver on the *Bluenose* found much more; the keel had been gouged and splintered severely, but not through sabotage. The damage had been done when the boat had sat on the rock at low tide. Walters called for an hour's

TURMOIL IN GLOUCESTER: 1922   *III*

postponement while the diver pared down a 12-foot (3.6-metre) section of the shoe. By the time the two boats met off the breakwater for the eleven o'clock start, the wind was puffing up a fresh nor'westerly breeze. Morrissey was still feeling poorly and had brought Captain Al Malloch, one of Gloucester's great "drivers," aboard to help him out. Both the boats, under four lowers, killed time dodging around the HMCS *Patriot* before the start.

When the cannon fired, the wind had flopped to a mere twelve knots, catching the boats well behind the line. The start was a poor one; the boats crossed the line more than a minute behind the gun. The *Bluenose* took an early lead by several boat lengths, moving faster than her rival in the long ocean swells. The day seemed to be right for the Nova Scotians when the wind picked up to real fishermen's weather, at times topping thirty knots. "Captain Morrissey's *Ford* appeared in the puffs much the tenderer, heeling down until her lee rail was in the water. The *Bluenose*, standing up straight in the gusts, slowly drew away, all the way down the shore," wrote Leonard Fowle of the *Boston Globe*.[40] On the second leg the *Ford* fared better when the wind eased off to about ten knots and she chased down the *Bluenose*. From his position on the cabin roof, hunched over to ease the pain of his hernia, Morrissey kept an eye on his sails while Al Malloch handled the wheel. Just as the *Ford* was about to overhaul her rival, the wind picked up slightly and gave the Lunenburger a chance to escape. When Walters characteristically spat on his hands and gave his wheel a hard spin at the second mark, the *Ford* almost overhauled the *Bluenose* again. The Americans were not quite as efficient at shifting the staysail as were the Canadians, and "as the boats were only seconds apart, quick sail handling counted heavily and the *Bluenose* gained 20 yards."[41]

On the third leg, the *Ford* gripped onto the stern of the *Bluenose* as if attached by a tow line, never more than one hundred yards behind. When the wind rose again, however, the *Bluenose* took off. There was only a minute between them when they passed the next mark, but the Nova Scotian was back in her element. The *Ford* hung on, only a few hundred yards behind. "Both vessels were carrying too much sail, as the wind hardened again and they were smothered in the puffs; but neither skipper would start a halyard and both hung on to their kites and drove them while the steel rigging hummed."[42] At this point in the race, the crew of the *Ford* noticed a small split in the staysail and had to cast off the halyard to bring it in. They had barely smothered the billowing sail on the deck when, with a blistering crack, away went the top ten feet (three metres) of the fore topmast. The rigging held, but the broken mast carried off the fore gaff topsail and the ballooner. The crew worked like demons to clear away the mess and haul in the loosened sail. She seemed to sail better with her top-hamper gone, but was still well behind her opponent. Seeing the problems on board the *Ford*, Angus, in a show of sportsman-ship, quickly hauled in matching sails, so both were now smoking along under the same set of canvas. Jerry Snider, on board the *Ford*, described the scene on deck as she bravely fought towards the finish.

Driving her to the limit she was awash from for'ard of the fore rigging to the taffrail. When she dipped to the heaviest puffs she had a roaring millstream of water on her decks extending inboard ten feet from the scuppers. The upper deadeyes of her shrouds are away above a man's head as he stands on the deck. She was heeled until these were buried in the broken water of her track. The gangway between her cabin house and the lee rails is three or four feet wide and house and rail are each two feet or more above the quarterdeck. This gangway was filled to the brim with roaring water and it swirled up three feet or more past the lee side of the house, nothing could be seen on the lee rail except one little piece of the bow.[43]

The *Bluenose*, on the other hand, barely had her decks wet as she crossed the finish more than seven minutes ahead of the *Ford*. The *Boston Globe* reporter lamented: "Today's meeting proved conclusively that the *Henry Ford* is no match for the *Bluenose* in a breeze from 15 to 30 knots in strength. While the Nova Scotian stood up and seemed to enjoy the puffs, the harder the better, the *Henry Ford* was close to being overpowered along toward the close."[44] When asked later about the weather on the course, Angus replied in his characteristically cocky manner, "Well I tell you, I never wore no coat or oilskins and if there was any spray flyin' I never felt it. Certainly not the kind of weather you look for a topmast to go in. Leastaways, ours didn't."[45]

Although the controversies over sail cutting and the disallowing of races raged on, the series was officially over and Nova Scotia the winner of the cup. Four races had been run, the *Ford* proving herself better in lighter airs and the *Bluenose* standing up to a "fisherman's wind." The relative merits of each vessel would be talked about long and hard over the coming winter.

The dissent, misgivings and generally ugly mood that accompanied the races did not go away. The *Ford* lodged four official protests against the *Bluenose*. First,

there had been no American observer on board the *Bluenose* during the last two races. The original observer, Russell Smith, had resigned, and the new man had failed to appear. As this was found to be the committee's responsibility and not Captain Walters's, this protest was not allowed to stand. Second, a replacement staysail used in the final race had not been measured. The first one had been blown to pieces when Ernie Hiltz had his mishap. It had been replaced by a smaller, older sail, which was found acceptable by the committee. The third protest concerned the material used in the sail canvas of the *Bluenose*, reputedly of finer quality than that used by an ordinary fisherman. Since her arrival, remarks had been made about the fine Egyptian-cotton yacht sails given to Walters by an English admirer. Speculation had been further fuelled by the set of sail covers on her booms, a highly unusual and suspicious feature in the eyes of fishermen, as no other banks schooner carried them. This charge was quashed when the sail was inspected and found to be of a common grade. The last protest accused the *Bluenose* crew of shifting ballast between races, but as no evidence of this manoeuvre could be found, this charge was also dismissed. The fact that all four protests came to naught did nothing to dispel the bitterness felt by both sides and only served to convince their opponents that the Americans were sore losers.

Astonishingly, Captain Morrissey expressed a desire for one more race. "I raced after winning the first two times. We have now won two each. I hope Angus will meet me again."[46] Jonathan Raymond raised $2,000 for the matchup, but Walters, satisfied that the best boat had won two races in a "fisherman's breeze," flatly refused to entertain the idea. The race committee felt it had performed its functions and would not act further on the matter. Suspicion around the series continued to fester. Members of the race committee were accused of having rigged the series in favour of the *Bluenose*. When Captain George Peeples, the committee chairman, got wind of a rumour that he had bet on the *Bluenose*, he posted a $100 reward for anyone who could prove it. Most believed too many yachting interests had become involved in the event, and the only hope of continuing the series lay in yachtsmen and their fancy rules being excluded in the future.

Walters had no desire to remain in these unfriendly waters and wanted to pick up his winnings and head home as quickly as possible. He had lost all interest in competing against the *Mayflower* and announced unequivocally that he would not race again in the United States that year. Then rancour turned to grief when an

‹ **ANGUS WALTERS** poses for cameramen at the wheel of the *Bluenose* the day after winning the highly contentious 1922 series against Clayton Morrissey and the *Henry Ford*. A news reporter compared the atmosphere in Gloucester to that of a war zone, with citizens boiling over with anger at the outcome of the series. Walters vowed never to race in American waters again. *Leslie Jones, Boston Public Library*

announcement was made during a noon-hour banquet to present the prize money and trophy to Walters and his crew that Bert Demone, Walters's nephew and *Bluenose* shipmate, had been found dead, face down in the mud at the foot of a wharf behind the Olympic Theater. The night before, Demone had requested money to go ashore, but Walters had turned him down, feeling that, as tempers were high in town, his crew would be safer aboard. Despite Walters's warning to stay close to the boat, Demone headed ashore. What transpired remains a mystery. Walters always maintained his nephew must have got hold of some liquor and probably fell in with a bad crowd, one of whom shoved him off the wharf, drowning him. A police inquiry later found no evidence of foul play. For Walters, added to the trouble about the races and the two men he had in hospital—Ernie Hiltz with his broken leg and Randolph Stevens with appendicitis—this news was more than enough reason to end the celebration. He recalled his crew and sent the *Bluenose* home under the command of his mate, Ammon Zinck, while he remained behind to escort the body of his nephew. It was a sad departure, perhaps appropriate for a bitter and disappointing series. Not a whistle blew nor bell rang out as onlookers silently watched the black-hulled schooner slip out of the harbour, her ensign flying halfway down her peak.

At that moment, the future of the series looked remarkably bleak. Fred Wallace, the eminent editor of *Canadian Fisherman* magazine, wrote years later in his book, *The Roving Fisherman*, "After the acrimony and ill-feeling engendered by the races of October 1922, I lost all interest in the event. Skippers and crews were all right. It was the newspapers and sports writers and yachting enthusiasts, by injecting their ideas into the business, that ruined it."[47]

NOTES

1 *Evening Mail*, October 27, 1921; Story, *Hail Columbia!*, p. 43; *Atlantic Fisherman*, June 1922, p. 17

2 *Evening Mail*, October 27, 1921

3 George Hudson, *Boston Sunday Herald*, February 5, 1922

4 Dunne, *Thomas F. McManus*, p. 323

5 *Atlantic Fisherman*, June 1922, p. 18

6 Garland, *Adventure*, p. 23

7 *Atlantic Fisherman*, July 1922, p. 5

8 Ibid., p. 6

9 Backman, *Bluenose*, p. 42

10 *Evening Mail*, September 30, 1922

11 Jerry Snider, *Evening Mail*, October 9, 1922

12 Ibid.

13 Ibid.

14 Ibid.

15 Ed Millet, *Halifax Herald*, October 13, 1922

16 *Halifax Herald*, October 16, 1922

17 See Appendix, (4)

18 *Boston Globe*, October 21, 1922

19 Ibid.

20 Leonard Fowle, *Boston Globe*, October 22, 1922

21 Ibid.

22 Edgar Kelly, *Halifax Herald*, October 23, 1922

23 Merkel, *Schooner Bluenose*, p. 37

24 Fowle, *Boston Globe*, October 24, 1922

25 Snider, *Toronto Telegram*, October 24, 1922

26 *Boston Post*, October 25, 1922

27 Kelly, *Halifax Herald*, October 25, 1922

28 Garland, *Eastern Point*

29 Snider, *Toronto Telegram*, October 25, 1922

30 *Boston Globe*, October 25, 1922

31 Snider, *Toronto Telegram*, October 26, 1922

32 Ibid.

33 *Boston Globe*, October 25, 1922

34 Snider, *Toronto Telegram*, October 26, 1922

35 Ibid.

36 Ibid.

37 *Maclean's*, June 15, 1950, p. 48

38 Snider, *Toronto Telegram*, October 26, 1922

39 Ibid.

40 Fowle, *Boston Globe*, October 27, 1922

41 *Gloucester Daily Times*, October 26, 1922

42 *Yachting*, November 1922, p. 258

43 Snider, *Toronto Telegram*, October 27, 1922

44 Fowle, *Boston Globe*, October 27, 1922

45 Backman, *Bluenose*, p. 43

46 *Boston Globe*, October 27, 1922

47 Wallace, *Roving Fisherman*, p. 422

‹ **THE *COLUMBIA*** was the last all-sail schooner to be built for the American fishery. Even though most American schooners had been motorized and turned to the fresh-fish trade, *Columbia*'s backers felt there was still a dollar to be made in salt fish. It was obvious that her primary function was to beat the Canadians, but, as she was built as a salt banker, there could be no argument about her being a true fisherman under the race regulations. *Author's collection*

7

"I AM NOT A SPORTSMAN": 1923

IF THERE WAS ANY lingering ill will in 1923 after the turmoil of the previous series in Gloucester, it did not appear in the popular press. There was too much public interest to allow the International Fishermen's Cup series to be overshadowed by bad feeling, and the Americans also wanted another opportunity to win back the cup. The papers were full of stories anticipating the upcoming series and celebrating the last. Ironically, one New York newspaper went so far as to suggest that the 1922 series should be nominated as the sporting event of the century. The Fishermen's Cup had often been favourably compared to the illustrious America's Cup, which was now held infrequently, depending on the whim of Sir Thomas Lipton. Enthusiasts were eager for an ocean race that could be counted on to run like clockwork every fall, and so far the Fishermen's Cup had done exactly that for three years running. The perception that it was a working man's race gave it greater credibility with the general populace, and the uproar of the previous year was generally dismissed as growing pains. The Fishermen's series had all but eclipsed the "millionaire's races," and most believed they could go on indefinitely.

One man still with an axe to grind was Captain Larkin of the schooner *Mayflower*. His long battle for acceptance into this select group of fishermen had been denied time and again. After he had finally fixed a match with the *Bluenose* for the end of the 1922 series, he arrived in Gloucester only to find that Walters had sent his ship home. Fit to be tied, Larkin fired off a telegram accusing Walters of reneging on the deal and challenging him again, this time for a purse of $5,000. "I have tried for two solid years to get this man to race," Larkin declared in an open letter to the papers.[1] Larkin attempted to embarrass Walters into a match, but Angus, playing to the hometown crowd, countered that it was he who had been slighted. "For two years the master and owners of the *Mayflower* have studiously ignored our offer to race the *Bluenose* against the *Mayflower* for a side bet of ten thousand dollars, vessels to sail from Newfoundland to West Indies with equal cargo of fish, proceeding to Turk's Island, load equal cargo of salt and return to Newfoundland."[2] A frustrated Larkin finally gave up his attempts to race the *Bluenose* over a measured course and never followed up on Walters's offer. In a move that seemed to substantiate the international race committee's original claim that she was no fisherman, the owners of the *Mayflower* decided she was not commercially viable, and in March 1923 had her hauled up on the marine railway in Gloucester, an engine installed and her lofty spars cut down to a workmanlike size.

Another schooner was under construction in Essex over the winter. Ben Pine had wanted to compete with his own boat ever since his first taste of racing with Marty Welsh on the *Elsie*. Thus far, his two attempts had yielded disappointing results. His first had been with the beautiful but short-lived schooner *Puritan* and his second with the *Elizabeth Howard*, which had proved incapable of beating the *Henry Ford*. Former members of the Manta Club agreed to finance the building of a new schooner and again engaged Starling Burgess, the designer of both the *Puritan* and the *Mayflower*, to draw up plans. Contrary to the American practice of the time, which favoured building boats for the fresh-fish industry, Pine decided his vessel would be a true salt banker. He believed there was still money to be made in that market, and that this would no doubt discourage any argument about whether his boat was a true fisherman. Her owners declared emphatically that she was built for banking, pure and simple, but it was also clear she was a prime candidate for Fishermen's Cup honours. The new schooner, *Columbia*, was built at the A.D. Story yard in Essex. As with the *Henry Ford* before her, Arthur Story invested in her.

Pine was an interesting character in Gloucester. Although he never really spent much time on schooners, he was an invaluable member of the fishing community. Born in Belleoram, Newfoundland, in 1883 (then a British colony separate from Canada), he had moved to Gloucester when he was only ten years old.[3] Like many of his compatriots from the Maritimes, he no doubt believed the future in New England looked brighter than that offered by his Newfoundland outport settlement. As a "rag and bone" man servicing the maritime industry, he scoured Gloucester Harbour, buying dories and selling and salvaging anything that could make him a dollar. He would occasionally go fishing to supplement his income but spent most of his youth developing a keen business sense as a junk dealer. In 1905 he went into a trading partnership with Joe Langsford, selling ship supplies and buying shares in fishing vessels. By 1922, he had started the Atlantic Supply Company, a ship's chandlery that also managed a fleet of schooners. Pine often went into partnership with a fisherman by jointly purchasing a schooner and equipping it from his chandlery. If his partner needed dories, sails, trawls, line or any other equipment required in the running of an offshore boat, Pine supplied it, marking it up against his co-owner's side of the ledger. After a few years, the partner might want to sell his share—only to find that he had little value left from his original purchase. Pine could thus cheaply buy out his partner and add a new boat to his private fleet.

Although Pine was a steely businessman who drove a hard bargain and knew the value of a dollar, when it came to schooners he was soft to the core. He loved them, and he loved the industry. He must have been able to foresee the end of the all-sail fleet, because there was an urgency in his desire to make his mark as a racing fisherman in those twilight days of sail. His utter lack of experience as master of a fishing schooner did not deter him in the least. He appeared to have a natural talent for ship handling by virtue, some said, of just being born a Newfoundlander. Whatever it was, he felt completely comfortable at the helm of a big banks schooner, and he had the tenacity and ambition needed to compete. The fact that "Piney" was not a true fisherman did not seem an issue in the fishing community of Gloucester, nor would it affect his participation in the International Fishermen's Cup series.

Crews began work on the *Columbia* in December 1922 and continued through one of the most vicious winters in living memory. Sea ice choked the harbours, and the Cape Ann peninsula was swept with snowstorms. In spite of the slow progress caused by the weather, the sweet, graceful lines of the hull of the 141-foot (43-metre) schooner soon emerged. In March, when normally milder temperatures should have allowed work to speed up, another snowstorm put the builders further behind schedule. When the grey-and-white hull was launched on April 17, there was little time left before the deadline of April 30 in which to complete the rigging and fitting. The vessel was quickly towed to Gloucester and, in record time, masts were stepped, rigging was hung and the ship fitted out and readied for sea by April 26. She left under the command of Captain Alden Geele, to pick up a crew and a load of dories in Shelburne, Nova Scotia. Carrying only a minimum of sail, she was a disappointing sight to the spectators in the harbour, but because of the time constraints and the necessity of putting in a season of fishing before the races, there had been no choice. She had no mainsail or topsails and carried only a small triangular storm sail, a foresail, jumbo and jib. After arriving in Shelburne, where he picked up twenty-four dories (for a much lower price than in the United States), Geele was forced to wait for crew until another storm abated. Crews for fishing schooners were becoming increasingly hard to find in Gloucester, and the skippers and owners relied on Nova Scotia men to fill the depleted ranks. The *Columbia* finally put out to sea on her first fishing trip on May 8. Pine applied to the international committee in Halifax for dispensation caused by the delays, and received assurances that his entry would be accepted.

In Nova Scotia, another contender for the international series was launched in late April from Mahone Bay. Captain Albert Himmelman, on the *Independence*, had lost the Canadian elimination races to the *Bluenose* in 1921. Rather than watch from the sidelines, he had signed on as part of the *Bluenose* racing crew and sailed with Walters against both the *Elsie* and, in 1922, the *Henry Ford*. Himmelman, brother of Tommy Himmelman, was a successful and popular fishing skipper who loved to race and was determined to captain his own craft to victory. In the fall of 1922 he sold the *Independence* and ordered a new craft, the *Keno*, to be built at the John McLean and Sons yard in Mahone Bay. Having studied the *Bluenose*, Himmelman was determined to build an even faster boat. Walking her decks he had been heard to say, "She'll be a foot or so narrower than this one and she won't have the shoulders on her."[4] At 140 feet (42.7 metres), the *Keno* was very similar in size to

the champion, but delays in her construction meant she did not get onto the banks until late spring—too late to qualify. So Nova Scotians would have to wait another year to see what stuff she was made of. According to Jerry Snider, writing in the *Toronto Telegram*, her passage from Lunenburg to Louisbourg in Cape Breton "was the fastest ever made by such a vessel in the memory of living man."[5]

Gloucester was gearing up for a big birthday bash in 1923. It was the three hundredth anniversary of the founding of the community, and the city fathers were planning a week-long celebration to begin on August 25. The centrepiece of the tercentenary festivities was to be a locally run fishermen's race that would, with any luck, successfully erase the memory of last year's debacle. Attempting to demonstrate to the trustees of the international event how to run a fishermen's race properly, Gloucester's was declared open to all fishing schooners, regardless of size, with no limitations on ballast or sail area. Notice of the event went out to all comers from Maine to Newfoundland. The great America's Cup contender Sir Thomas Lipton was asked to donate a cup for the race.

Although half a dozen owners initially expressed interest, only three boats participated. Ben Pine's *Columbia* was unfortunately out of the running as she had suffered damage in a collision with the French beam trawler *La Champlain*, while sitting at anchor off Sable Island. The *Columbia* had been struck on the port side and her forward rigging, bowsprit and bulwarks were damaged, and some of her seams had opened up. She was towed to St. Pierre and temporarily patched up but was clearly not going to be repaired in time for the contest. Unable to resist a race, Pine borrowed the *Elizabeth Howard* once again and entered her. Two Boston boats, the *Yankee* and the *Mayflower,* considered it, but bailed out at the last moment. Captain Clayton Morrissey would be there with the *Henry Ford* if he could get back in time from fishing, and a brand new schooner, the *Shamrock*—fresh from the Story yard in Essex—would also race. She had been built for the O'Hara brothers of Boston, who had hired Captain Marty Welsh to skipper her. No Canadian or Newfoundland boats attended.

Weather conditions on the day of the race, a Wednesday, were so miserable—thick fog and little wind—that officials were forced to postpone until the next day. The contenders did their best on Thursday in a light, eight-knot wind, but it became a drifting match, ending two miles off the finish line when the time limit expired. On Friday, weather at the beginning of the race was not much better. The three vessels started well, within thirty-five seconds of each other, but coasted over a glassy sea towards the first mark. The *Ford* took an early lead and kept it throughout the race, with the *Howard* challenging when the wind freshened through the latter part of the race. The *Shamrock* fell behind right from the start— to no one's surprise, since the schooner was only a week old and Welsh had not had time to try her out or adjust her trim. On the windward beat of the second leg, Pine capitalized on Morrissey's mistake of standing too far inshore, cutting down the *Ford*'s two-minute lead. For the first time in the event, both vessels were scuppering as their lee rails dipped. The race continued to be close, with Pine pressing his vessel for every second of gain, finally crossing the finish line only fifty seconds behind Morrissey. The Lipton Cup and the $1,000 purse were Morrissey's, and Pine and Welsh both came away with the $800 apiece for second and third prize. More entertaining than the actual race was watching Sir Thomas Lipton being dragged from pillar to post in Gloucester for photo opportunities and receptions. The race may have been a fairly lacklustre affair, especially when compared with "the race it blew" of 1892, but it did revive interest in the upcoming international series in Halifax. Talk about the town was focussed now on the absent *Columbia* and how she might perform against the *Henry Ford* and the *Bluenose*.

The *Columbia* returned in mid-September from her misadventure with the French trawler. It appeared after the collision that the crew had thought their schooner was about to sink and had abandoned ship. According to Dana Story,

> Captain Geele ordered the crew to return and save her. Believing their ship was doomed, the crew refused the order. For one of the two times in his long career as a master, Captain Geele was forced to threaten the men with his pistol. He assured them he would use it unless they returned and manned the pumps. In the face of this threat the men re-boarded the vessel and were able to lower the water and keep ahead of it while the trawler which had struck them towed *Columbia* to St. Pierre.[6]

Once back in Gloucester, the *Columbia*'s cargo of salt cod was off-loaded and her repairs completed. The American Fishermen's Cup race committee dearly wanted an elimination race between the *Henry Ford* and the *Columbia*, but as the *Ford* had returned to sea, time was slipping away. On October 14 the Americans appealed to the trustees in Halifax for a postponement, and the Canadians agreed to delay the event until October 27. The Americans were in a quandary. Still awaiting the return of the *Ford,* they held a meeting on October 17 in the Master Mariners Association rooms in Gloucester and decided they would give the *Ford* twenty-four hours to return, after which the *Columbia* would be chosen to contest the 1923 Fishermen's Cup by acclamation. The following day at noon, and only a few hours before the *Columbia* was due to become the certified challenger, the *Henry Ford* sailed into the harbour with 90 tons of fish on board. As soon as Captain Morrissey stepped ashore, he was accosted by members of the committee and grilled about his willingness to race.[7] Unaware of the negotiations and debate that had preceded his arrival, Morrissey announced he was rather cool to the idea. The previous year's series had soured him. He had an enormous amount of work to do in unloading his ship and felt that the *Columbia,* skippered by the enthusiastic Ben Pine, should be Gloucester's challenger.

That night, after another meeting of the race committee, Pine finally persuaded the reluctant Morrissey to compete. With little time and even less inclination, Morrissey set about readying his ship to race on Sunday, October 21, only a week before the international series was to begin. All through Friday and into the night the shore crew worked to remove the fish from the *Ford*'s hold, and on Saturday riggers installed a borrowed topmast and replaced a boom. Although there was no time to haul the *Ford* out and clean her bottom, she was as ready as she was going to be by Sunday morning. The frantic preparations built up the excitement in the town, and any ill will held over from 1922 evaporated with the frenzied pace of events. There was a genuine feeling of optimism, very similar to that of the 1920 race, when the *Esperanto* had been similarly rushed into service.

Regrettably, after all the anxiety, preparation, pleading and cajoling, the elimination race was a bust. Morrissey's *Ford* did not live up to the expectations placed on her, and Pine's *Columbia* effortlessly led the way through a listless race that ended unfinished. After five and half hours of sailing over the thirty-one-mile course, the committee decided to cancel the race before the boats were near the end. The *Columbia* was leading the *Ford* by almost twenty minutes, and it was obvious to all that she should be the challenger. On the following Tuesday morning, amid tremendous cheering, the *Columbia* left Gloucester, accompanied by the uss *Bushnell.* The noise of the crowd had barely died away when the schooner came up hard on Great Round Rock off the Dog Bar breakwater. She was hurriedly escorted back to the harbour and put up on the ways, where a twelve-foot (three-and-a-half-metre) section of her shoe was found to be badly splintered. It took the rest of the day, in heavy rain and high wind, for workers to repair the keel. Wednesday's departure was postponed because of storm-force winds, so Pine and the *Columbia* could not begin their trip until October 25. Faced with the further delay, the trustees agreed to move the opening race date to Monday, October 29.

In Nova Scotia, planning for the series was in its final stages. Requests had been made to competitors for a fleet elimination race, but none had entered, leaving the *Bluenose* to defend the cup unchallenged. Walters had finished off another successful season on the banks with a record catch of 213 tons of fish, making him the season highliner of the Lunenburg fleet. The *Bluenose* had been well prepared. She was hauled out of the water, scrubbed, painted, ballasted and trimmed by many willing hands under the careful supervision of Captain Walters and William Roué. Walters had decided the vessel was too deep during the 1922 series, particularly in the stern, so he lightened the weight of ballast by about ten tons. The *Bluenose* and Walters had by now become household names across Canada, and William Roué, although still working at his family's carbonated-water plant in Halifax, was steadily gaining a reputation as a naval architect. The prominent firm of Ford and Paine in New York asked him to join it as an associate member. He agreed to supply designs to the New York firm but remained based in Halifax, and did not become a full-time boat designer until 1929.

The *Columbia* and the USS *Bushnell* made the 360-mile trip to Halifax in just thirty-eight hours, in good time for the first race. The bickering started almost immediately. Questions were raised over the eligibility of the American boat and the credentials of her skipper. The trustees responded quickly by stating that, in their opinion, "no question regarding the eligibility of Capt. Pine has arisen, and he was designated to handle the *Columbia* in the match if he so desires."[8] Angus Walters then insisted the American boat be hauled out and measured, just as his boat had been for the two previous years.

> We are going to finish this series without a hitch and without ill-feeling if we can. We are not worrying about technicalities. All we ask is a fair field and no favors. We do not want any of the trouble and hard feeling we had at Gloucester last Fall. The request that the *Columbia*, a new vessel, be hauled out and measured is quite an ordinary one.[9]

Trouble about the *Columbia*'s eligibility had been brewing throughout August and September. After the 1922 series the trustees had seen fit to further amend the regulations, adding new rules concerning the tonnage and the freeboard measurements.[10] The American race committee accused the Canadians of stacking the deck in favour of their own boat, and the Canadians responded by insisting that the owners of the *Columbia* send the ship's drawings to be inspected by the race officials. After much correspondence, the Americans yielded and sent off the plans. The trustees found the *Columbia* to be a few inches short of the freeboard dictated by the new regulations, but at length they agreed to waive the new rule. They assured the *Columbia* associates that they would accept the measurements of the vessel at face value and nothing further would be required before the race. So it was an already highly annoyed Ben Pine who reluctantly agreed to a compromise that, should he win, his vessel would be put under the tape.

On Monday morning, the competitors were greeted by a brooding October sky. It was dark and rainy, with a fresh breeze from the west. The harbour was full of pleasure craft huddled about the start line, and hordes of citizens under umbrellas gathered on the headlands. The *Columbia* was first to make sail, leaving her berth at the Pickford and Black wharf shortly before eight o'clock, followed by the *Bluenose*, which left from the Plant wharf. Both vessels jogged under four lowers and awaited the fifteen-minute gun. Signals from the flagstaff on the breakwater indicated course number 2. According to the *Gloucester Daily Times*, both skippers seemed tentative and "unduly gun shy, particularly so with the Yankee as she gingerly approached the line. Seldom in an International trophy race have skippers gone about their work in such a leisurely fashion."[11] With a Canadian Air Force service plane roaring overhead, the *Bluenose* crossed the line first, five boat lengths ahead of her rival and one minute, twenty seconds after the gun.

It was a close reach down to the Inner Automatic Buoy, with a squally wind and wicked puffs coming down off the land. The *Columbia* buried her lee rail in one puff and the sea washed over her deck as high as her cabin top, reminiscent of the *Henry Ford* the previous year. Her crew quickly eased sheets and stood her up again. The *Bluenose* gained on the first leg and passed the mark one minute, sixteen seconds in the lead. American observers on board the warship *Bushnell* looked on in dismay as the Canadian boat seemed to be walking away with the race. After both vessels left the confines of the harbour, they faced a stiffer breeze and a choppier sea. Easing the sheets on the broad reach to the Outer Buoy,

DURING THE FIRST race off Halifax in 1923, Angus Walters in the *Bluenose* was crowded towards the rocky shore when he attempted to overtake the *Columbia* to windward. Ben Pine continued to pinch his rival towards the shoal marker off Duncan's Cove, but an undeterred Walters ran inside the marker and overtook the *Columbia*. Forced to either run ashore or turn into the *Columbia*, he chose the latter and struck the American boat with his main boom. The collision set off a storm of protest and indignation from both parties. *Author's collection*

Walters made further gains, passing the next mark more than two minutes ahead of the *Columbia*. Thus far, the *Bluenose* had proved to be the better vessel on runs and reaches. When the boats rounded the second mark and headed towards the Sambro Lightship Buoy, the wind picked up and moved around to the southeast and a heavier sea tumbled in from offshore. The Yankee was finally in her element and both boats revelled in the weather, pounding along a starboard tack with sheets flattened. With water streaming over her bridge, the committee boat *Lady Laurier* had a rough ride, frequently disappearing in the hollows of waves.[12]

Things began to get exciting when the *Columbia*'s superior windward ability allowed her to point higher than her rival and sail as fast. After two long tacks towards the Sambro Buoy, Ben Pine attempted to seize the windward berth between the *Bluenose* and the next mark. Pine drove his vessel as far offshore as he dared before coming about, forcing Walters to over-stand the mark. The Americans' superior handling of sail allowed the *Columbia* to come about in half the time of her rival. Past the buoy, the *Columbia* gained the lead for the first time in the race but by only a few seconds.

On the long eleven-mile reach back to the Inner Automatic, the *Bluenose* attempted to regain the weather berth, sailing slightly behind her opponent, her bowsprit never more than a few yards from the *Columbia*'s stern. To the spectators ashore it began to look like a repeat of the 1920 race, when Marty Welsh and Tommy Himmelman had fought a duel alongside the shoals of Devil Island. Pine pinched his vessel higher towards the shoals off Chebucto Head with Walters tenaciously hanging on and gradually inching his vessel ahead, until her bow began to overlap the American on her port side. Pine pinched higher, forcing the race closer to the shore and farther from the course line. The Canadian observer on the *Columbia* described the scene: "Both vessels were tearing towards the Inner Automatic buoy, with the iron fangs of Chebucto Head gnashing at them close aboard. *Bluenose* was regaining ground she had lost by over standing, and the *Columbia* kept luffing her... until both vessels were almost on the rocks."[13] With the *Bluenose* threatening to overtake the *Columbia*, Pine fought hard to hold on to his position, pushing the *Bluenose* closer towards the shore. "The schooners tore along, the *Bluenose* not more than a biscuit toss from the Three Sisters, one of the most dreaded shoals on the coast." When they barrelled down on Bell Rock Buoy, marking another inshore shoal, members of his crew reported that Pine all but "scraped the whiskers off the buoy" in an attempt to force Walters to fall off under his stern. Undeterred, the Lunenburger shot through the "green waters inside the buoy" and committed the *Bluenose* to the dangerous path of passing between it and the shoal.[14] Continuing her gains, the *Bluenose* overlapped her rival and steadily began to overtake her. Unwilling to give his opponent an inch, Pine kept his course and deliberately kept on luffing his rival towards the shore.

On board the *Bluenose*, the Halifax harbour pilot shouted to Albert Himmelman, spelling off Angus Walters at the helm, that he must bear away from shore. "Bear away and we strike him," Himmelman replied. "Strike him, or we strike the rocks," was the pilot's terse response. It was becoming obvious to all that the *Bluenose* had no choice, so she bore off with eased sheets, allowing the booms to run free in the now-following breeze. Walters doused his staysail and flung his foresail to port, wing and wing. Pine could have fallen off but continued on his course until the vessels converged, the eighty-one-foot (twenty-four-metre) boom of the *Bluenose* looming towards the *Columbia's* afterdeck. The great wings of the Nova Scotian swallowed *Columbia's* wind, stalling her as she crossed her bow. When the *Bluenose* surged ahead, the main boom, standing out forty feet (twelve metres) to leeward, struck the main shrouds of the *Columbia*, scraping clear and hitting the fore shrouds, buckling the one-inch-thick (twenty-five-millimetre) sheer pole in half like an iron hoop. The boom then skidded forward, catching on the jib stay and holding there, actually towing the challenger for a minute or two before being wrenched free. On board the *Bluenose*, the drag on the boom end unshipped the jaws from the mast, sending the boom forward several feet past the mainmast and leaving the mainsail hanging like a broken wing. With Herculean effort, seven brawny Lunenburgers manhandled the massive boom back into place.[15]

The *Columbia* recovered her speed and resumed the chase, but the *Bluenose* turned the last mark just over one minute ahead. Along the last six-mile broad reach up the harbour, the *Bluenose* once again showed her superior ability on the reaches and gained a few more seconds, crossing the finish one minute, twenty seconds ahead. The two ships received a tumultuous welcome from the crowd. The race had been one of the most stubbornly contested in the history of the International Fishermen's Cup series. The *Columbia* was, without a doubt, a good match for the Nova Scotian, and her determined skipper, Captain Ben Pine, every bit the equal of the tenacious and obstinate Angus Walters.

The *Columbia*'s crew and supporters cried for blood after being fouled by the *Bluenose*, believing it had cost them the race. But, although it was clear that the Lunenburg boat had struck them, Ben Pine refused to lodge a protest. Both boats had been on a beam reach, with the *Bluenose* gaining steadily, when the incident occurred. It stood to reason that the *Bluenose* had to have been even with or slightly forward of the beam for her to start taking the American's wind when she bore off and crossed. Pine had forced Walters's hand by crowding him farther into the shore off Duncan's Cove, but according to rule 6 of the race regulations he was obliged to give sea room only after being hailed by the other vessel. This, he insisted, had not happened. However, as both boats had Halifax pilots aboard, neither could argue that they were unaware of their proximity to shore and of the dangers close by. Pine would have been blind not to have realized his opponent would either have to alter course immediately or risk piling up on the shore. His own course was a good forty degrees away from the course line to the next buoy. He had chosen to continue crowding his rival in order to keep the weather berth, instead of easing his sheets for the run to the buoy.

Walters and Himmelman, on the other hand, felt they had cause for protest. Whether or not they had actually hailed for sea room remains unclear, but it appeared obvious from the film footage taken from an aircraft above the race that, minutes before the incident, the *Bluenose* had already overtaken the *Columbia* and was quickly running out of sea room. It was indisputable that Pine remained on course while the *Bluenose* bore off towards him, indicating that he was willing to incur a collision rather than give way. In the Canadians' minds, Pine's refusal to give way had caused the collision. Both sides decided in the end that there would be no advantage in pursuing the matter. The sailing committee made it clear that there would be no similar occurrences in the future, however, by drafting a set of "special rules" to cover the rest of the series. It listed all the buoys and specifically ordered that all of them be passed to seaward.[16]

On Tuesday, dense fog and lack of wind caused the postponement of the second race. Pine used the day off to trim his vessel. He was unhappy with her steering and thought she was sluggish in her turns. Captain Geele had brought this to Pine's attention during the fishing season, but Pine had not considered it a serious problem until now. He also thought the surface area of the rudder was inadequate and hired a diver to spike planks to it. H.R. Silver, the chairman of the trustees, advised him that such an action, while the series was underway, was

unwise. Pine relented, but he and his crew had another problem to deal with: They were upset with their Canadian observer, Jerry Snider, and wanted him removed. Snider, who had been the observer on the *Henry Ford* the previous year, was a well-known reporter for the *Toronto Telegram* and often wrote in the Halifax papers. His partisan and inflammatory account of the race had incensed the American crew and, charging that he "had a camera aboard and took copious notes concerning the tactics of the Yankee crew," they complained that his presence on board affected morale. His "observations both during and after Monday's race, proved very obnoxious to the men."[17] The race committee thought it prudent to have him replaced, and was roundly applauded by the Gloucester crew.

More favourable conditions seemed likely for Wednesday's race, as the remnants of a gale that had whipped up through the night left heavy rain and a light northwest breeze. Pine's alterations to the *Columbia*'s trim appeared to improve her performance in the light airs, and she outpaced the *Bluenose* throughout the race. After the boats had taken three and half hours to cover less than half the course, however, the sailing committee acknowledged there was no possibility of finishing the contest and called it off. Ironically, the wind picked up to fifteen knots soon after the committee boat hailed the vessels and sent the racers scurrying back into harbour. Had timing been better, it would have made for a splendid race. The *Bluenose* came to life and easily overhauled her rival as they headed up into the harbour.

On Thursday morning, the men had their mug-up early so that they could dry out the sails left sodden after a heavy overnight downpour. The clouds were scudding across the sky and the air was raw, with a fine breeze of about twenty knots blowing from the northeast. Conditions seemed made to order and the course chosen for the day was number 2, the same as for the first race. Both schooners crossed the start within forty seconds of each other, and the *Bluenose* had a thirteen-second lead on the run for the Inner Automatic. Pine's attempt to work his boat to windward of the *Bluenose* failed due to lack of speed. The wind grew stronger, and the sea began to build as they passed the Inner Automatic, leaving the fleet of spectator boats pitching and rolling in the waves behind them. As they neared the second mark, the Outer Automatic Buoy, the schooners had every stitch of canvas aloft and were now outpacing the steamer *Lady Laurier*, which was moving along at twelve knots. Only the Canadian destroyer *Patriot*, which carried the race officials, could keep pace with the flying fishermen. The *Columbia* was splitting the oncoming waves, throwing off sheets of green water to either side, and the *Bluenose*'s fuller bow was smashing into the seas and sending off a blinding smother of foam.[18]

Both boats jibed and heeled over hard around the second mark, "a feat calling for heroic courage considering the half gale and the nearly 10,000 feet of canvas, hard as iron, under tons of pressure, that spired 150 feet above the sea."[19] Blocks squealed as the crews manned the sheets and the massive eighty-foot (twenty-four-metre) booms were hurled from port to starboard, coming up hard on the shock-absorbing preventers. It was the roughest day of the series, with a wind blowing thirty knots. The *Bluenose* quickly righted herself as she made the mark one minute, twenty seconds ahead of the *Columbia*. On the run for the Sambro Buoy, both boats were wing and wing, wallowing and rolling in the growing seas. The American had a harder time of it as her main boom dipped and dragged in the combers, which affected the quality of her steering. Since her mainsail was cut much higher on the foot, the *Bluenose* did not drag her boom. The effort required to maintain the course took its toll. On board the *Columbia*, Ben Pine and another crew member struggled with the wheel, "as no one man has the physical strength to steer a wildly rearing vessel of some 260 tons displacement hour after hour."[20] Although the *Columbia* had been slowly gaining on her rival, she lost ground when her fore topsail was taken in too soon at the Sambro Buoy.

The sea around the buoy was rough and choppy, with stiff squalls picking off the crests into sheets of spray. The eighteen-mile stretch for home would be a real test for both as they made the close-hauled thrash to windward. The vessels stood out for a long starboard tack towards the Sambro Ledges, and there the *Bluenose* showed her best performance of the day. The *Columbia* seemed to have trouble with the wind and fell off course badly as her crew struggled to clew up the fore-topsail, which had sagged to leeward. Walters kept pinching his vessel on the wind, pointing higher, footing faster and finally leaving his rival half a mile behind. Neither boat could make the mark, and both were forced to tack as they approached the Inner Automatic Buoy, but when the *Columbia* came about, a wave swept over the lee rail, carrying crew member Steve Post into the sea-foamed scuppers and washing him over the side. Five men grabbed him by his oilskins as he swept past the quarter, dragged him back on board and threw him on the cabin roof. He suffered only scratches and bruises, commonplace on a banks schooner.

The *Bluenose* had problems of her own. The wind—shrieking through the rigging and exerting tremendous pressure on the masts—had parted a backstay to

the main topmast. The thick wire whipped and flailed about the deck, coming within inches of the American observer and several others. It then snaked about the stern of the vessel, where the captain was stationed. The *Gloucester Daily Times* reported that "it caught a turn about Capt. Angus Walters's arm as he crouched at the steering wheel and held his ground in the face of death. This wire, almost as thick as one's wrist, could sever his body yet the plucky Lunenburger hardly flinched, fists gripping throbbing spokes and the mad sea a maelstrom."[21] The crew quickly took in the staysail until the wire could be secured, but in the process the main topmast became badly sprung. The *Bluenose* remained firmly in the lead past the final mark, but the *Columbia* fought back during the continuous series of tacks up the harbour to the finish. After nearly five and half hours of hard sailing, and well over fifty miles of ocean covered, the big Lunenburger crossed the line only two minutes, forty-five seconds ahead of her rival. It was by far the strongest challenge for the championship yet. Ben Pine had given the *Bluenose* the toughest competition of her career and pushed her to the limit, but she had prevailed. The reception at the finish was extraordinary, as the city and harbour erupted into a cacophony of whistles, horns and sirens.

A celebration banquet was scheduled that night at the Halifax Hotel to present the trophy and prize money, but early in the evening it became clear that something had gone wrong. Shortly before the banquet was to have begun, an announcement had been made that representatives of the *Columbia* had lodged a formal protest with the sailing committee concerning the day's race. All the events of the evening were put on hold while the committee convened. H.R. Silver made a brief announcement that there was now some doubt as to the outcome of the race because of the protest, and he asked for co-operation and patience from the crowd as the committee worked through the process. Pine had accused Walters of passing one of the buoys—the Lighthouse Bank—on the wrong side, and both men were asked for an account. Walters admitted he had passed on the landward side of the buoy in question, simply because he had missed it. He said "that he did not see it in time to pass it on that side, and that if he had so seen it he would have passed the buoy on the seaward side."[22] Since the action contravened the new special rules, which had included the Lighthouse Bank Buoy as one that had to be passed to seaward, the committee had little choice but to rule in favour of the *Columbia* and disqualify the *Bluenose*. The committee, which that year consisted of three Canadians and two Americans, decided that since the

‹ **LAID OVER** and flying across the finish "like the hounds of hell were after her," the *Bluenose* wins her final race against *Columbia* by two minutes, forty-five seconds. The *Bluenose* proved to be the faster vessel in two races, but this victory was overturned by a technical protest. The 1923 series came to a premature end when Walters and his crew sailed off in disgust, leaving the series unfinished. *Wallace MacAskill Collection, Nova Scotia Archives and Records Management*

race series was now 1–1, there would have to be a third race, to be held on Saturday, November 3, which would give Walters and his crew enough time to repair the sprung topmast.

A furious Walters reported the decision to his crew who, to a man, vowed not to sail another race. In their minds, they had won the race fair and square and were not about to give any weight to ridiculous yachting rules. They had sailed the same "bee line" on a reach from the eastern side of the start line to the Inner Automatic Buoy as the *Columbia* had from closer to the western side of the line. Both vessels had covered the same amount of water to reach the first mark, and it had given them absolutely no advantage to pass on the wrong side. Walters said he would participate in another race only if the last one was declared "no contest" and Pine were denied the victory. The sailing committee could not support this demand. It insisted that a contest without rules was an invitation to chaos and the sacrifice of safety. If rules were not followed, the resulting "go as you please" affair would be better abandoned altogether.[23] Walters found himself in much the same position as had Clayton Morrissey the previous year. He, too, was implored by men of power and persuasion to race again for the good of the series. Premier E.H. Armstrong vainly tried to appeal to Walters, at one point trying to make light of it by saying, "After all, it was only sport," to which the peppery Lunenburger replied that it was "working sport."[24] It *was* hard work, and he suggested that if the premier did not think so, he should come aboard and see for himself. Men like Walters and Morrissey were unused to being told what to do; as sea captains, they made the decisions and did not stand for any argument. Morrissey had succumbed to pressure and agreed to race against his better judgement and the protestations of his family and crew; Walters showed his flinty resolve by belligerently digging in his heels. He would not race, and that was final.

A.H. Zwicker, the managing owner of the Bluenose Schooner Company, decided that if the present crew were unwilling to race, he would replace them with a scratch crew from Lunenburg. But Angus proved to be resourceful as well as stubborn, and he quickly ordered his vessel to sail for home. As the major shareholder and master of the boat, he had every right to do so, and at 1:30 PM on Friday he took a tow and slipped out into the stream. Captain Ben Pine was given the option of sailing the course alone on Saturday, but he declined. He was there to beat the *Bluenose*, and he took no joy in the idea of winning the cup by default. The international committee therefore had no other choice but to declare the 1923 series incomplete. It awarded the *Columbia* $2,500, which was half the prize money, and put the cup in the hands of the trustees until the next series. Pine left the next morning for Gloucester.

The series ended on a note of surprising civility when the American officials lavishly praised the Canadians for their efforts during the races. W.W. Lufkin, representing the president of the United States, said: "It has been a wonderful contest between two of the finest fishing vessels in the entire world, the most wonderful in the history of this great International sport." He congratulated the race committee for doing its best to leave "no stone unturned" in its efforts to avoid this unfortunate ending.[25] In the interest of continuing the series, the committee invited both parties to Gloucester the following year.

The press, on the other hand, had a field day. Not surprisingly, the *Halifax Herald* played down the affair as best it could, clearly siding with the *Bluenose* and characterizing the protest as a "trivial matter." The writers questioned the *Columbia*'s right to protest in what, in their opinion, should have been a matter between the *Bluenose* and the committee, adding that "any decision arrived at could never rob *Bluenose* of the honour of coming home in front yesterday."[26] Others were not so charitable. James Connolly, writing for the *Boston Post*, said Walters "may have been so overpowered by righteous indignation as to forget every obligation of a racing fishing captain in a contest of this kind, but the belief of the Gloucester men here is that he was overcome with cold feet."[27] The *Evening Transcript* in Moncton, New Brunswick, wrote that Walters "failed miserably to live up to the fine traditions of British seamen. He has proved that he is not worthy of the name of good sport."[28] Another *Boston Post* writer was more philosophical in his approach:

> There has been too much insistence on technicalities and too much disposition to win at all hazards. Somehow we cannot help thinking that the time honored idea of sport for sports sake, which has been a great virtue of the English speaking people, has suffered somewhat a decline... Most of us expected that the fishermen's races would develop the highest type of sportsmanship. That they did not is a sad reflection on both Americans and Canadians.[29]

The *Boston Herald* went even further by saying that, although it could not justify what Walters had done, it could understand:

> Before we talk about bad sportsmanship, Let us remember that the *Bluenose* is a fishing vessel, made primarily to catch fish and not to win an International race.

Even on the near perfect state, we should not look for the ethics and practices of the Tennis court and the Polo field on the decks of a deep sea fishing schooner.[30]

Walters tried to weather the storm of criticism directed at him and his crew, but the adverse commentary and editorials on the subject took their toll. On Monday, November 5, he made a public statement: "On reflection I regret the effects of my action. I was under great strain. I am a fisherman, not a sportsman. I acted hurriedly, and did not realize that other people were so largely interested." He offered to race the *Columbia* again. "I am prepared to correct the situation if humanly possible and am willing to meet the challenger *Columbia* under conditions to be agreed."[31] His statement was condemned in an editorial in the *Weekly Bulletin* of the Halifax Commercial Club. Walters's excuse for his behaviour as being that of a fisherman and not a sportsman was hardly justifiable, they wrote, and "should be resented by the fishermen in the spirit of fair play." In their opinion,

> adherence to rules should mark all phases of life whether in sport or in work. We can only say that Captain Walters and his crew have cast a reflection upon our fair Province from the effects of which we shall suffer for years to come. If it lay within our power we would disqualify them from ever taking part in any international races.[32]

After his return to Gloucester, Ben Pine was asked if there would be another race against the *Bluenose* that year. He replied, "We went 700 miles to race him and he ran away from us. No, Sir, there'll be no match for the *Columbia* this year. That's final. Tomorrow we get ready for fishing."[33] Whether or not another race could have been organized is doubtful. The international committee had washed its hands of the matter, declaring the series unfinished and repossessing the Herald trophy. What was certain was that the year's match, however sullied by controversy and accusation, was in sailing terms the finest, most exciting and most evenly matched contest in the history of the International Fishermen's Cup series. The second race had been lost on a technicality, but the *Bluenose* had outsailed the *Columbia* and Pine knew it. He also knew, however, that his vessel was quite capable of beating the champion, and he would not be satisfied until given another chance to prove it. The *Bluenose* and Walters had become a thorn in the side of the Gloucesterman.

NOTES

1   *Halifax Herald*, November 5, 1922

2   Ibid.

3   Newfoundland was a colony until 1949, when it voted to join Canada and did so.

4   Jerry Snider, *Lunenburg Progress Enterprise*, January 30, 1924

5   Ibid.

6   Story, *Hail Columbia!*, p. 93

7   *Atlantic Fisherman*, October 1923, p. 10

8   *Gloucester Daily Times*, October 27, 1923

9   *Halifax Herald*, October 29, 1923

10 See Appendix, (5)

11 *Gloucester Daily Times*, October 30, 1923

12 *Halifax Herald*, October 30, 1923

13 *Toronto Telegram, Halifax Herald*, October 30, 1923

14 *Boston Globe*, October 30, 1923

15 *Halifax Herald, Boston Globe, Gloucester Daily Times*, October 30, 1923; *Atlantic Fisherman*, November 1923

16 See Appendix, (5) (A)

17 *Gloucester Daily Times*, October 31, 1923

18 *Atlantic Fisherman*, November 1923, p. 15

19 *Gloucester Daily Times*, November 2, 1923

20 Ibid.

21 Ibid.

22 *Halifax Herald*, November 1, 1923

23 *Halifax Herald*, November 3, 1923

24 Gillespie, *Bluenose Skipper*

25 *Gloucester Daily Times*, November 3, 1923

26 *Halifax Herald*, November 2, 1923

27 *Boston Post*, November 3, 1923

28 *Evening Transcript*, November 4, 1923

29 *Boston Post*, November 3, 1923

30 *Boston Herald*, November 3, 1923

31 *Halifax Herald*, November 6, 1923

32 *Boston Globe*, November 9, 1923

33 *Gloucester Daily Times*, November 5, 1923

8

THE STORM YEARS: 1924–29

THE DISAPPOINTING OUTCOME of the 1923 series gave rise to a decision by the race trustees to forgo the 1924 series and give schooner racing a break. In a telegram sent to the American race committee, they explained "that the interests of the event would be best served by not having a race this year."[1] They also stated that when races resumed in 1925, Canada would be represented by "a boat and crew... prepared to abide by the decision of the International committee."[2] The reference was an obvious dig at Walters and his crew, whose actions had caused them great embarrassment. The trustees knew that the *Bluenose*'s position as cup defender was firmly established, and her supporters were legion—not only in Nova Scotia, but across Canada. They also knew Walters was unlikely to compete if the races were held in Gloucester. He had left no doubt after the 1922 series that he would never race in the American port again, and his anger over that series was still smouldering. Relations between the trustees and Walters were therefore understandably less than cordial. In fact, shortly after the 1923 series ended, the Bluenose Schooner Company sent a letter to the trustees stating that as it was entitled to the trophy and its share of the prize money, legal action would be taken unless both were handed over. Opinion in Lunenburg was that if any vessel were to race the Americans it should be the *Bluenose,* and no other skipper was likely to enter his boat if Angus Walters refused.[3] Tragically, Captain Albert Himmelman, who had built his schooner *Keno* specifically to compete against the *Bluenose,* had been lost at sea without a trace—along with the *Keno*—on a trip to Newfoundland in early January 1924. All in all, it looked highly unlikely that 1924 would see another fishermen's race.

The sad fact was that the once-large fleet of schooners in Nova Scotia was slowly disappearing, and there were fewer boats available for fishing, let alone racing. In 1920 the fleet had numbered 130 schooners, but by 1924 only 80 or so remained in service. Prohibition in the United States and in Canada opened up an illicit trade in alcohol smuggling, and in those economically hard times many boats were eagerly pressed into service. Rum-running was immensely popular with Nova Scotians, so much so that the once-proud fishing industry began to take a back seat. Trade magazines lamented that if the trend towards "bottle fishing" continued, there would soon be fewer fish to market.

After the fiasco of 1923, Captain Ben Pine was more determined than ever to win the international championship. He knew the days of the fishing schooner were coming to an end, and he wanted one more crack at the Fishermen's Cup before it all finished. His schooner, the *Columbia,* was the last to come out of Essex without auxiliary power and there was no question that although she had been expected to make money at the salt fishery, her main purpose was to beat the *Bluenose.* Most of the schooners in Gloucester, including the *Henry Ford* skippered by Pine's old friend Clayton Morrissey, had taken on engines, and large, reliable, steam-driven trawlers, with smaller crews, were steadily taking over the industry. But racing fever had taken hold of Pine and he determined to field a competitor, no matter what the cost. He did face obstacles. Although the *Columbia* had made a couple of trips freighting salt herring from Newfoundland, it was hard to convince investors there was much money to be made any more from the salt fishery. At the same time, it was getting progressively more difficult to find a crew that wanted to go dory fishing. The *Columbia* was not paying her way.

Pine was forced to dig deep into his own pockets to keep *Columbia* in racing trim while he tried to organize a race. There was some cause for optimism, as a new schooner named the *Haligonian*, designed by *Bluenose*'s William Roué, was under construction in Nova Scotia. On March 25, 1925, the *Haligonian* slid off the ways in Shelburne. She had been built for a group of Halifax businessmen as a viable challenger to the *Bluenose*, with hull and sail area nearly identical to the older boat. Most race aficionados had assumed the series would begin again in the fall of 1925, but the trustees were divided on its date and location. The Canadians felt a combined elimination and cup race should be held in Halifax in late November, an idea that had little appeal to the Americans, who wanted the usual series to be held in Gloucester earlier in the month. Talks remained deadlocked while the opportunity to hold the races passed. With no Fishermen's Cup for two years in a row, editorials predicted the demise of the series.

In 1926, it seemed Ben Pine's dream of beating the *Bluenose* would never be realized; the *Columbia* was sold at public auction in February. She had become a financial drain on her shareholders, and Arthur Story, who had built her for $35,000 three years earlier, foreclosed on the mortgage and bought her for the bargain price of $10,000. Undeterred, Pine found new partners and quickly bought her back in March. In April, he sent her off to sea again on a handlining trip to ensure compliance with the race rules. The outing was disappointing. Near the end of the month, she ran aground off Canso when seeking shelter from bad weather and was almost lost. Leaking badly, she was towed to Halifax for repairs. It was mid-May before the vessel was ready to fish, but after heading back to the banks, she found the fishing so poor that she was forced to return to Gloucester in July—a miserable showing for four months at sea.

In Nova Scotia, the Lunenburg fleet was hit by some of the worst weather fishermen had seen in twenty-five years. Storm followed storm, forcing many boats to return to harbour to replace lost and damaged gear. About ten schooners came home in early March with unused bait, causing further financial drain. The *Alachua* was lost, though her crew was saved, and the *Bluenose* was battered twice. The first time, she lost both her anchors, three hundred fathoms of cable,

her foresail and most of her fishing gear. The second occasion was even more dramatic. She was caught by a storm on April 24 when anchored off the Northwest Bar off Sable Island. A huge sea mounted her deck and parted her cable, carrying away fourteen stanchions and part of the rail and bulwarks. Under storm trysail, a reefed foresail and one headsail, Walters lashed himself to the wheel and struggled all night to hold her off the bar. The wind finally changed direction and he was able to drag her away from the deadly grip of Sable Island.

August has always been a time for bad weather on the banks. Hurricanes that develop in the south sometimes reach as far as the northern United States and Canada, whipping the banks with their vicious tails. What are referred to by the locals—with classic understatement—as the "August breezes" start as a whisper of wind off the African coast, move across the Atlantic Ocean with the trade winds and build in intensity until they become a tropical depression. Most fizzle out, but some, through the alchemy of atmospheric conditions, turn into the full-blown hurricanes that regularly harass the Gulf of Mexico and the eastern seaboard of North America. Occasionally one of these huge depressions makes its way farther north, cutting swaths through fishing fleets and battering northern coastlines. With no offshore weather broadcasting system in the 1920s, fishermen were always at the mercy of the elements. They depended upon a good eye and a barometer to give fair warning, but tropical depressions and hurricanes often move too swiftly to be detected early. By the time the glass drops, there is often nothing to be done but to hunker down and hope or pray for the best.

On August 7, 1926, hurricane-force winds of over one hundred miles per hour hit Sable Bank and battered the fleet. Known as "the Graveyard of the Atlantic," Sable Island is a sliver of shifting sands, twenty miles long and less than a mile wide. Its treacherous shoaling waters extend miles out from the exposed shore and have claimed more than 350 ships since 1583. So many have died that "wearing sand in your shirt" became a euphemism for drowning off Sable Island. Fishermen and merchant sailors alike dreaded and feared the island, which sits alone, 180 miles southeast of Halifax, but fishermen could not stay away; the rich and fertile fishing ground that surrounds the island provided them with a livelihood.

Boats at anchor in the shoal water off the lee shore of Sable faced a desperate situation on August 7, relying on the thin thread of an anchor hawser to keep

> SOMETIMES friendly but more often at odds with each other, the rival skippers of the *Gertrude L. Thebaud* and the *Bluenose* knew the value of publicity. Angus Walters's aggressive and fiery character contrasted greatly with that of the amenable and good-natured Ben Pine, something that played well with the media and kept interest in the races high. *Leslie Jones, Boston Public Library*

them from destruction. Schooners offshore in deeper water stood a better chance, but as the storms came up so quickly there was little time to secure the decks. Captain W. Conrad, aboard the schooner *Mary Ruth,* gave a detailed description of the devastation.

> At eight o'clock in the evening it started to blow. I had all hands on deck doing our best to secure everything... At 10:30 we parted cable. We hoisted a single reef foresail. In five minutes it went to pieces... shortly after that the wind came west—and we crossed the nor'-west Bar on Sable Island on an angle in eleven and twelve fathoms of water. And there is where the sea did its damage. The sea would break from the bottom and strike us. The deck was swept clean by the gigantic seas. It took our boats and all our moveable gear. It smashed the skylight; the cabin door and the cabin side. The stove and everything else was smashed. The cabin was half full of water and the men washed around in the cabin and beat to pieces. Two men were washed overboard. We just saved them—that was all. Nine men were injured with broken ribs and injured limbs and one man at the pump was half beaten to pieces with the terrific seas. George Locke, one of our best fishermen, was so badly injured that he has since died... It was the hardest thing I have ever endured in my life.[4]

Most of the vessels in the path of the 1926 storm were badly battered, but they survived. However, two schooners from the Lunenburg fleet were not so lucky. The *Sylvia Mosher* broke up in the surf on Sable Island, tumbling end over end until she lay smashed on the beach. Her remains stood there for years before the sand claimed them. Another, the *Sadie Knickle,* disappeared without a trace. Both crews, a total of forty-eight men, died in the wild weather of August 7. Ironically, though the storm of 1926 was the worst in living memory, the catch was the biggest on record, over 17,200 tons of fish. This, unfortunately, did not translate into profit, because of low fish prices and the expense of repairing the heavily damaged schooners.

A memorial service was held in October for the fifty-four men of the Lunenburg fleet who had perished that season. The families of fishermen were often hit harder by tragedy than those in other occupations, as family members frequently sailed together. It was not unusual to lose a father and a son or brother on one vessel. The service was attended by over seven thousand people, more than would have attended the annual Fishermen's Picnic, normally held at that time of year but cancelled in 1926 out of respect for the dead.

There had been efforts made earlier in the season to get the International Fishermen's Cup race going. Ben Pine attempted to draw out the Canadians by writing an editorial suggesting Gloucester was ready and willing to resume the series at any time. Angus Walters replied in his trademark manner, intended to get under the skin of the Americans: "Well, I'd like you to let Captain Pine and everybody else that doubts it to know that Nova Scotia doesn't have to get ready for Gloucester—Nova Scotia is always ready."[5] The Americans were becoming weary of trying to corner the stubborn Lunenburger, and their frustration began to show. "The thing that rankles is his arbitrary attitude. Why can't he take a win or a loss and display a semblance of sporting blood? Nobody would hold it against him if he got licked like a man. Neither would he be made the king of Kickapoo if he was to win" were a few lines from a lengthy article in the July issue of *Atlantic Fisherman*.[6] Soon after, a promising telegram arrived from the Canadians, saying there would be an elimination race in October and the winner would sail to Gloucester. The American race committee took this as a response to the challenge and sent word to Halifax that October 12 would be a suitable date.

In early September, Clayton Morrissey confronted Ben Pine at his Atlantic Supply Company office in Gloucester and proclaimed good-naturedly that he thought his *Henry Ford* was far superior to the *Columbia*, and he was willing to prove it. Pine responded to the challenge from his friend by enthusiastically agreeing to a race. Gloucester now had a contest—maybe not the one it was hoping for, but a race just the same. The race committee originally agreed upon October 2, 4 and 5, but then wisely changed the date to the following week, so as not to conflict with the upcoming baseball World Series. The Americans had not given up on an international event, but could not get any commitment from Nova Scotia. Captain Walters had cagily suggested he would be interested in a race if the "rules, committee and purse were satisfactory, but not otherwise," and he went on to say he believed any race should be held off Halifax.[7] On September 30, the following message was received by the Nova Scotians:

> American Fishermen's Race Committee invite the entry of the *Mayotte* [another recently built schooner that had shown good speed], the *Haligonian*, and the *Bluenose* in an open fishing schooner race to be sailed off Gloucester

October 11th, 12th and 13th. Races open to all vessels of the North Atlantic, to be sailed fishermen's orders, no restriction, sails, rig or crews. Valuable silver trophies and generous cash prizes. Gloucester schooners *Columbia* and *Henry Ford* have entered. Kindly answer. Signed W.A. Reed.[8]

This began a series of correspondence between Gloucester and Lunenburg that could only be characterized as voluminous, with the Americans leaving no stone unturned in their attempts to entice the schooners from Nova Scotia.

The owners of the *Bluenose* and the *Mayotte* replied immediately and briefly that it would be utterly impossible for them to attend, but gave no explanation. The owners of the *Haligonian* responded by saying: "Thanks for the telegram. Damage to sails and rigging occasioned by stranding at Canso makes it impossible for the *Haligonian* to compete in your contest as cost of suitable equipment too expensive." Undeterred, the Americans offered up aid. "We are allowing Gloucester schooners $1000 each expense money for conditioning vessels. Committee will allow owners *Haligonian* $1000 for same purpose in order to have city of Halifax represented."[9] H.L. Montague, representing the owners, wired back that although they "cordially appreciate your very generous offer," they needed a day's postponement of the race in order to be able to participate. The race committee met and reluctantly decided it could allow no further delays. Montague then replied that "every effort being made dispatch *Haligonian* Friday morning. Hope succeed... will telegraph when vessel sails." The citizens of Gloucester, who had been following the discourse in the local paper, found reason to be optimistic that there would be a Nova Scotian boat in their upcoming series. Both Morrissey and Pine agreed to race the *Haligonian* even if she arrived too late for the main event. "They would race for money or peanuts and settle their supremacy and let the fastest boat take on the *Haligonian*," reported the *Gloucester Daily Times*.[10] The bubble burst when a telegram arrived the following day: "Regret advise that although everything possible had been done cannot arrange berth on slip and complete sails for time to race *Haligonian* next week." In a last futile attempt, the Americans offered up an available slip in Gloucester for the Nova Scotian boat, but this, too, was declined. William Roué, the designer of the *Bluenose* and the *Haligonian*, was so disgusted with the pettiness and the unenthusiastic response from Nova Scotia that he commented it would be "very poor advertising for this Province... They are calling our bluff... and we are allowing them to do it. The humiliating thing about the whole business is that it will appear Halifax cannot afford to send a schooner, even when Gloucester is putting up the money."[11]

The following day, an announcement was made in Halifax that there would be a provincial championship race on October 16 between the *Bluenose* and the *Haligonian*. Many embittered Gloucestermen believed that, after all the back-and-forth and dangling of carrots, the holding of their own series was the real reason for the reluctance of the Nova Scotians to sail south. Mr. Corbett, the chairman of the Halifax race committee, suggested that the winner of the Nova Scotia series might challenge the champion of the Gloucester races. Pine and Morrissey were willing to await the outcome and take on the challenger. When asked if he would compete against the Canadians, Morrissey replied that "he would race the Nova Scotian for a brass can and that Captain Pine undoubtedly feels the same."[12]

Over the Columbus Day holiday the two Gloucester boats, the *Columbia* and the *Henry Ford*, faced off against each other before huge crowds drawn to the peninsula by the fine weather. The *Columbia* prevailed, beating the *Ford* in two closely matched races and taking the open championship. Pine immediately sent a telegram to the Halifax newspapers:

> Will you please announce through the columns of your paper that I hereby challenge the winner of the Provincial Fishing Vessel Contest to be sailed in the near future off Halifax, to a race the week of October 25th off Gloucester, best two out of three, for prizes $2500 and $1500 under conditions which governed the race series just concluded here.[13]

Curiously, at a well attended reception that followed the Gloucester races, Pine appeared to bow out of future competition when he announced his "racing days were over and that never again would he hold the wheel of a racing vessel in a formal contest."[14] He went on to name Clayton Morrissey as his successor should the *Columbia* enter the International Fishermen's Cup race. Both he and Morrissey booked passage to Halifax to watch the Nova Scotians race in the provincial championship.

Captain Moyle Crouse, the master of the *Haligonian*, welcomed a match with the Yankees with open arms. "Race Ben Pine off Gloucester?" he said. "Sure why not?" Angus Walters, on the other hand, gave the challenge a more predictable reception: "Off Boston, perhaps. Off Halifax, maybe. But off Gloucester, never!"[15]

Captain Joe Conrad, the master of the *Canadia,* was unimpressed with the attitudes coming from his side of the border, and in a letter to a friend wrote: "I saw in one of the papers last week where both the *Haligonian* and *Bluenose* could beat the *Columbia* with the foresail and jib down. All I hope is that *Columbia* beats her [*Bluenose*]. They are no sports there, only bags of wind."[16]

The first provincial race, held on Saturday, October 16, had an ideal start with a fine fifteen-knot breeze behind the boats. A crowd of thousands held its collective breath as it watched the *Haligonian* cross the start line two seconds before the gun went off. Both vessels were immediately informed of the false start, but as Walters declined to protest, the race went on. A confident Walters had earlier predicted the victor. "I don't like to make any prophecies. But I'll tell you... bring a couple of boxes of good cigars down to meet us when we get in after tomorrow's race. I and my boys will have them half smoked before *Haligonian*'s got a line ashore."[17]

The *Haligonian* held her lead until the first buoy, after which the *Bluenose* took over and surged ahead. She continued to be ahead throughout the forty-mile course and crossed the finish in four hours and sixteen minutes, beating her previous record for the course by a quarter of an hour. The *Haligonian* crossed the finish a full half an hour later. No one had expected such a thrashing, and the same question appeared to be on everyone's mind. "The city seemed to be one huge interrogation mark... The poor *Haligonian* never seemed to get going at any stage in the race... She appeared listless, 'sick'—labouring under some kind of burden all the way."[18] Her size and shape were comparable to the *Bluenose* but had not translated into similar speed and, as her sails seemed a good fit, her trim would have to be improved in order for her to make a better showing. After William Roué, the designer of both boats, had observed every move, a shift was made in her ballast.

On Monday, the *Haligonian* looked to be in better shape and got off to a good start by leading the *Bluenose* across the line. Her advantage was short-lived, however, and the *Bluenose* once again pushed ahead in the twenty-knot breeze. After the wind hauled due north on the last leg, the schooners took so long to make way, tacking repeatedly, that the time limit had expired by eleven minutes when *Bluenose* finally crossed the finish. "No race" was declared. Although the *Haligonian*'s performance had been better this time, she had still lost by the considerable margin of twenty-two minutes, leaving her followers wondering where the difference lay between these almost identical boats. After the race, Angus Walters

decided he had had enough and announced that his vessel had proved her superiority and he should be allowed to take the trophy and go home. The officials disagreed and insisted the races be completed. Perhaps tempered by lingering guilt over his behaviour after the 1923 international series, Angus relented. The third race was a repetition of the second, with neither vessel completing the course before the allotted time. Once again, the *Haligonian's* skipper, Crouse, got the better start and maintained the lead for a short period during a luffing match that took them far off the course line. After the first mark, Walters began to draw ahead. When both vessels jibed around the second mark, Crouse foresaw danger and called for sea room. The *Bluenose* refused to alter course and was struck by the *Haligonian* on the starboard side, breaking two stanchions. Both boats told different stories about the accident, but neither skipper filed a protest. In the end, Walters led his rival across the finish by thirty minutes, leaving the *Haligonian's* supporters again scratching their heads. Some blamed her dismal showing on the fact that she had run aground off Cape Breton earlier in the year; perhaps the damage to her hull had been more severe than believed, possibly leaving it twisted. In any event, a frustrated Walters was becoming weary of the contest and declared that, as he had beaten his rival three times and his crew was tiring of the races, he would head for home. Once again the race committee stood its ground and, in the end, sportsmanship prevailed.

The fourth and final race of the series was the closest. The wind was lighter, and from the northwest at the start. It hauled around to the southwest later on, allowing the racers to sail "downhill" all the way on runs and reaches. The lack of windward work, which was always *Bluenose's* best point of sail, probably accounts for the closeness of the race. She won by just over six minutes and held onto the championship of the Nova Scotia fishing fleet, decisively beating her rival in all four races, two of which were declared official. When Walters finally sailed for home with the silver cup and the prize money, he left the backers of the *Haligonian* wondering what they should have done differently.

While they were in Nova Scotia, captains Pine and Morrissey had used every opportunity they could to promote the international series. After the first provincial race on Saturday, Pine had restated the challenge: "We want an International Race. We are prepared to race the winner of this series off Gloucester for The Halifax Herald International Trophy and the prize money called for by the International Race regulations."[19] After the *Bluenose* victory, he continued to press but insisted the race be held off Gloucester. Walters repeated his refusal to race there: "I made a solemn vow that I would not race off Gloucester again and I cannot be expected to break it. I am ready and willing to race off Halifax."[20] He insisted that this was not just a matter of personal preference but was more to do with the inferiority of the Gloucester course and the fact that it was time to have the series off his home port of Lunenburg. In the end, neither moved from his respective position, and Walters began the dismantling of his boat for winter lay-up.

Apart from Ben Pine and some of his friends on the American race committee, few cared to pursue the competition further. The dull and predictable series off Halifax, added to the losses suffered by the fleet during the "August breezes," had had a decidedly dampening effect on public interest. Pine put the disappointment of 1926 behind him and set his sights on 1927, swearing that, if all else failed, he would send his schooner to Halifax in the fall and stand by in the harbour until he had a race.

On August 24, 1927, hurricane-force winds again tore across Nova Scotia and the offshore banks. Apple orchards in the Annapolis Valley were torn up and barns flattened, and on the coast, fishing stages were ruined and an unknown number of boats smashed. In a repeat of the "August breezes" of 1926, the fleet on Sable Bank was hit hard, and those ashore prayed and braced themselves for bad news. *Canadian Fisherman* magazine reported:

> In a few days vessels that had been fishing around Sable Island, where the storm was at its worst, began limping into port, with their sails gone and their decks swept of everything and their captains and crews telling of marvellous escapes from the treacherous sand bars...Some vessels were so near destruction that the sand from the bars washed over their decks.[21]

The second day after the storm, the battered schooner *Edith Newhall* arrived back in port after a narrow escape. Her captain, Gordon Mosher, related that his vessel had been caught in the storm while fishing near the treacherous Northeast Bar and that when the gale struck he was forced to sail right over it. Huge seas, tossed up from the seabed, crossed his decks and tore away hatches and skylights before flooding the engine room. Waves broke the main boom and stanchions and carried away the light boxes in the rigging. When they arrived in port, the crew reported they had passed a lot of debris from another vessel also hit by the storm.

Angus Walters had to head back for repairs to the *Bluenose*. She had been able to ride out the storm in open water, losing only an anchor cable and trawls and having her sails badly ripped. Walters commented on the ferocity and sudden appearance of the storm: "There was no canvas ever made to stand such a gale. In all my seagoing experience I've never seen the barometer go down and come up as quick as it did on that occasion."[22]

The difficult part for those ashore was the waiting. With no radio communication, there was no way to find out if something was wrong with a boat at sea. If a schooner was undamaged, its crew would simply continue fishing and not come in until the holds were full or the bait gone, so it could be weeks, even months, before anyone knew the fate of these vessels. Schooners heading home often carried letters from other boats to be posted ashore, and the masters and crews would pass on the latest news from the banks, but all a desperate family could do was to wait and hope for the return of their men or for news of their safety.

The first sign of tragedy arising from the August 24 storm appeared on September 3 when the steamer *Albertolite* sighted debris in the water. It found a sea chest belonging to a crew member of the *Joyce M. Smith,* a schooner that had carried eighteen men. By mid-September, it became clear that three more schooners from the Lunenburg fleet were missing: the *Clayton Walters,* the *Mahala* and the *Uda R. Corkum.* All were overdue and, by the month's end, presumed lost. A total of eighty fishermen perished. In those two years, 1926 and 1927, 130 fishermen from Lunenburg had lost their lives to the sea. The 1927 storm had travelled to Newfoundland's shores, striking without warning on a clear, cloudless day. Winds of more than ninety miles per hour had taken five schooners, the *Vienna,* the *John C. Lochlan,* the *Hilda Gertrude,* the *Annie Healey* and the *Effie May,* all of them lost with all hands.

In Gloucester, the storm did no more than dump heavy rains on the Cape Ann peninsula, so it did little to arouse concern for the fleet at sea. Then news began to trickle in about the destruction caused by the path of the storm across Nova Scotia, and soon Gloucester boats returned home with tales of their own narrow escapes from disaster. One of Ben Pine's schooners, the *Marion McLoon,* was lost on the Nova Scotia shore. She had dropped anchor in Yankee Harbour, near Whitehead, where she had seemed snug and secure until the wind suddenly began to howl. The crew rushed up on deck just in time to see the anchor windlass pulled clean out. They desperately tried to secure the hawser around the foremast, but were driven ashore before they could finish. As one of the crew recounted:

‹ **THE *COLUMBIA*** and *Henry Ford* fight it out off Gloucester in 1926 in an "open" championship the Canadians declined to contest. The *Columbia* won hands down, but both skippers, Ben Pine and Clayton Morrissey, headed to Halifax in a fruitless attempt to entice the Nova Scotians to race the *Columbia* and resume the International Fishermen's Cup series. *Cape Ann Historical Association*

The waves were dashing all over her, and it was not possible to stay on deck, nor was it possible to launch a boat and get ashore. There was about 150 feet of boiling water between us and the rocks and the old craft was pounding her life out. We took to the rigging and there we hung praying, and praying, that the wind would stop.[23]

After three hours, the wind died down and the crew made it safely ashore, though the boat could not be salvaged.

Another schooner arrived at the Boston Fish Pier with her flag at half-mast. The popular skipper Alvaro Quadros had been swept from the deck of his schooner during the height of the storm. Members of the crew had been fighting for their lives, with the decks awash and water pouring in the fo'c'sle and aft cabin, and it was hours before anyone noticed their captain was gone.

Pine also had his beloved schooner *Columbia* at sea. She had been out since July 2, on her second handlining trip of the season. When reports of the storm arrived in Gloucester, they did not concern Pine, who was confident that his boat and her master, Lewis Wharton, could ride it out. Even when he heard early news that debris, battered dories and oars bearing the *Columbia*'s name had been recovered on Sable Island on September 13, Pine could not believe they came from his boat; he had recently sold a load of old *Columbia* dories and suspected those found had come off another schooner. Reports from another master that placed *Columbia* on Western Bank later in the summer indicated to Pine that she was too far away from Sable Island to have arrived there before the storm. The *Columbia* was not expected back in port until the first week of October.

As hope for the return of the missing Canadian schooners began to fade, anxiety about the *Columbia* grew. The American coast guard cutter *Tampa* was dispatched to Sable Island to search for clues to her fate. Bits and pieces of dories and oars were found on the island but nothing conclusive. An undaunted Pine refused to give up hope. Finally, on October 27, a local haddock boat, the *Mary Sears,* arrived at the Boston Fish Pier with a dory that had the name "Columbia" painted on her side and, inside, a bait knife with the letter "M" carved on the handle and known to have belonged to a crew member of the *Columbia*. This was irrefutable evidence that something awful had happened to the schooner, and the amount of sea growth on the bottom of the dory was an indication that it had occurred some time before. Pine was finally forced to acknowledge the loss of his treasured schooner and her crew of twenty-two. The *Columbia*'s crew was mostly Nova Scotian, adding more names to the province's list of victims of the August breezes, and bringing further misery and grief to the families.

The two years of tragic losses hit the industry hard, especially in Nova Scotia. Gloucester had steadily surrendered to the pressures and demands of modernization, and its fleet had been taken over by steam-driven trawlers that required smaller crews and could work year-round in almost any weather. There were few fishing schooners left in American ports, and their numbers were quickly dwindling. Most of the remaining schooners had had engines installed and their masts cut down to convert them into trawlers. In Canada, however, the banks schooner still dominated the industry, and fishermen accustomed to traditional methods were resisting the introduction of mechanization to their fleet. However, two disastrous seasons brought about a change in attitude and direction in the fishery. Now that an alternative technology was available, most men, particularly those new to the industry, were no longer willing to risk their lives in a dory when they could work from the relative comfort and safety of a trawler. As fewer schooner men remained wedded to the old ways, even the best fishing skippers, like Angus Walters—men whose reputations could guarantee a crew—came to the realization that the glory days of the fishing schooner were numbered. Modernization was expensive; it cost thousands of dollars to install an engine in a vessel, which took years to pay off, but no crew meant no fish.

The following year, a postscript was added to the story of the *Columbia*. In the early morning hours of January 1, 1928, the steam trawler *Venosta* was dragging the bottom about forty miles southwest of Sable Island when her trawl became entangled in wreckage. When the men hauled it up, they saw it was the hull of a schooner. Her top masts, boom and bowsprit were gone, but apart from that, she was in remarkable condition. There was little sea growth, and most of her rigging appeared intact. Even the paint on her hull was in good shape. The stunned crew watched in disbelief for a few minutes before the heavy steel cables parted and the ghostly apparition slid back into the sea. Although she was never positively identified, those who had known the *Columbia* were certain that this was indeed the famous Gloucester schooner.

Ben Pine's obsession with fishing-schooner racing seemed to wane after the sinking of his pride and joy. His favourite racing mate, the *Henry Ford*, was also gone; she had run aground and broken up on Whaleback Reef off Newfoundland on June 16, 1928. Perhaps it was time to admit that his dream of beating his rival would remain a dream. To add insult to injury, the Canadian government immortalized the *Bluenose* on a postage stamp in 1928, a reminder to Pine of his failure every time he received a piece of Canadian mail.

Modern trawlers may have been the future of fishing, but the sight of them could not hope to match the silent majesty and beauty of a fleet of schooners under full sail. Promoters could still count on a race's appeal to the viewing public, and in 1929 the beating of the drum for another series began. Gloucestermen still loved a schooner race and the American committee reconvened to organize a local event. There were a few older schooners available, but none was of the class of the *Henry Ford* or the *Columbia*. Four entered, the most famous being the *Elsie*, which had raced against and lost to the *Bluenose* in 1921. Pine entered his schooner the *Arthur D. Story*, built in Essex in 1912, and announced that, contrary to his assertion in 1926 that he was retiring from racing, he would be taking the helm. The other two were the *Thomas S. Gorton*, the oldest (1905), and the *Progress* (1913), which at ninety-six feet (twenty-nine metres) was the smallest. The *Progress* was originally to be skippered by Captain Marty Welsh, who, after his doctor advised him to stay ashore, gave up his position to Captain Manuel Domingoes. The fact that the schooners were four old workhorses did not diminish the race in the eyes of the public; after three dry years (and six years since the last international race), the public was hungry for a return to racing. Subscription money poured in, and the required amount of $20,000 was quickly met, then exceeded.

The competition was held during the last days of August, but light winds plagued the racers. The first and second races ended without completion after passing the seven-hour time limit. The third race, held on Labor Day, was won by the little schooner *Progress,* an unlikely victor considering her size. Captain Domingoes trailed Ben Pine on the *Arthur D. Story* for thirty miles before he overhauled him, taking the lead and winning the race by ten minutes. With no assurance of better conditions for the following days and unwilling to see the American open series become a prolonged and dull affair, the committee put an end to it and gave the cup to the *Progress,* allowing victory celebrations to begin. Officially, the series was reduced from a best of three to a one-off in the interests of restoring normality to the fishing industry, but it is more likely that the contestants and organizers were anxious to get on with the party.[24] The races may have been disappointing, but they reawoke "race fever" in Gloucester, and plans were soon in the offing to build another contender to challenge the Nova Scotians once again.

NOTES

1 *Canadian Fisherman*, October 1924, p. 281
2 Ibid.
3 Ibid.
4 *Canadian Fisherman*, September 1926, p. 274
5 *Atlantic Fisherman*, July 1926, p. 7
6 Ibid.
7 *Gloucester Daily Times*, September 29, 1926
8 *Gloucester Daily Times*, September 30, 1926
9 *Halifax Herald*, October 1, 1926
10 *Gloucester Daily Times*, October 6, 1926
11 *Gloucester Daily Times*, October 5, 1926
12 *Gloucester Daily Times*, October 7, 1926
13 *Gloucester Daily Times*, October 13, 1926
14 *Halifax Herald*, October 13, 1926
15 *Gloucester Daily Times*, October 14, 1926
16 Letter from Joe Conrad, October 21, 1926, Maritime Museum of the Atlantic
17 *Maclean's*, June 15, 1950, p. 48
18 *Halifax Herald*, October 18, 1926
19 Ibid.
20 *Halifax Herald*, October 22, 1926
21 *Canadian Fisherman*, October 1927, p. 303
22 Story, *Hail Columbia!*, p. 151
23 *Gloucester Daily Times*, August 29, 1927
24 *Atlantic Fisherman*, September 1929, p. 17

9

THE LIPTON CUP: 1930

AFTER THE INTERMINABLE difficulties of the latter half of the 1920s, it seemed to
many that the cup races were beyond revival. There were no schooners in
Gloucester or Boston able to compete against the Canadians, and there
was little incentive to build new boats. In Gloucester, an elderly insurance man
from New York named Louis A. Thebaud came to the rescue. After spending a
few weeks each year with his family in a cottage near Rockport just up the coast,
Thebaud had bought a summer home close to Gloucester. Bored with the tedium
of summer life, he engaged a local garage owner, Joseph Mellow, to act as his
driver and companion. Through Joe, Thebaud was introduced in 1929 to the Master Mariners Association, where he learned about the fishing industry and was

captivated by the stories of schooner racing and the long-standing rivalry between Gloucester and Lunenburg. The thrill and passion of these tales must have struck a chord, because he immediately wrote a cheque for $2,000 to go towards financing the local schooner races to be held that summer. Before he left the hall he was not only granted membership in the elite club of fishing skippers but was also put on the race committee and given the honorary title of captain.

Mellow took Thebaud down to the wharves, where he became friendly with the local skippers and crews, turning up regularly to chat and listen to tales of the sea. Ben Pine frequently took the old man out fishing and further broadened his knowledge of the fishermen's races and the role played by the *Columbia* before her tragic loss. Thebaud spent hours on the docks observing preparations for the upcoming races, and when Mellow casually remarked that it would be nice to have a schooner that could race the Canadians, Thebaud jumped at the idea. On September 12, he turned up at Mellow's garage with a cheque for $10,000 in his hand. Mellow's confused reaction got a quick response from Thebaud: "Don't you remember after the races on Labor Day, when we agreed there wasn't a good racer here in Gloucester; well here's $10,000 toward a vessel that CAN race. Speak up now; who shall I make the check out to?" Mellow stammered, "Make it out to Ben Pine and myself."[1]

This windfall resurrected Pine's hopes of beating the Nova Scotians, but, after looking around at prospective purchases, he and Mellow decided there was only one schooner capable of racing, and that was the *Mayflower,* the only American "racing fisherman" still afloat. She had been sold to the British government, which had coppered her bottom and was using her as a freighter in the West Indies. Inquiries were made, but the asking price of $28,000 was considered too much for the eight-year-old schooner. When they told the news to Thebaud, he instantly wrote them a cheque for an additional $20,000 and told them to build a new one. The dumbfounded duo were further astonished when Thebaud's wife entered and handed them another cheque for $10,000. The pair headed back to Pine's Atlantic Supply Company offices to talk things through. One thing was clear: this schooner was going to be built to race, and any consideration of her being a fisherman was almost an afterthought.

In spite of the generosity of the Thebauds, $40,000 was not enough to cover the expense of building a schooner. Fortunately, their friends were persuaded to join in: Wetmore Hodges, a wealthy Gloucester businessman, Bassett Jones, an electrical inventor from New York, and Thebaud's brother-in-law, Robert H. McCurdy, each invested $5,000. Ben Pine and his pal Joe Mellow enthusiastically paid the difference up to $73,000, making the boat the most expensive fishing schooner ever built. Normally, fishing vessels were financed by selling $100 shares, which were usually bought by those close to the industry, but this project was quickly becoming a rich man's hobby.

Frank Paine, the Boston designer of the *Yankee,* an America's Cup contender (not the Boston schooner of the same name), was engaged to draw up the plans. The new vessel was to be called the *Gertrude L. Thebaud* after the principal owner's wife, and any pretensions that this was to be anything but a racer were put to rest with Paine's design. *Rudder* magazine reported there were substantial differences between this schooner and the average Gloucester boat. "The *Thebaud* is more cut away forward and her after sections are quite yacht-like."[2] The *Gloucester Daily Times* wrote that she "has an underbody like a yacht, in fact closely [resembling] that of the *Yankee.*"[3] And *Yachting* magazine added that the design followed "more or less, the lines of some of [Paine's] recent yachts, though of course a more burdensome vessel."[4] She was equipped with all the amenities, such as electric lights, and her cabin was of solid mahogany, a luxury unheard of on a banks schooner. Her holds were small—she carried far less than the *Mayflower,* which had been barred from racing in part for just that reason. Had the *Thebaud* been built five years earlier, her eligibility for the Fishermen's Cup would have been out of the question. Identifying her as a bona fide banks fisherman was little more than a charade, but by 1930 it seemed no one cared to notice. In the early years of the Depression, and with schooner fishing representing a dying way of life, the spectacle and tourism potential of another International Fishermen's Cup race was clear on both sides of the border; there seemed little to be gained by quibbling about the qualifications of the contestants. However, it looked as though the race of working men in working schooners was about to be reduced to the "pink tea" variety, in total opposition to the original intent.

On St. Patrick's Day, March 17, 1930, three months after the keel was laid in the A.D. Story yard, the slender hull of the *Gertrude L. Thebaud* slid down the ways into the Essex River. Huge crowds were on hand, and every available parking space in town was taken. It was a grand occasion, flavoured with nostalgia, as the *Thebaud* was one of the last schooner hulls to be built in this historic yard. The Thebauds themselves were unable to attend because of preparations for a trip to Europe. The vessel was 124 feet (37.8 metres) long, 99 feet (30.2 metres) on the waterline with a 14-foot, 8-inch (4.5-metre) draft, smaller than the *Bluenose* by 19 feet (5.8 metres) and carrying 3,000 fewer square feet (278 square metres) of sail. Those who knew boats predicted she would be fast in light to moderate weather, but likely would be beaten by the *Bluenose* in a heavy blow; still, they hoped she would prove more nimble than her older rival. Although the *Thebaud* was rigged with topmasts and carried more than 7,000 square feet (650 square metres) of canvas, her main source of propulsion was a 180-horsepower Fairbanks Morris diesel engine. In the months after her launch, little effort was made to prove she was a sailing fisherman. Unless she was racing, she seldom unfurled her sails.

Enticing the competition from Nova Scotia to race once again proved difficult. The American race committee wanted a match with the *Bluenose*, if only to be able to take the contentious Angus Walters down a peg or two. Walters still had a habit of goading the Americans whenever possible. The previous March, after making a voyage from Lunenburg to Halifax in record time, he had boasted: "From now on I will refuse to race the *Bluenose* against any other vessel unless we take the mainsail off of her. Otherwise there would be no interest in it for me. If we race a United States craft we will probably tow an anchor over the side as well."[5] Just when it seemed possible that the Lunenburg schooner might race in the fall, she ran aground off Argentia, Newfoundland. Walters's brother, John, had taken her there on a caplin-bait trip in June, prior to heading out to the banks. She went ashore at Point Riche at the entrance to the harbour and sat there, grinding her bottom on the gravel beach, for five days until the Canadian government hospital ship *Arras* pulled her off. Although there appeared to be no serious damage, this did nothing but strengthen Walters's resolve not to race.

With well-heeled investors eager for a contest, the American race committee continued to pressure the trustees in Halifax for a race in October. Ben Pine had been actively wooing the wealthy yachting fraternities of Gloucester, Marblehead and Newport by organizing exclusive sailing excursions on the *Gertrude L. Thebaud*. An exhibition race between the *Thebaud* and the America's Cup contender *Yankee* was under consideration. Sir Thomas Lipton, back in the United States to challenge for the America's Cup for the fifth and final time, was persuaded to donate another huge silver cup for the proposed fishermen's race. Any idea of sending the *Thebaud* off fishing was almost an afterthought to drumming up support for the coming event. Finally, a delegation was sent off to Halifax to see what could be done.

> UNDER FOUR lowers, the *Bluenose* is laid over so far that her keel is exposed during the second race of the 1930 series. With winds blowing over forty knots, the schoonermen finally had the "fishermen's wind" they had all been hoping for. Unfortunately, as the high winds had flattened the highliner poles marking the course, making them difficult to see, the sailing committee decided to call off the race, much to the fury of Walters, who was by that time well in the lead. *Leslie Jones, Peabody Essex Museum*

After lengthy discussions, agreement was reached in August that not one but two races would be held in the fall. Walters was persuaded to race Pine off Gloucester in early October on condition that the championship of the International Fishermen's Cup was not at stake. It would be an exhibition race only, and the "true" Fishermen's Cup race would be held later off Halifax in October or early November. Walters insisted the agreement be drawn up and all conditions of the exhibition race spelled out. If they were "not strictly adhered to by the Gloucester signatories, then all races [would] be called off."[6] Even the proposed name, the International Fishermen's Challenge Trophy, was considered too contentious and was changed to the Lipton Cup. (This would be the third Lipton Cup; the first was donated in 1907 and the second in 1923.) Gloucester had succeeded in getting a race, but only on Walters's terms.

After the grounding in Newfoundland in June, the *Bluenose* continued to fish on the Grand Banks, returning to Lunenburg in early September. Walters was anxious to inspect her hull and found that half her keel and some planking had been damaged and needed to be replaced. Over the next two weeks the schooner was repaired and groomed, had a new set of sails cut and part of her rigging replaced. A fishermen's regatta held in Lunenburg on October 1, 1930, was the finale of a three-day Fisheries Exhibition, and four vessels were entered to race: the *Haligonian,* the *Margaret K. Smith,* the *Alsatian* and the *Bluenose.* For Angus Walters, it was an opportunity to fine-tune his vessel before heading out to Gloucester. In his typically arrogant fashion, he requested that his competitors be given a ten-minute handicap because of the *Bluenose's* superior speed. This show of hubris proved unfortunate, as the *Haligonian,* under the command of Captain Moyle Crouse, put on a fine show for the first time in her existence, beating the *Bluenose* by eight minutes. "It was easily seen here that the *Haligonian* had advanced to a new place in the contest and was calling upon all observers to sit up and take notice... When he came about he put the *Bluenose* and *Smith* well to leeward, making it impossible for either schooner to get anywhere near him for the finish," reported the *Halifax Herald.*[7] Keen disappointment was felt by the legions of loyal *Bluenose* supporters, who were left to wonder whether the old champion was still fit to be representing Canada in the upcoming Gloucester race. All hoped the *Bluenose* would show better form in more favourable winds. Meanwhile, her international rival was on the marine railway in Gloucester having her engine removed in preparation for the contest.

The *Bluenose* set off for Gloucester in convoy with the *Arras* and the Canadian naval destroyer *Champlain*, but quickly lost sight of both in the heavy seas. When the wind picked up, she broke her foresail gaff during an attempt to jibe, and the crew took an hour to repair it. She continued with reduced sail but still beat the government ships to harbour. Upon her arrival in Gloucester on the night of Sunday, October 5, after a thirty-five-hour run from Lunenburg, she received a boisterous and rousing welcome, in stark contrast to the solemnity and melancholy that had accompanied her last departure from the port, in 1922. The following night, the crews from the rival schooners and the *Champlain*, along with local military, coast guard and several marching bands, paraded together through the town in a torchlit procession. Putting their differences behind them, skippers Angus Walters and Ben Pine looked forward to a promising and uncomplicated contest in their exhibition race for the Lipton Cup.

On Wednesday, October 8, 1930, the competition almost ended before it started when the *Gertrude L. Thebaud* ran into trouble the day before the first race. She had been out on the course for a trial run when her hull sprang a serious leak. One of several problems that had plagued her construction had been a shortage of full-length timbers. The shorter timber used meant more butt-ends, which tended to work open at sea, causing serious leakage.[8] The crew had been puzzled by the lifeless and unresponsive handling of their vessel and found, when they went below, that there was three feet (a metre) of water in the hold. Five miles off Thatcher's Island, she was taking on water at such an alarming rate that three pumps were unable to keep up with the flow. She immediately headed for home and was lucky that the marine railway was free when she arrived—had she been farther offshore, it is doubtful she would have made it back. The worst leak came from a weak seam in the deadwood in the stern, but at least a dozen other seams had also opened. A six-foot (two-metre) plank and another, smaller insert were replaced near her bow. Pine took the incident in stride and appeared confident his boat would be on the water the following day, "dry as a bone."[9]

With the Columbus Day holiday on Monday and an American Legion convention in nearby Boston, Gloucester was in a festive mood and expecting up to thirty thousand visitors over the weekend. A small fifteen-mile triangular course, which would be followed twice by the schooners, promised to give shore-bound spectators an optimal view. The local press went to great lengths to inspire enthusiasm for the contest, describing the vessels as the "two fastest fishermen on the North

Atlantic, manned by crews of hard-bitten, frost-touched men of the sea," adding that "for anyone that wants a two-fisted, he-man, crest-crushing and wave-breaking contest, 100 per cent satisfaction is guaranteed all comers."[10] It was ironic that the race being touted as a true test of fishing schooners and fishing captains included a vessel owned by a junk dealer, a taxi man and a wealthy insurance broker. Nevertheless, the races were billed as the highlight of a well-planned weekend, and wireless reports from a U.S. Coast Guard boat following the race were to be broadcast live from a Boston radio station. Overwhelmed with the fanfare and flattered to be on radio for the first time, a jocular Walters threatened to stay: "It's wonderful the way they received us, and if things keep on, the women folk down in Lunenburg shouldn't expect us home until Christmas."[11]

The first race began on Thursday morning and both boats got off to a sluggish start. Once on the course, however, the *Thebaud* took off like a whippet and quickly established herself in the lead position. The *Bluenose* staggered behind, her new set of sails so hopelessly stretched out of shape that a *Yachting* magazine reporter commented they "looked like insufficiently re-cut circus tents."[12] Local fishermen watching from the shore agreed she carried a "clumsy suit of sails." Even when the gaffs were raised as high as they could go, they remained baggy. The stretching of her sails was later blamed on the high winds she had encountered on the trip to Gloucester. Nonetheless, Walters gamely chased the *Thebaud* along the roundabout course and, at times, the *Bluenose* showed some of her old class, when she was able pick up speed to twelve knots. But the die was cast, and the *Thebaud* seemed only to be toying with her before delivering the knockout punch. "It was a walkaway and disappointing to racing experts. But to those who sought only spectacle, there was nothing to moan about... Leaning on the shoulders of a 15-mile breeze, both boats gave an unforgettable picture as they dug into the water and sent the spray flying," wrote John Griffin of the *Boston Post*.[13] The *Gertrude L. Thebaud* romped home fifteen minutes, thirty-seven seconds ahead of the *Bluenose*, to an enthusiastic reception from the hundreds of boats that lay along the finish line.

As soon as he was alongside, Walters had the huge 4,000-square-foot (370-square-metre) mainsail unbent and sent ashore with his two topsails and foresail. He personally supervised the cutting of the sails and removed as much as five feet (one and a half metres) from the foot of the mainsail and a similar amount from the others. He also ordered ten tons of ballast removed.

‹ **DURING THE SAME** race as in the photo on page 167, the *Gertrude L. Thebaud* was less successful at coping with the high seas and wind and was unable to keep up with her opponent. On several occasions, she could not properly answer her helm and became caught in irons, forced to watch her rival soaring ahead. *Leslie Jones, Peabody Essex Museum*

The next two races were abandoned for lack of wind. In the first of these, on Saturday, the *Thebaud* got the jump on the *Bluenose,* leading across the starting line by about a minute. She opened up the lead in a disappointing wind that never picked up above eight knots and occasionally fell away to nothing. Every time there was a light puff, the *Thebaud* would respond like a yacht and spring ahead. But by the end of the first half of the course it had become obvious that, barring a full gale, the vessels could not possibly finish in time. The *Bluenose* seemed to sail better with her recut sails but still could not gain sufficiently on her rival. Walters's reaction to an announcement that the races would resume the next day, a Sunday, was emphatic: "We never fish on Sunday and we won't race on Sunday."[14] The race was rescheduled for Monday, when once again the boats were beset by light airs. The *Thebaud* once more beat the *Bluenose* to the gun and led at the start by one minute, but on the close reach to the first mark the Lunenburger began, astonishingly, to overhaul her rival. Foot by foot, she worked her way up, turning the mark thirty-seven seconds in the lead. On the next leg and in the lightest breeze the *Thebaud* worked up alongside the *Bluenose,* "so close that the rival crew could nearly shake hands with each other." In response to a ribald hail from the Americans, the high-spirited Nova Scotian crew pelted their rivals with a barrage of Annapolis Valley apples.[15] Camaraderie was high between the crews, but the wind was not as friendly. An hour and a half later, the race was called for the second time.

This series was developing into one of the longest to date, and Tuesday morning promised more of the same weather, so the race was cancelled well before the start. The Lipton Cup was turning into a listless, drawn-out affair that satisfied no one, sailors and onlookers alike. However, later that day thickening clouds heralded a possible change in the weather.

What the previous races lacked, Wednesday's contest had in abundance—wind, and plenty of it. In contrast to the pleasant but dull days that had characterized the series thus far, this day was dark and stormy, with driving rain and winds raging from twenty-five to forty knots. For the first time, the weather was worthy of fishermen; it "had enough weight and teeth and punch in it to suit the toughest sail-dragger who ever raced a schooner."[16] It was a race that Ben Pine was sadly obliged to miss; he had been ordered to stay ashore by his doctor because of a sinus infection, and he had turned over the helm to Captain Charles Johnson. The strong northeasterly and torrents of rain had reduced visibility to a few hundred yards when the *Thebaud,* sheeted hard to windward, flew across the start, forty-six seconds ahead of the *Bluenose*. *Thebaud* took off like a runaway freight train, heeled over so far that her keel was visible from the press boat, and a grey-green sea washed over her deck. The *Bluenose* was hard on her heels and "charging after her like a mad thing."[17] John Griffin of the *Boston Post* described the dramatic scene: "The crews were clinging to whatever was handy, and probably the most unenviable position in the world at that moment was occupied by the men who went aloft in the swaying rigging. Great tumbling seas smashed against the side of the schooners and climbing aboard, rushed down the decks and slid swishing off the stern."[18] This was, perhaps, the race both sides had been waiting for: one that would finally settle the question of which schooner was the fastest in wind that could honestly be called fishermen's weather.

The *Bluenose* had been built for conditions like this, and she was revelling in it. The six-mile beat straight to windward going towards the first mark was obscured by fog and rain, and the battle between the two went largely unseen by the observers ashore. Johnson was having difficulty tacking his vessel in the heavy weather, and three times she was caught in irons, allowing her rival to forge ahead. The *Bluenose* made for the slim, flagged highliner pole that marked the first turn six minutes and one mile ahead. On board the *Thebaud,* one huge wave after another was washing over the deck and the crew was desperately trying to hang on. One crew member, Carlin Powers, was washed over the side by one wave and tossed back by the next. Another, Kellogg Birdseye, was saved from being thrown overboard only because his foot had tangled in a line, holding him long enough to be rescued. The *Thebaud* lost a further six minutes on the run down to the second mark and fell two miles behind.

Trouble began for the *Bluenose* when she failed to find the third mark, a slim pole with a red flag on top. The committee boat, which was supposed to keep station close to it, had also been unable to locate it. The Nova Scotian continued searching for the mark and fell well off to leeward on a broad reach, in the area the eighteen-mile mark should have been, and all the time the *Thebaud* was closing in. The marker might have been blown flat on the grey heaving seas or simply have broken loose. Whatever the case, the sailing committee called off the race, blaming the heavy rain that continued to obscure vision. Whether this was a disastrous mistake is a moot point, but it brought to a premature end the only race so far that had offered the kind of excitement and drama expected of a true fishermen's race, and which many have compared to the legendary "race it blew" of 1892.

The two skippers were furious, and both were scathing in their criticism of the committee's decision. Walters quite rightly noted that the visibility at the beginning of the race had been equally poor and added that fishermen were quite used to finding buoys in poor weather. "Let us stay out there until something blows away. That's our hard luck. We were perfectly satisfied to carry on," he said during a long harangue that scorched the air in the committee room.[19] Captain Knickle of Lunenburg, a Canadian member of the committee, attempted to pour some oil on the troubled waters by acknowledging that, though the sailing committee had had no right to call off the race, it was probably the correct thing to have done, pointing out that "the men of both boats were wet and cold and if the race had continued we might have lost a man or two from one of the vessels."[20] In an attempt to mollify the two skippers, the committee decided that for future races, a boat would be stationed at each mark.

The next day the boats lay idle, in order to give Walters a chance to repair damage to the crosstrees of the foremast. One of the "hams" that supported the rigging had splintered and the *Bluenose* had come close to losing her foremast. Walters emphatically denied there was anything seriously wrong with his vessel and claimed the *Bluenose* would have finished the previous race with no problem. A gang of carpenters worked until early the following morning to replace the splintered piece.

The final race was held on a beautiful sunny Friday morning, October 17, with a fifteen-knot nor'westerly blow and no sea running. The *Thebaud* again led at the start, but by only a boat length, with the Lunenburger slightly to weather and gaining. The Gloucester boat seemed slow to respond to her helm and had trouble making headway. Walters quickly overtook his rival and, after twenty minutes, was three boat lengths ahead, running with the wind and with sheets well off. The *Bluenose* was a minute ahead in a freshening breeze at the first mark and held her own on the next six-mile leg to the southwest mark, adding a further fifteen seconds to her lead. After rounding the second mark, disaster struck the *Bluenose*. Walters mistakenly elected to head inshore on a port tack on the first windward leg of the race. Almost immediately, adverse currents that ran the shore caught the *Bluenose* and pushed her farther leeward of the buoy. Johnson wisely stayed on the starboard tack and ran farther offshore, steering clear of the inshore tidal movement. This action won him the race. With one more tack, he was able to make the third mark, while Walters continued to struggle against inshore currents. After

> THE *GERTRUDE L. THEBAUD* leads the *Bluenose* across the finish in the 1930 Lipton Cup exhibition series off Gloucester. After a seven-year hiatus from international competition, Angus Walters and the *Bluenose* suffered their first defeat at the hands of the Americans. This was a sad moment for Walters, but he accepted it graciously and blamed himself, not his beloved schooner, for the loss. The stage was now set for a resumption of the International Fishermen's Cup series the following year off Halifax. *Mariners' Museum, Newport News, Virginia*

four lengthy tacks, the *Bluenose* finally made the buoy fifteen minutes behind the *Thebaud* and gallantly tried to make up the difference, gaining on every leg of the second turn around the course. But the damage done to her chances was irreparable, and the *Gertrude L. Thebaud* sailed home the winner, the *Bluenose* crossing the finish eight minutes behind. A humbled Angus Walters would later admit that because of his mistake the *Thebaud* had beaten him rather than his boat.[21] He deeply regretted straying from the old racing wisdom of staying between the other fellow and the mark and not splitting tacks. No one, however, could argue that the result was not fair and square, and the victory gave Gloucestermen every reason to celebrate.

Bill Taylor of *Yachting* magazine argued that the series was not so much a celebration of speed and strategy as a homage to a quickly disappearing way of life:

> The interest in the races off Gloucester lies not in the extreme speed of the vessels nor in the exhibition of consummate racing tactics, but in the spectacle itself and its traditions—in that the few remaining commercial sailing vessels can still scare up the will and the way to put on a race at all.[22]

All things considered, the 1930 Lipton Cup series was a good-natured affair, unmarred by the wrangling and bitterness that had marked the previous decade. The proposed resumption of the International Fishermen's Cup series that was planned for Halifax in November was postponed to the following year. The trustees felt that in view of the economic hard times and the necessity of raising funds through public subscription, holding another race so soon after the Lipton Cup could not be justified.[23]

NOTES

1 Frank Jason, "Avast Ye Lubbers," *Boston Post,*
   March 16, 1930
2 *Rudder,* December 1930, p. 60
3 *Gloucester Daily Times,* October 5, 1930
4 *Yachting,* December 1930, p. 108
5 *Bridgewater Bulletin,* March 19, 1929
6 *Halifax Herald,* September 1, 1930
7 *Halifax Herald,* October 2, 1930
8 Dana Story in conversation with the author,
   October 2003
9 *Boston Post,* October 9, 1930
10 Ibid.
11 *Gloucester Daily Times,* October 7, 1930
12 *Yachting,* December 1930, p. 81
13 *Boston Post,* October 10, 1930
14 *Halifax Herald,* October 13, 1930
15 *Gloucester Daily Times,* October 14, 1930
16 *Halifax Herald,* October 16, 1930
17 *Atlantic Fisherman,* October 1930, p. 15
18 *Boston Post,* October 16, 1930
19 Ibid.
20 Tom Horgan, Associated Press, October 16, 1930
21 *Halifax Herald,* October 20, 1930
22 *Yachting,* December 1930, p. 108
23 *Canadian Fisherman,* November 1930, p. 24

10

THE REVIVAL: 1931

THE GREAT DEPRESSION that began in 1929 hit the fishing industry hard, especially in Lunenburg, where the demand for salt cod had been on the decline for the second half of the 1920s. This was due in part to the expansion of the fresh-fish market in the United States, but also to fierce competition in salt cod from Iceland and Norway, which had effectively closed out Nova Scotia from its traditional markets in the West Indies, South America and Europe. Although Lunenburg's cod was still considered the finest available, other countries had improved the salting process and were now able to undercut Lunenburg's prices. The fresh seafood market in Canada was not yet a viable option, and duties on Canadian fish made the American market prohibitive. The lean years took a heavy toll on the Lunenburg fleet, forcing many owners to sell or lay up their boats. Three years after 1929, when there had been over seventy boats in the fleet, there remained only twenty-six.[1]

Angus Walters laid up the *Bluenose* for the first time in her career in 1931. She had always been a highliner, consistently catching impressive amounts of fish, but with the dramatic drop in price, it was cheaper to stay ashore no matter how much was caught. South of the border, things were not much better. The market was steadier but the prices still miserably low. Trawlers had squeezed all but the few remaining schooners out of business, and even the venerable old *Elsie* had turned to greener pastures, serving as a summer training vessel for Sea Scouts. Despite an adequate halibut-fishing season, the *Gertrude L. Thebaud* could not pay her way, and she too was laid up before summer's end.

When talk of a 1931 Fishermen's Cup series surfaced, interest in Gloucester was lukewarm until Louis Thebaud once again stepped up to the plate. Though his friend Ben Pine thought better of it, reminding him that "times are hard" and "people are not interested enough to subscribe money," Thebaud pulled out his cheque book and offered $5,000 to get things moving.[2] Pine turned the money over to the American race committee, urging it to immediately challenge the Nova Scotian fleet. When this was received by Halifax in mid-September, it was immediately accepted. With his beloved *Bluenose* laid up, Walters was more than willing to take on the Americans, seeing this as an opportunity to redeem his poor showing of the previous year and to win a substantial purse that could help pay his expenses. He knew inadequate preparation and his own poor racing strategy had let the *Bluenose* down in 1930. There would be no excuses this time: his vessel would be properly groomed and ballasted, with her sails well cut and in perfect condition. The course off Halifax would, in his opinion, be a far better one; it would be deep-sea course, not the tiny roundabout circuit offered by Gloucester with its "baby buoys" that went missing in a breeze. A civic appeal went out in the press in Nova Scotia for a subscription fund—a further $6,000 was needed to help cover the expenses and prize money.

Contrary to Pine's pessimistic view of the public's likely response, the promise of a new series was welcomed with enthusiasm, offering as it did an escape from the dreary economic realities of day-to-day life during the Depression, with its collapsing businesses, soup kitchens, idleness and despair. Races and other forms of entertainment were hugely popular during those hard times and the citizens of the fishing communities, so badly affected by the Depression, saw in the Fishermen's Cup race an occasion for optimism and hope.

After the *Esperanto* had beaten the *Delawana* in the first series of 1920, Americans had thought of themselves as rightful owners of the cup, never truly reconciling themselves to its loss to the *Bluenose* by the *Elsie* in 1921. There was still the lingering feeling that they had been "robbed." It had been nine long years since the *Bluenose* had last won the series in 1922, and this time she would be facing a competitor that had already proved her worth in the Lipton Cup. The dominance demonstrated by the *Thebaud* in the previous fall's races gave Gloucestermen cause to anticipate that the Fishermen's Cup would finally be returning. And, for the first time, the date of the races did not have to be determined by the fishing season, as both boats were available and in port. October 17 was agreed upon—earlier than usual, but, with the benefit of better weather and a bit of luck, it would attract larger crowds.

Both skippers began to prepare seriously for the contest. Angus Walters took the *Bluenose* out on a trial run against the schooner that had just won that year's Lunenburg fishermen's regatta, the *Alsatian*. In fairly light winds, she showed fine form, handily beating the *Alsatian* on all points of sail. When asked about his chances against the Americans, Walters replied with customary bravado that "the wood is not yet growing of the vessel that will beat the *Bluenose*."[3] Ben Pine took his own boat out of the water and gave her a thorough overhaul. The *Boston Post* reported of the *Gertrude L. Thebaud:*

> A corps of workmen swarmed over her, smoothing her seams and painting her sleek hull. Below the waterline she was painted a ruddy copper, red as a fish's gills. Along the waterline a boot top of bright green contrasted pleasingly with her more subdued under body. A coat of glistening black hid the scars the fishing banks had left on her topsides.[4]

Pine expected more wind on the Halifax course and consequently wanted more ballast on board. Her designer, Frank Paine, reluctantly agreed to deepen her with more pig iron, as long as her waterline length, then 99 feet (30.2 metres), grew no longer than 101 feet (30.8 metres). When she was measured in Halifax before the first race, she taped in at 103 feet (31.4 metres), well within the rules of

the deed of gift but an obvious indication that she was a much heavier vessel than she had been the previous year.[5]

Pine arranged a trial match with the *Elsie*, probably the only other schooner left in the port of Gloucester that could put up a challenge. With borrowed top-masts and a crew of Sea Scouts, the *Elsie* seemed not to have lost her old form and gave the *Thebaud*'s backers a fright. In the first race, the *Elsie* started late but within fifteen minutes forged ahead and took the lead. The *Thebaud*, looking sluggish in the brisk southerly wind, finally bounced back, narrowly taking the win by only two and a half minutes. This was a cause of much concern in Glouces-ter to those who had expected far more from the *Thebaud*. "It was a severe blow to Gloucester hopes of recovering the blue ribbon of the North Atlantic fishing banks," reported Tom Horgan in the *Boston Post*.[6] The *Thebaud* looked in better form during the second race and beat the *Elsie* by more than eight minutes, but the margin of victory had been augmented by a mishap; a broken backstay had forced the crew of the *Elsie* to douse her topsails. Confidence in the *Thebaud* was not restored until her trip north to Halifax on October 13. Skippered by Captain John Matheson, the *Thebaud* clocked an impressive 365 miles in just over thirty hours, mostly under four lowers, making astonishing speeds of between twelve and fifteen knots. The crew was ecstatic about her performance and felt they could have pushed her even harder had they not wanted to avoid taxing the rigging and sails before the race. They were so sure of the trouncing they were about to give the *Bluenose*, they felt sorry for her.[7] Ben Pine could only hear about the trip; he had been forced to go by rail because of his recurrent sinus troubles, though he would skipper the *Thebaud* on race day.

On October 17, thirty thousand spectators arrived on the shores of Halifax to watch the great sea challenge. An easterly gale had blown hard all night but blew out by morning, leaving a nasty, steep swell rolling across the course. The race was a stern-chase from the start for the *Thebaud*. The *Bluenose* crossed first and within ten minutes had opened up a lead of several boat lengths. She appeared to rise easily with each swell and work her way well to windward on the beat down to the first mark. Her rival, on the other hand, could not overcome the boisterous seaway and plunged and butted into each swell. She looked as if she was "wallow-ing around like a punch-drunk prize fighter," according to reporter John Griffin of the *Boston Post*.[8] Those aboard the official spectator boat, the *Lady Laurier*, watched as the Lunenburger sailed away from her rival, and they predicted the

< **WITH THE SHEETS** hauled bar-taut and sailing close to weather, the crew of the *Blue-nose* struggles to stay upright on a heaving, wave-swept deck while working lines at the mainmast. *Edwin Levick, Mariners' Museum, Newport News, Virginia*

result long before the first buoy was reached. They quickly lost interest in the race and "devoted all their time to being seasick" as the wildly tossing government steamer tried to keep pace with the lead boat. The *Bluenose* tore around the course, leading the *Thebaud* by more than four miles, but with about six miles left to the finish, Walters hit an ebb tide and the wind died, leaving him barely half an hour to beat the clock. This he failed to do, leaving the committee to call an end to it and saving the *Thebaud* from an ignominious defeat.

The second day of the series, Monday, October 19, seemed far more suited to the American sailer. The sea was flat and smooth, with a fresh offshore breeze. After the first race, Ben Pine had realized belatedly that his increased ballast was hindering his boat and he wished to have it removed, something the rules did not allow after the series was underway. His appeal to the race committee to grant a dispensation depended on his getting the consent of his rival. Walters refused and pointed out that the American skipper had had plenty of opportunity before the series to properly adjust his ballast; he had raced the *Elsie* off Gloucester, sailed up the coast and made several trial runs around the Halifax course. All Pine could do was attempt to improve the *Thebaud*'s performance by shifting the ballast on board, and initially this appeared to work. He outmanoeuvred Walters and took off from the start, twelve seconds ahead. For the next half hour, the *Thebaud* stood her ground and both vessels were neck and neck until the big Lunenburger came through on the weather side of the *Thebaud* and got down to business. By the first mark, in a wind of twelve to fourteen knots, she was four lengths ahead and steadily gaining. In contrast to the *Bluenose* ploughing forward under a great press of sail, the *Thebaud* appeared to be standing still, her dismal performance causing one wag on board the press boat to shout for her to pull up her anchor.[9] The only thrill left in the contest was packed into the last few miles when Walters again had to fight the clock. At 3 PM the *Bluenose* was off Thrumcap Shoal, only four and a half miles from the finish, and she had forty-five minutes to go before the time limit expired. Walters threw his vessel from one tack to another, fighting his way up the harbour and finally making the breakwater a mere six minutes and thirty-one seconds before time ran out. When the cannon roared, "Captain Angus smiled and his men tumbled about the deck in handsprings," wrote the correspondent for the *Boston Post*.[10] Steam whistles, horns and sirens screeched approval. A dejected *Gertrude L. Thebaud* arrived thirty-two minutes later and was given, upon arrival at her dock, three rousing cheers from the *Bluenose* crew.

A disappointed Ben Pine took the defeat graciously, but he knew his vessel, in its over-ballasted state, was no match for the Lunenburg flyer. He explained that he had sailed against the wishes of his doctor as he did not want his alternate, Captain John Matheson, to bear sole responsibility for the *Thebaud*'s defeat, which he felt certain was coming.[11] Pine's health was deteriorating and he would not sail again in that series. Angus Walters revelled in the *Bluenose*'s obvious superiority, but complained about his competition. "You know, it was kinda lonely out there today, *Thebaud* wasn't any company—in either race, for that matter—and a feller don't get much fun out o' racing the clock all the time."[12]

Conditions for the next race on October 20 were a repetition of the first's, with the sea as smooth as a ballroom floor and a good sailing breeze from the northwest. The *Bluenose* crossed the line first, fifteen seconds after the gun, with the *Thebaud,* this time under John Matheson, only seconds behind. Both vessels settled into the seventeen-mile run to the Sambro Lightship Buoy with their sails wing and wing. There appeared to be little or nothing to choose between them. Though the conditions were virtually identical to those that had brought her defeat the day before, the *Thebaud* surprisingly held her own. Hope sprang up in the Gloucester camp when, for the first time in the series, she seriously challenged the ten-year-old Lunenburger. After jockeying back and forth to the buoy, never more than a couple of boat lengths apart, the *Bluenose* finally came alive in the windward thrash for home. Slowly and steadily, the *Thebaud* fell astern while the *Bluenose* ate up the wind on her tacks down the harbour and, an hour after turning the Sambro Buoy, she left the *Thebaud* several miles behind. The *Bluenose* surged home in five hours, six minutes, well under the time limit, with the *Thebaud* crossing twelve minutes later. The American boat had proved handier in the second race but was still no match for the Nova Scotian.

The crowds went wild in Halifax and Lunenburg in celebration of their heroes, the victorious team of Walters and the *Bluenose*. The usually staid *Yachting* magazine summed it up:

> The *Thebaud* is a good vessel, but the *Bluenose* is a better one…Gloucester had sent a boy to do a man's job, and a boy with his pockets full of pig iron at that. In perfect trim, the *Thebaud* could probably beat the *Bluenose* she met last year at Gloucester. But it was a different *Bluenose* she met this time…and a *Bluenose* better sailed. Angus was taking no more chances on splitting tacks. He had the

Thebaud covered all the time, no matter how far back she was, and he sailed his vessel with the loving touch of a master playing an old violin.[13]

Captain Ben Pine did not go away empty-handed. Not only did he receive his portion of the prize money, but he was also praised for his enthusiasm and competitive spirit. The premier of Nova Scotia, G.S. Harrington, in presenting him with a silver cup marking his ten years of participation in fishing-schooner racing, remarked:

> Captain Pine, may I tell you with genuine sincerity how much we all appreciate your fine sportsmanship, as displayed in these great contests almost from their inception…We all realize the sacrifices you have made and the greatest of these is your devotion to your duties and the handicap of ill health.[14]

The *Bluenose*'s success was, to her fervent supporters, as much a vindication as a triumph. All the bitterness and ill will that had permeated the previous decade seemed to dissolve into the past. However, the victory was bittersweet. There was an underlying feeling of sadness about the series. People sensed the inevitability that the races—and the life they represented—were coming to an end.

NOTES

1 Balcom, *Lunenburg Fishing Industry,* p. 51
2 *Boston Post,* September 17, 1931
3 *Halifax Herald,* October 15, 1931
4 *Boston Post,* October 12, 1931
5 *Yachting,* December 1931, p. 39
6 Tom Horgan, Associated Press, October 9, 1931
7 *Evening Mail,* October 14, 1931
8 John Griffin, *Boston Post,* October 18, 1931
9 Ibid.
10 Griffin, *Boston Post,* October 19, 1931
11 *Boston Post,* October 20, 1931
12 Backman, *Bluenose,* p. 49
13 *Yachting,* December 1931, p. 40
14 *Halifax Herald,* October 21, 1931

‹ **PICTURE-PERFECT** and escorted by two police launches, the *Bluenose* departs Toronto Harbour in September 1934 on her way out of the Great Lakes and back home to Nova Scotia. She had been invited to represent Canada at the World's Fair in Chicago the previous year. *Library and Archives Canada*

11

THE LAST FISHERMEN'S
RACE: 1938

THE GREAT DEPRESSION settled heavily over North America in the early 1930s. The fishing industry on both sides of the border was faltering and many boat owners were forced into bankruptcy. At best, most considered themselves lucky to be able to cover operating costs and provide a subsistence wage for their crews. Even those former fishermen involved in the illegal liquor trade were forced to look elsewhere for income when Prohibition in the United States ended with the repeal of the Volstead Act in 1933.

Trading on their celebrity status, the *Gertrude L. Thebaud* and the *Bluenose* both took on new roles. The *Thebaud* began to function as an emissary for the ailing fishing industry. She sailed to Washington in April 1933 carrying a large delegation of prominent fishing skippers and industry chiefs from most of the coastal ports in the New England states to meet the newly elected U.S. president, Franklin D. Roosevelt. They provided his administration with a detailed report on the industry and requested they be included in the government's labour programs, which were then being instituted to reinvigorate the American economy. The *Thebaud* and her complement of hardy, nearly legendary fishing captains were welcomed to the United States capital with much excitement. "The *Thebaud* party while in Washington received honors usually reserved for the highest potentates. Crowds stormed the navy yard where the *Thebaud* was tied up to inspect the vessel."[1] The visitors were wined and dined in Congress and even had tea with Eleanor Roosevelt in the White House, leaving with hope and promises that the administration would do all it could to provide assistance by developing a national market for fish products. The *Thebaud* also made appearances in New York at the famous Fulton Market to help stimulate sales.

In Canada, there was much talk of preserving the *Bluenose* as a training ship for merchant and naval services, but neither the federal nor the provincial government was willing to contribute any funding. As the *Bluenose* began to fall on hard times, Angus Walters soon realized he could capitalize on the celebrity status of his vessel. He found a public eager to pay to sail on his schooner, and so began a new career touring his vessel for profit. The *Bluenose* spent the next few years on intermittent charters as well as fishing. In 1933 Walters was invited by the Canadian government to take the *Bluenose* to Chicago for the Century of Progress Exposition. This was the first time the schooner had travelled to the Great Lakes, and Walters found she had enormous appeal to the citizens of communities that bordered the waterway. He had her fish holds gutted and replaced with cabins on the starboard side and a showcase of the Lunenburg fishery—complete with scale models and exhibits—installed on the port side. She was funded by a newly formed company of businessmen, Lunenburg Exhibitors Limited, who saw this as an opportunity to promote Lunenburg sea products.

In Chicago, she tied up near her old rival, the *Gertrude L. Thebaud,* representing the state of Massachusetts at the exposition. Like the *Bluenose,* the *Thebaud* had had her fish pens removed and extensive alterations made to accommodate guests, crew, and exhibits on loan from the Cape Ann Historical Association. The mass appeal of both schooners was obvious as hordes of visitors, more than 2,500

a day, descended on them. There were many calls for a race between the two old combatants, but neither skipper was interested.

Walters had his hands full, committing his vessel to a busy schedule of charters, until he ran afoul of a dissatisfied customer who sued him for not adequately catering to his needs. Although the case was eventually thrown out of court, it brought the vessel to the attention of the U.S. customs and excise service, which began to investigate the schooner for customs infractions. Chicago's sinister side came uncomfortably close to the *Bluenose* when a gangster shootout resulted in a bullet-riddled body being dumped astern of her in the early morning. It could be that Angus felt safer in a hurricane at sea than spending a winter in Al Capone's Chicago; he decided in late fall that it was time to head home.

Back in Canadian waters, the *Bluenose* was met by Walters's old newspaper chum, Jerry Snider, who persuaded him to stay for a while in Toronto. Snider had arranged a berth for the boat and a hero's welcome for Walters in Canada's largest city. Over the spring and summer, the *Bluenose* continued in her new career as a showboat for hire. Although she was very popular, she did not meet with the same success as in Chicago, and by the fall of 1934 Walters and his partners decided there was little profit to be made in staying any longer. They headed back home to fish.

In 1935 the *Bluenose* was once again in demand, this time as Canada's ambassador to Great Britain, to attend the silver jubilee of King George V's coronation. Angus made the passage to Plymouth in seventeen days. There, the *Bluenose* found herself anchored among the long lines of British battleships to be reviewed by the king, where her presence was noted and appreciated. Walters was later summoned to the royal yacht to be received by His Majesty and his three sons. The diminutive fishing skipper from Lunenburg found himself sought after by the British elite. He was wined and dined and had the time of his life swapping tales with the rich and famous. When his boat was challenged to a friendly match against a schooner from the Royal Yacht Squadron on a course around the Isle of Wight—where the America's Cup races had begun—he could hardly refuse. The *Bluenose* was clearly outclassed by the refined racing schooner *Westward*, but even so the feisty Walters figured she had given her a run for her money. After this successful foray into British society, he left for home on September 11. The bad weather that accompanied his departure turned steadily worse, until he and the crew were forced to heave to in hurricane-strength winds. Walters later proclaimed the weather was the worst he had ever encountered at sea. For four days they were pounded by fierce headwinds that caused considerable damage to the vessel, and a week after departing England, the Nova Scotian schooner limped back to Plymouth for repairs.

Both the *Bluenose* and the *Thebaud* survived the lean years of the 1930s by making ends meet in any way they could. They continued to fish, bringing in reasonable catches but for paltry returns. In 1936, in an attempt to remain competitive, Walters finally succumbed to the indignity of having diesel engines installed in his beloved schooner, at a cost of $12,000. His efforts to have his vessel officially recognized as a national treasure, with a permanent berth as a museum ship, failed to arouse interest with either local or provincial governments. South of the border, Ben Pine had little more financial luck with the *Thebaud,* as fish prices remained miserably low. In 1937, he chartered his vessel to the renowned Arctic explorer Donald MacMillan for use on a lengthy scientific expedition to the Arctic. After having given so much entertainment and excitement to a generation, each boat seemed to be fading into oblivion.

Two things occurred in 1937 that brightened prospects for both. The likeness of the *Bluenose* was minted onto the Canadian ten-cent piece (where it remains to this day), breathing new life into Walters's campaign to preserve his legendary boat. The other event was the resurrection of Gloucester's glory days of schooner fishing by Hollywood, when MGM Pictures made the Rudyard Kipling classic, *Captains Courageous,* into a movie starring Spencer Tracy as Manuel, a Portuguese fisherman. The story revolved around the character of a spoiled rich brat, played by Freddie Bartholomew, who falls off an Atlantic liner en route to Europe. He is rescued by Manuel, who is out fishing from his dory, and taken back to Manuel's schooner, the *We're Here.* The hard-working, fair-minded skipper has no intention of making a special trip into port to return his errant cargo and puts the little stranger to work gutting fish. The moral lesson taught to the rich child by the industrious, no-nonsense fishermen on board a Cape Ann schooner resonated with the American public, still suffering from economic hard times. The high drama of the last scenes of the movie rang especially true, when two genuine Gloucester schooners, the *Oretha F. Spinney* and the *Imperator,* were used to portray the boats in the film, racing neck and neck under full sail with the sea guttering over the leeward rails. Even today, the excitement of watching the two old schooners race is a powerful testament to the magnetic attraction of the power of sail.

The enormous success of the movie rekindled Gloucester's love affair with schooner racing. The members of the Master Mariners Association met in December to discuss the possibility of reviving the International Fishermen's Cup series. The American race committee was resurrected after seven years of dormancy, and the indefatigable Ben Pine happily threw in his hat. The Halifax trustees were contacted but were not seriously interested in taking part, instead officially handing over the race trophy to Angus Walters and leaving the decision in his hands. Angus was happy to have the chance to race, not only to see his beloved schooner once again in the spotlight, but also to benefit from the occasion by having her fitted out and, with any luck, using the prize money to help pay off the cost of her engines. The Bluenose Schooner Company was in financial difficulty and had not been able to come up with adequate funds.

The American race organizers felt they could better capitalize on the event by having a best-of-five series run off two locations, Gloucester and Nahant Bay, near Boston. A longer series in both locations would maximize the tourism potential. They promoted the series to be held in 1938 as an idyllic romp into a bygone age with two legendary skippers squaring off for battle one more time. Steadfastness and courage under the banner of true competition would be the order of the day. Hoping for a friendly contest that would be in keeping with the romantic spirit of the movie, they neglected to take into account the reality of the personalities involved, more specifically that of Captain Angus Walters, who was there not to entertain the public but to win.

Pine himself still had an axe to grind, and seven years had done little to soften his fierce desire to beat the combative Lunenburger. Walters made his intentions clear the moment he arrived in Boston in October 1938. When the mayor greeted the *Bluenose* from the deck of a U.S. Coast Guard cutter and invited Walters to a luncheon in his honour, Angus declined, saying to his crew, "Let them spout. I'm getting ready to race."[2] Nor was he about to keep silent about his views on the organization of the race. When the race committee let it be known it had decided on a short course to enable the race to be better viewed from the shore, Walters went ballistic and fired off the first of a series of broadsides at the race committee, and in particular its chairman, Captain Lyons. Calling it a "merry-go-round," Walters said "he would positively not allow his vessel to be sailed over any course that required going over it twice to complete a race."[3] He was no doubt remembering his defeat at the hands of the *Thebaud* on a twice-around course

‹ **IN 1935**, Angus Walters and the *Bluenose* were invited by the Canadian government to attend the silver jubilee celebrations of King George V's reign. The sight of such a small fishing craft among the fleet of battleships on review at Plymouth in England delighted the king, who insisted on an audience with the Nova Scotian fishing master. Walters can be seen with cap in hand behind the large gentleman on the far right. *Times* (London)

at the exhibition race in 1930. He went on to protest the lack of Canadians on the committee and found fault with the regulations being used. He let his full fury fly when he accused Captain Lyons of being unfit for the post of chairman, telling him to go back to the farm where he belonged.[4] As the "shrapnel burst and the storm of words raged," Captain Ed Proctor of the committee dug in his heels, remarking that he "saw no reason why [the panel] should buckle under to suit Angus." However, a compromise was needed, and in the end the seven-member committee agreed to a variety of long and short courses and reduced its American membership to three, adding two Canadians. Proctor resigned in disgust but later changed his mind. Ben Pine said that although he would go along with any arrangement, he found the fact that there were no Gloucester fishermen on the committee insulting. All this did not bode well for the future tone of the event, and the cantankerous Angus Walters had just begun. Denying he was making life difficult, he said "he would race in a puddle of brimstone for a counterfeit Chinese centime to settle the championship once and for all."[5] Initially, at least, the combative attitude of the Canadian skipper played well with the press, and reports of the controversy drove up enthusiasm and interest in the series.

The first race was held on October 9 off Nahant Bay. The *Bluenose* was the odds-on favourite going into the race, as most felt the smaller *Thebaud* had little chance against the big Nova Scotian defender in spite of her showing in the 1930 Lipton Cup. The race began in light winds, which picked up quickly into a brisk northwest breeze. The *Bluenose* shot off at the start and secured the weather berth, leaving the *Thebaud* trailing badly eight boat lengths behind. The schooners carried every inch of canvas and flew around the short, eighteen-mile "merry-go-round" course that Walters so despised. Neither would shorten sail, even though both were labouring under the heavy press of wind and shipping huge deck-loads of water. The *Bluenose* blew out one of her foresails on the first leg, but this did not slow her down. It was a wonderful race for the thousands of spectators who were able to view it in its entirety from the shore and hear the crisp, booming sound of rippling canvas on every tack. The Gloucester mistress soon found her legs and began seriously battling the Lunenburger, advancing on each turn, taking only thirty seconds to come about while the *Bluenose* took more than a minute. On the last leg, about three miles from the finish, a sharp crack was heard from aloft on the *Bluenose*. Walters was forced to douse both his fore and jib topsails to ease the pressure on a fractured fore-topmast. The accident slowed the *Bluenose*, but she had already been overtaken by her rival when the mishap occurred. The *Thebaud* soared across the finish nearly three minutes in the lead. With surprising good humour, Angus congratulated Ben Pine, saying: "It was a great race, the finest I have ever sailed and there are no complaints. You know, two boats can't win and Ben sure knows how to sail."[6]

The *Thebaud*'s win was totally unexpected, and it galvanized the American public and the crew. Few had seriously expected her to beat "the big brute from Lunenburg," though the *Thebaud* had never looked so good. She was in great trim, properly ballasted, and her new suit of sails, hand-stitched by Marion Cooney, fitted like a glove. Americans suddenly felt confident of her chances of victory over the Canadians. Despite the glorious sight she made at sea, the *Bluenose* was showing little of her previous form. She seemed far too tender in the gusty wind, rolling heavily and exposing too much weather bilge. When she had arrived from Lunenburg, Walters had had her engines as well as tons of iron ballast removed in preparation for the races. Her seventeen years of life as a fisherman had taken their toll: her sea-ravaged hull had run aground, battled innumerable storms and soaked up so much water over the years that it was now hard to determine her proper ballasting needs. As it was, she was longer on the waterline than she should have been for the competition. She was also hogged—her bow and stern sagged distinctly from the middle—and the strain of the overhang at either end was giving way to gravity. Most boats of her age were retired from fishing and had been sold off to freight cargo in the south.

The next race moved to Gloucester, and then came the first of a barrage of protests from the Americans that the *Bluenose* was breaking the rules by being too deep on the waterline. A survey revealed she was a full fourteen inches longer than permitted. When they had measured her in Boston, Walters had cunningly kept his crew out of sight below decks, moving the men to the stern when the measurer was at the bow and to the bow when the measurer was at the stern, thus making her appear farther out of the water, and therefore lighter than she actually was.[7] In answering the charge, Angus shot back that the *Thebaud* was also in violation by having 50 square feet (4.6 square metres) over the allowable limit of sail, whereas he was nearly 800 square feet (74 square metres) under. Captain Lyons, tired of the protests, insisted the races continue with both vessels in "as-is" condition, and they would discuss the differences at a later date.

The race of October 11 was called off due to lack of wind, but only after it had been allowed to continue for nearly the entire six hours. (The race duration varied between six and seven hours, depending on the course for this series.) Both

Walters and Pine were furious that it had been allowed to continue when it had taken the schooners more than four hours to cover one twelve-mile leg. At one point, a bored Ben Pine called over to Walters, "Hey Angus, you haven't a canoe aboard, have you?"[8]

The schooners did not sail on the twelfth, as both were invited to the dedication of the brand new Gloucester Community Fish Pier. At the time, it was a state-of-the-art facility with a freezer capacity of nearly 1,600 tons of fish and capable of producing 50 tons of ice daily, paid for by federal, state and local money under the Public Works Administration. Thousands toured the new building as well as the *Bluenose* and the *Thebaud*, which were tied up alongside. While the officials and politicians made their speeches on the dock, the fishermen were having their own private party on board the *Bluenose*. *Thebaud* crewman Sterling Hayden gave a delightful description of the party in his book, *Wanderer*:

> From the fish hold of the *Bluenose* come the sound of a trumpet muted by the three inch pine… Fishermen guard each hatch, for the party below is by invitation only—given by the crews of the schooners in their honor, and maybe that of the press. No one else is welcome… Here ninety men are assembled out of the sun, away from the politicians and tourists, the kids and the wives. They're assembled this day to bury some hatchets and kill a few kegs of rum. Up and down this cave long bundles of sails are spread, with flags nailed to the inner hull. Hymie Rodenhauser [sic], one of the *Bluenose*'s mastheadmen, straddling a keg in a cradle, is blasting loose with his trumpet. A bedlam of laughter and singing and wild gesticulations seen through a pall of smoke… A figure bursts into the hold, blowing the cook's tin whistle. "All right, you bassards, up, up, everybo'y up on the goddam deck! Hear me? The governor's gonna make us his honorin' speech, an' the mayor wants every friggin' one o' you on th' deck… An leave the booze down here… An' no more friggin' noise! Hear?" No one moves. "Drink up!" roars O'Toole. You can hear the Legion band playing the National Anthem. All rise. When the Anthem expires, they sit.[9]

Clearly these hard-bitten fishermen had their own agenda, which was to drink and have fun, with no interest in the ceremonies going on outside.

The second official race occurred on October 13 off Eastern Point, in light winds that only occasionally reached eighteen knots. It was a decent sailing breeze, much

> ›SMASHING INTO a head sea, the *Gertrude L. Thebaud* momentarily stalls, spilling wind from her jib. Such conditions made for dramatic moments during the series. *Peabody Essex Museum*

suited to the *Bluenose,* and she quickly overhauled her rival and finished twelve minutes in the lead, despite blowing out her staysail. Among the spectators was a very seasick Greta Garbo, a guest aboard a pleasure yacht. Both race skippers were infuriated at the use of trawl buoys to mark the course; these marks disappeared in the swells and were easily confused with the other fishing markers strewn over the water. Pine had so much difficulty locating the buoys that, at one point, the *Thebaud* wasted two tacks in overshooting one mark by more than two miles. Walters wired friends in Halifax: "We won despite the baby buoys."[10] The captains also objected to a new rule that all crew members had to stay on deck during the entire race so that there could be no one below shifting ballast. The series now sat at 1–1, with the next race scheduled for the following day. Because of unfavourable conditions, this race was postponed six times before it was finally sailed.

If the captains were the ringmasters of the show, the men who worked the topsails were the acrobats entertaining the masses. Working eighty feet (twenty-four metres) aloft, men like Fred Rhodenhiser, the main topman of the *Bluenose,* constantly wowed the crowd. Rhodenhiser would casually do a tightrope act across the spring stay between the two masts and inform the public that it was no more difficult to do than walking across the deck. The masthead man of the *Thebaud,* Sterling Hayden, attracted many admirers, primarily women, to the docks to watch his displays of fine seamanship aloft and enjoy his handsome good looks. The local paper, the *Gloucester Daily Times,* plastered his photo across the front page with a headline proclaiming "*Thebaud* Sailor Like Movie Idol," calling him a "Fine Masculine Specimen." Hayden was a superb sailor and navigator, but he was eventually drawn to Hollywood, partly due to the Associated Press reporter Tom Horgan, who arranged a screen test for him.

The next two attempts to race off Gloucester were called off due to light airs. Argument then erupted between the rival skippers and the committee about the location of the next race. The committee wanted it moved to Nahant Bay to satisfy Bostonians' desire to see the race closer to home, but Pine vehemently refused to move from Gloucester. He had hauled out the *Thebaud* to repair a splintered shoe after bumping a ledge in the harbour, and he was determined to have the next race off his home port. Walters was expecting to race off Nahant Bay and had already moved the *Bluenose* to an East Boston boatyard to have a new bowsprit installed. The wrangling continued for three days while the boats were being repaired. The committee was at first deadlocked over what to do, but it finally capitulated to Pine's demand and ordered the *Bluenose* to return to Gloucester. A furious Walters responded: "What do they think I have here, a Halifax ferry boat? I'll have to get a passenger license to navigate between Boston and Gloucester."[11] A disgusted Canadian member of the race committee, Wallace MacAskill, resigned and headed back to Halifax, announcing that his membership on the committee was superfluous. An unexpected visit to the *Bluenose* by John Roosevelt, a son of the American president, managed to calm the waters somewhat and caused Walters to tone down his robust attacks.[12] Leonard Fowle, writing for the *Boston Globe*, could not resist parodying the latest developments:

> The reason for the latest postponements was the inability of Capts. Ben Pine and Angus Walters, who are rivals for the hero's role, to promise to produce their feminine leads, *Gertrude L. Thebaud* and *Bluenose,* on the same stage tomorrow. Captain Ben Pine stated he could not bring his fair lady to Boston in time for a start off Nahant and Capt. Walters was equally certain that his Nova Scotian beauty could not possibly rise early enough to reach Gloucester.[13]

Finally, on Wednesday, October 19, both boats were on the line and ready to race off Gloucester. Captain Cecil Moulton had replaced Ben Pine as master of the *Thebaud,* as Pine was again suffering from a recurrence of his sinus infection. Walters was impatient to race, saying he had spent far too long lying alongside. "I've spent enough time tied up here to the dock for the average Nova Scotia boy to become a full-fledged master in sail."[14] The day held great promise; a spanking twenty-knot breeze was blowing in from the southwest and both crews were more than ready. Suddenly, it was all over before it had started. Five minutes before the starting gun sounded, a bronze composition nut that held the steering wheel in place broke on the *Bluenose,* and the heavy, cast-iron Lunenburg Foundry wheel clattered to the deck. Walters hoisted his ensign to half-mast indicating his boat was disabled, and the race was once again postponed. The vessels returned to port to allow him to repair the damage.

Walters also had a ballast problem. He knew he would need more weight deep in the *Bluenose*'s belly if he were going to race successfully in any substantial wind, but his waterline was already too long. He and his crew had begun surreptitiously loading forty-pound iron ingots in the pre-dawn hours, in clear violation of the rules. Captain Ed Proctor heard a rumour concerning ballast-shifting and had

been closely watching the *Bluenose* over a period of five nights in an attempt to catch the crew in the act. On the night of October 19, he sprinkled sand over a big pile of ingots sitting in a shed on the Pew wharf and asked the night watchman, Manuel Silva, to keep an eye on them. At 4:30 AM on October 20, Proctor received a phone call from the watchman telling him the door to the shed had been opened during the night; when Silva had gone to investigate, he had scared off about fourteen men. In the morning, Proctor found footprints of rubber boots in the sand and several tons of ballast missing. He took his findings to Captain Moulton, who delivered a protest to Captain Lyons on board the committee boat *Thetis*, demanding an investigation. Lyons brushed the complaint aside, saying he had had enough of protests and talk "about a little ballast," and he ordered the race to continue regardless.[15]

The news of the nocturnal ballasting episode spread quickly, and Gloucestermen prayed for the light wind that would work against the *Bluenose*. Their prayers may have been answered too well, for once again the race was cancelled after four and a half hours due to insufficient winds. The *Bluenose* had appeared sluggish during the race to that point and the *Thebaud* was in the lead by more than ten minutes when it was finally called off. When the boats returned to harbour, suspicions were aroused when a zealous "Angus watcher" saw Walters dock at the newly dedicated Community Fish Pier instead of at the Pew wharf. This turn of events was reported to Ray Adams, a friend and associate of Ben Pine's at the Atlantic Supply Company who later became his wife. She sped down to the fish pier and apparently caught Walters and his crew in the act of unloading ballast. When Miss Adams asked Angus outright what he was doing, he admitted he was removing ballast he had loaded that morning.[16] He said it was his ballast and he could do with it as he pleased. The open admission left Captain Lyons with little option but to order the boats be measured again and to postpone the race set for the following day. Miss Adams arranged for the police to guard the *Bluenose* through the night until the measuring was completed.

Walters telegraphed the boat's designer, William Roué, asking him to hurry down from Halifax to help with the problem of bringing his vessel back up to a 112-foot (34-metre) waterline. Instead of removing any more iron ballast, which was located deep in the hull, Roué told the crew to rip up the deck and take out five oil tanks, three air tanks, a generating plant and about five tons of other equipment, explaining that "she was carrying too much weight above the waterline. With that

< **THE OPENING** of the new Gloucester Fish Pier provided a brief pause in the 1938 series, and the two famous fishing schooners were a main attraction. As thousands poured across the decks of the *Bluenose* and the *Gertrude L. Thebaud,* the rival crews danced, sang and drank in a private party in the hold of the Nova Scotian boat. Over several kegs of rum, the crew members buried the hatchet for a brief while, before resuming the battle for the Fishermen's Cup. *Cape Ann Historical Association*

weight carried high she was tender and sluggish."[17] He later acknowledged that, in the condition she was then in, it was impossible to give the *Bluenose* adequate ballast for a stiff breeze while still holding her up to the required waterline. She was old and hogged, and her waterline was simply not straight any more.[18] The Americans took great delight in seeing the much lighter *Bluenose*, judging that she would now be far too tender in a breeze to carry much sail and prayed for wind. Any vestige of friendliness between the competing crews had been severely tested by this time, and when Angus was asked to comment, he responded: "They've pushed me too far. I will now give them a beating they won't forget."[19] Frustrated by all the delays, one of the *Bluenose* crew, Sam Shaw, facetiously remarked: "We can only stay in this country six months under the immigration laws and our time will soon be up."[20]

The protests from the Americans seemed to have backfired when, on October 23, a rejuvenated *Bluenose* sailing the "merry-go-round" course off Gloucester outraced her rival by nearly seven minutes. Judging from her performance, it might have been better for the *Thebaud* if the *Bluenose* had been allowed to go on loading ballast, as the Canadian boat now appeared to be in her best trim since the start of the series. As Lester Allen of the *Boston Post* wrote, the *Bluenose* swooped by the *Thebaud* "like a hawk over a chicken yard."[21] A grim, determined Walters had worked his crew like automatons, squinting hard at the sails and roaring out orders that sent the men madly scurrying about the vessel. The defeated crew of Gloucestermen returned to Boston licking its wounds, the series now heading towards the finish with the Canadians up 2–1.

The following day, the Americans evened the score by beating the *Bluenose* over an irregular thirty-five-mile triangular course off Boston. Although the *Thebaud* trailed the *Bluenose* for the first leg of the race, her victory was all but assured on the second twelve-mile leg to windward in a piping southerly breeze. The *Bluenose* had problems with her gear. On the first tack to windward, the block on the fisherman's staysail fouled and would go neither up nor down. As sails lashed and flogged about, Fred Rhodenhiser clung precariously to the spring stay high above the deck and struggled to clear the block. When the *Bluenose* rounded the second mark, a backstay parted and Walters was forced to come up into the wind to lower the jib topsail, which cost him valuable time. The breeze fluctuated in velocity from eight to twenty-five knots, and whenever the wind strengthened, the *Thebaud* drew away from the big defender.[22] At times both vessels were logging twelve to fourteen knots, and the crews were working waist-deep in the green water along the lee rail. It was no picnic on board the *Thebaud* as she hurtled through the smother of sea and spray. Aloft, Sterling Hayden and Jack Hackett fought their way out to the end of the mainsail gaff in the howling wind to secure a block that was threatening to tear away. Lester Allen described the scene: "From afar the yellow oilskinnned figures of the *Thebaud's* crew seemed to swim around, while working at the leeward gear, like little yellow dabs of butter on a smoking oyster stew."[23] When the *Thebaud* finally crossed the finish, there was some confusion about on which side of the mark she should pass, so having gone past on one side, Moulton came about and repassed it on the other, just to be sure. The lead she had on her rival varied from three to five minutes, according to different sources. The committee boat had great difficulty keeping up with the racers and became lost in the rain and fog, so the finish was not officially timed. When asked how he won, a gloating Moulton said, "The *Bluenose* simply couldn't take it."[24] Walters blurted out: "*Thebaud* beat us—enough said."[25] Echoing the simmering tension between the two competitors, the vessels turned their sterns to each other and went off in opposite directions. The *Thebaud* headed back to Gloucester and the *Bluenose* to East Boston, where it was reported the police had their eyes on her to make sure no more ballast was shifted.[26] Through blinding rain squalls and a boisterous sea, the crew of the *Thebaud* had put the *Bluenose* crew on notice that they were still in the game.

With the series now even and the Americans on a roll, Moulton was furious when the committee cancelled the race the following day. Storm warnings posted all along the coast forced Lyons to call it off to protect the men and vessels. Ben Pine, now out of hospital, charged that Lyons should have consulted the rival skippers beforehand. "Captain Lyons has sent us out day after day when there was no wind and we knew we could not finish, but when everyone knew there would be a breeze he called it off and he wouldn't if he had to pay the expenses of one of these vessels."[27] Both Moulton and Pine went on to accuse Lyons of everything from being seasick to being in collusion with Walters. Their protests concerning the weather appeared to be well founded, since the day passed with clear skies and a twenty-eight-knot northwest breeze, possibly the best conditions since the series had opened.

The fifth and deciding race was held off Boston on October 26. The two old competitors again squared off for the final act in a two-decade-old drama, the likes of which would never be seen again. The previous day, both skippers had been involved in the repair of their vessels. Walters had the broken stay and frayed gear to mend, and Moulton, leaving nothing to chance, had had the *Thebaud* hauled out for the fourth time in the series to have her hull scraped and painted. The *Bluenose* crossed the start fifteen seconds ahead of the *Thebaud* when the gun boomed at noon precisely. On the first leg of the thirty-six-mile triangle, Walters sent his charge plunging out past Graves Light with every inch of canvas flying. As the *Thebaud* trailed slightly behind, Walters's small figure, in its trademark faded blue sweater, could be seen behind the heavy Lunenburg Foundry wheel, carefully adjusting direction one spoke at a time. Under a moderate southwest breeze, the *Bluenose* ripped along at eleven knots and gradually pulled farther away, yard by yard, from her rival. On board, the crew huddled under the windward rail, no one stirring but all ready to move at a moment's notice.

On the second leg, the *Thebaud* began to chase down her rival and for the first time started to gain on her. Cecil Moulton, who would have much preferred a good blow, nursed every ounce of the 15-knot wind that flowed across her sails. As Lester Allen described it, Moulton "had an odd trick of rocking back and forth like a lad on a sled, trying to urge his vessel on—and throughout yesterday's race, with eyes cocked up at the fluttering leech of the mainsail, he rocked and rocked and rocked."[28] Conditions on the first two legs did not allow for a luffing match or a strategic tacking duel. Both crews sat idle during the long reaches, except to trim a sail now and then. This part of the race belonged to the skippers, who used all their knowledge and skill to coax every bit of speed they could out of the wind.

The real fight began on the last leg to the finish, when the two big schooners had to work the nine-mile beat to windward. The *Thebaud* crew, which had been far quicker at sail handling than their rivals, found themselves matched on this point for the first time. There was simply too much at stake, and both crews worked with clockwork precision. When they tacked around the last buoy, Walters kept his boat well to windward and was able to point higher than his rival. He sailed so close to the wind that his sails were constantly on the verge of luffing and losing air. The crews went to work in earnest for the first time during this part of the race as both vessels tacked again and again. When the wind freshened to twenty knots, the *Thebaud* was able to gain a little ground on each tack, but she ran out of time. The *Bluenose* was out of reach and flew across the finish two minutes, fifty seconds in the lead. In the closing minutes, the topsail halyard of the *Bluenose* had parted. Had this happened earlier, the result might

have been different, but breaking so close to the finish it did not matter. Lester Allen was magnanimous in his praise of the Lunenburg skipper, writing that Walters and the *Bluenose* were an unbeatable combination. "Walters sailed a magnificent race… He didn't miss a strategic bet anywhere along the 36-mile course. At all times he was the master of both the *Bluenose* and the *Gertrude L. Thebaud*."[29]

The Gloucestermen were disconsolate. There were no smiling faces or caps tossed in the air, only silent groups of men braced against the heel of the deck, with thumbs in the suspenders of their oilskins, silently examining their boots. Each knew this had been the last chance to take on the Nova Scotians.

On the *Bluenose*, the crew were already into the rum and prepared to party. When they made their way into the dock in East Boston, Fred Rhodenhiser, the indomitable foretop man, tooted a merry parody of "The Music Goes Round and Round" on his trumpet, while the crew sang lustily and loudly some uncomplimentary verses about the "merry-go-round" course their skipper so detested.[30] The *Bluenose* had retained her title of Queen of the North Atlantic and her triumphant skipper, Angus Walters, could not have been happier. "Today's race was beautiful, but if the *Thebaud* couldn't beat the *Bluenose* today, she never could and never will."[31]

Although the racing had finally ended, the accusations and recriminations continued. From the start Captain Lyons, the chairman of the race committee, had come under intense criticism from both sides for his handling of the series. A highly disgruntled Cecil Moulton wasted no time in accusing him of favouritism and blamed him for the result. "*Thebaud* was not beaten by *Bluenose*, but by Capt. Lyons. He sent us out day after day when there wasn't enough wind for a real race and kept us in port when there was a good breeze."[32] In Moulton's opinion, the final race was nothing but a drifting match, with no windward work, which favoured the *Bluenose*. "Angus says they haven't got a vessel here that can beat the *Bluenose*, does he? Well, all I can say is that there is no boat can beat him in a drifting match. The *Thebaud* is a racer, not drifter."[33] Captain Proctor, the Gloucester member of the race committee, supported Moulton and agreed that the *Thebaud* was robbed of victory by being forced to stay in port every day there was fishermen's weather. An equally irate Ben Pine said he would never again challenge for the International Fishermen's Cup. "We took two races sailed in a good breeze. *Bluenose* got three sailed in weather I don't consider fit for a fisherman's race. I don't want any more of it."[34]

Walters had also had enough of the series and was glad to see it over. In a brief statement to the press, he said, "I will never sail *Bluenose* again in American waters in a race with an American vessel. I have been treated unfairly. All the tricks they tried on me in Gloucester didn't do them any good, and I'm through with them for good and all."[35] Unfortunately, his problems with the race committee were only just beginning. The promised prize money plus expenses, totalling $9,000, were unavailable as meagre donations and poor sales of subscriptions to the race fund had left the organizers struggling to come up with funds. But Walters had entered into the series with a contract stipulating that he would be paid in full, and he was not about to leave without it; nor was Ben Pine about to let Walters depart with any money until he had received his own share. As John Griffin said in the *Boston Post*, "It would take the talents of the proverbial Philadelphia lawyer to set things in order, and even then it is doubtful that all hands would be satisfied."[36] To make matters worse, the International Fishermen's Cup, which had been on prominent display in a Boston department store window, went missing.

News of the trophy's disappearance brought great amusement along the waterfront in Gloucester. Although no one admitted to stealing it, most thought it had been "borrowed" as a prank. Pine said he had no interest in the trophy and had only raced to "beat Angus," but, he added, "it was a great joke that the trophy was gone, and wondered how Angus could ever convince the Nova Scotians that he had beat the *Thebaud* if he couldn't produce the trophy."[37] The insurance company that held a policy on the cup put up a $500 reward for its return, with no result. Walters was not amused and told the race directors, "You better get it back or else." He ordered the *Bluenose* to depart for Lunenburg, "before she too disappeared."[38] He was not about to wait around to have the engines installed, either, as he did not "want to have anything more to do with Gloucester." In fact, at the time Angus probably felt the same way about Boston; to add insult to injury, a confidence man there robbed him of $10 he had put down on a new suit.

Cecil Moulton could not shake off his bitterness over the outcome and refused to let things rest. He desperately wanted another chance to take on the *Bluenose* in "real fishermen's weather" and sent a telegram to Walters, stating, "I hereby challenge you to one race over your own course in Massachusetts waters in any breeze of 25 miles an hour or more velocity. You and I put up $500 each and race under deed of gift. Put up or shut up. Winnings go to winning crew."[39] Walters was unmoved and replied through the press that he had "more important things on his mind now," referring to his upcoming marriage to Mildred Butler of

Halifax. Nonetheless, he could not resist a jab at Moulton and upped the ante: "Five hundred dollars, Bah! That's only poker money those Gloucester folks are talking about. Let's get this thing settled for once and for all. Let's race for $5,000, from Boston to Bermuda, around the island and back to Halifax, winner-take-all. Let them think that over instead of spouting about chicken feed."[40] Neither challenge was accepted, and both skippers adamantly refused to negotiate.

At the same time, Walters—still in Boston—was basking in the attention given to him as victor, secure in the knowledge that the International Fishermen's Cup was now his forever. He was wined and dined and, at a victory dinner put on by the Canadian Club at the Chamber of Commerce in his honour, his rivals, Ben Pine and Cecil Moulton, as well as Captain Lyons, were all on hand to congratulate him and his crew. If there was any ill feeling between the rival skippers at that point, it was well hidden, as each congratulated the other for fine sportsmanship. Walters was invited to speak to the Massachusetts House of Representatives, and told the assembled politicians he was confident the prize money would be forthcoming and the trophy soon found. The opportunity to speak before the house, he said, had given him the greatest pleasure he'd had since arriving in Boston. The representatives gave him a rousing round of cheers and enthusiastic applause. Walters was by now enjoying his reception so much that he made hints he might return with his new bride to settle in the city.

The errant trophy finally resurfaced, mysteriously appearing unharmed on the Boston doorstep of the New England Home for Little Wanderers. The culprits were never identified, but there was a rumour the Boston press had been responsible. No one was more puzzled than Elizabeth Beyer, the matron of the home, when she found the parcel on her steps on Halloween morning. Like a foundling child, the cup lay carefully wrapped, with a bottle of cod liver oil beside it and a poem reading:

> Here's to Angus, good old sport,
> Whose challenge sort of takes us short.
> Send us a gale that blows at thirty,
> And we'll bet our shirts on little Gerty.[41]

The irony of the 1938 series was that, in a reversal of roles from their previous encounters, the *Gertrude L. Thebaud* was probably the better boat in a strong breeze and the *Bluenose* better in light airs. From the beginning of her career,

<CARRYING LESS sail and almost twice the age of her rival, the *Bluenose* manages to creep up on the *Gertrude L. Thebaud* during a race off Gloucester in 1938. That Fishermen's Cup series became the longest and most contentious in the history of these races; it also turned out to be the last. *Leslie Jones, Boston Public Library*

the *Bluenose* had made her name in heavy-weather sailing and was always considered at her best going to windward in a strong blow. She had beaten the *Elsie,* the *Henry Ford* and the *Thebaud* over long courses in heavy weather. Only the *Columbia* had come close to matching her, boat for boat, in a gale of wind. The *Thebaud,* on the other hand, always seemed out of trim and improperly ballasted until the 1938 series. In 1930, during the second race of the Lipton Cup series, she floundered so badly in the forty-knot breeze that she was caught in irons and barely able to manoeuvre before the race was abandoned, while the *Bluenose* had soared ahead. But in 1938 it appeared the *Thebaud* was in her prime, giving the best performance of her career, far superior in a strong breeze than her opponent. The *Bluenose* was by then too old and sea-worn to be racing at all, but she had honours and a skipper's pride to defend—and engines to pay off. She was now a very different boat than she had been the last time she raced, in 1931. If the final race of 1938 had been run on October 25, when the wind was blowing hard, the series might have had a different outcome. The *Bluenose* needed the lighter air to race effectively because her lack of proper ballasting made her too tender for a strong breeze. Even Ed Kelly, the *Halifax Herald* writer who had followed the *Bluenose*'s career from the time she was built, admitted she was too old and too tender for racing:

> Imagine it! *Bluenose*—the "heavy weather vessel"—wanting a "light breeze." We would have called it ridiculous, if we had not realized by then it was true... Heavily handicapped by years, woefully out of condition, in no shape to do what she used to do, this splendid old Champion came through yesterday with the greatest triumph of her long career.[42]

With the trophy now handed back to him, Walters returned home to a hero's reception, though still without the promised prize money. It would take months, and the help of lawyers, to sort out the financial wrangling. In the end, Walters received only a portion of his winnings and expenses.

NOTES

1 *Atlantic Fisherman,* May 1933, p. 5

2 *Boston Post,* October 8, 1938; Hayden, *Wanderer,* p. 218

3 *Gloucester Daily Times,* October 6, 1938

4 Ibid.

5 *Boston Sunday Post,* October 9, 1938

6 *Boston Post,* October 10, 1938

7 Cameron, *Schooner,* p. 60

8 *Halifax Herald,* October 12, 1938

9 Hayden, *Wanderer,* p. 221

10 *Halifax Herald,* October 14, 1938

11 *Boston Globe,* October 17, 1938

12 Ibid.

13 *Boston Globe,* October 18, 1938

14 *Boston Post,* October 19, 1938

15 *Gloucester Daily Times,* October 21, 1938

16 *Gloucester Daily Times,* October 21, 1938; *Halifax Herald,* October 22, 1938

17 *Boston Post,* October 24, 1938

18 *Halifax Herald,* October 27, 1938

19 *Boston Sunday Post,* October 23, 1938

20 *Boston Post,* October 21, 1938

21 *Boston Post,* October 24, 1938

22 *Halifax Herald,* October 25, 1938

23 *Boston Post,* October 25, 1938

24 Ibid.

25 *Halifax Herald,* October 25, 1938

26 *Gloucester Daily Times,* October 25, 1938

27 *Halifax Herald,* October 26, 1938

28 *Boston Post,* October 27, 1938

29 Ibid.

30 Ibid.

31 *Boston Herald,* October 27, 1938

32 *Gloucester Daily Times,* October 27, 1938

33 *Boston Herald,* October 27, 1938

34 Ibid.

35 Ibid.

36 *Boston Post,* October 28, 1938

37 *Gloucester Daily Times,* October 28, 1938

38 *Boston Post,* October 28, 1938

39 *Boston Post,* October 28, 1938

40 *Halifax Herald,* October 29, 1938

41 *Gloucester Daily Times,* November 1, 1938

42 *Halifax Herald,* October 27, 1938

12

IN THE WAKE

AS BITTER AND ACRIMONIOUS as the 1938 series was, the competition did serve as a swan song for the schooner fishery. The sight of tall spars marking a harbour beyond a headland was by then already becoming a distant memory, and the end of an era could not have come with more finality than with the beginning of the Second World War. Even as the *Gertrude L. Thebaud* and the *Bluenose* were facing off for their first race of the 1938 series, the prime minister of Great Britain, Neville Chamberlain, was attempting to negotiate a peaceful resolution to Nazi aggression with Adolf Hitler in Germany. Despite the fuss and fanfare, to most of the world riveted to news of events in Europe, the last Fishermen's Cup races were really only a bit of nostalgic entertainment for some.

In 1939, Angus Walters had a tough time trying to keep his vessel afloat financially. The marauding German U-boats had effectively closed the sea lanes off North America and the banks fishery had entirely collapsed, leaving the *Bluenose* and the rest of the Lunenburg fleet no option but to remain tied up at the dock. The Bluenose Schooner Company could not make payments on her engines, so the mortgage was foreclosed and the *Bluenose* went up for auction on November 14, 1939. Walters had retired from life at sea in 1939 and taken up dairy farming, but he could not bear to part with his treasured schooner. One hour before she was due to go under the auctioneer's hammer, he rescued her with $7,000 of his own savings. "I think it a disgrace the schooner be threatened with the auction block. I still will protect the *Bluenose* with all that I have as she has served me so faithfully to be let down," the impassioned skipper later declared.[1] He continued to lobby hard to have her taken over by the government and preserved as a national monument, but without a groundswell of support, there could be little hope of success. He appealed to his own community and beyond to help save her, and he tried to organize a nationwide campaign to sell non-dividend-bearing shares at a dollar apiece. The timing could not have been worse. An old fishing schooner in Lunenburg could not compete with a world war. By 1942, Angus could no longer afford to keep his schooner and was forced to sell her to the West Indies Trading Company Ltd. for $20,000; she was put to work as an itinerant freighter carrying cargoes of rum, bananas, sugar, dynamite and fuel oil throughout the Caribbean. It is not hard to imagine his grief when he cast off her lines in May 1942 and, knowing he would likely never see her again, watched her go. "We've seen a lot together in fair weather and foul, and the *Bluenose* was like a part of me," he said after she departed. He remained bitter that the province and his own community had failed to preserve the schooner that had served so faithfully for eighteen years and brought fame and glory to Lunenburg, Nova Scotia and Canada.

As Walters predicted, the *Bluenose* did not return to Nova Scotian waters. Her new career in the West Indies was a short one, coming to an abrupt end in January 1946 when she struck a reef off Haiti and sank. Too late, her loss finally struck a nerve in Canada, and as the *Halifax Herald* lamented, "her passing is a national sorrow; the ignominy of her death, a national shame."[2] As a Lunenburg resident put it more poignantly years later, "*Bluenose!* You know how Loun'burg feels? Like somebody just buried their mother. Home now after the funeral, they sit in the kitchen and remember they didn't treat her very good when she was alive."[3] In a letter to the *Chronicle Herald* in 1953, Walters wrote, "I feel it is to the shame of the Province and the town of Lunenburg, and the citizens who were in a position to have set up the *Bluenose* as a permanent memorial of a fast dying way of fishing that she was allowed to go South to founder and to rest on a bed of rocks."[4]

Sadly, the sinking of the *Bluenose* seemed to be part of a pattern affecting the schooners that took part in the International Fishermen's Cup series; many of them came to similar tragic ends. Her rival, the *Gertrude L. Thebaud,* passed the war years on loan to the United States Navy, acting as a flagship for the Corsair fleet of volunteer pleasure boats that patrolled the Atlantic and Gulf coasts looking for German submarines. In the spring of 1944, with a wheelhouse added and bowsprit removed, she was returned to her owner. As Ben Pine had little use for his anti-quated schooner, he sold her to a New Yorker who sent her south, like the *Bluenose,* to cart cargo around the Caribbean and South America. She left Gloucester for the last time in May 1945 and met her end not far from her famous rival, smashed against a breakwater in Laguaira Harbour, Venezuela, in February 1948.

Both schooners from the first series of 1920 were lost, the *Esperanto* off Sable Island in the summer of 1921 and the *Delawana* in a storm off Guysburo County in April 1924. The little *Elsie* foundered in the Gulf of St. Lawrence in January 1936, and the *Henry Ford* broke up on Whaleback Ledge on the west coast of New-foundland in June 1928. The *Columbia* never did race the *Bluenose* again after the 1923 series, and she sank with all hands, off Sable Island, in August 1927. Many of the vessels that competed in the elimination races, or were built to compete, also met with disaster. Both the *Puritan* and the *Keno* had their racing careers cut short before they had a chance to prove their worth, the *Puritan* sinking off Sable Island in June 1922 and the *Keno* on her way to Newfoundland in January 1924. Others, such as the *Uda R. Corkum,* the *Mayotte,* the *Mahaska,* the *Arthur James,* the *Elizabeth Howard* and the *Elsie G. Silva,* fell victim to the sea in one way or another. The tragic endings were blamed on the jinx of the Fishermen's Cup races, but in reality they were no different from the fates of many fishing schooners at the time. One need only remember the monuments to drowned fishermen in Lunen-burg and Gloucester to realize how many schooners and men were lost at sea.

Despite the sometimes heated bluster of their public comments, Ben Pine remained friendly with Angus Walters and had a cordial relationship with his rival until his death at the age of seventy in February 1953. He was buried in Gloucester under a headstone that bears an image of his favourite schooner, the

Columbia. Although he never sailed as a working skipper on any of the fishing boats he owned, his title of "captain" was well earned through his untiring efforts to promote an industry he loved and his almost single-handed efforts to keep schooner racing alive through the late 1920s and the 1930s. He was plagued with illness and could not always be at the wheel when he wished, but he always showed great sportsmanship and, given the opportunity, a masterful handling of his schooners. His one remaining regret was that he never had a second chance to take on his nemesis, the *Bluenose,* with the *Columbia,* which he considered the finest and fastest fishing schooner ever built.

On July 24, 1963, Angus Walters watched history repeat itself at the Smith and Rhuland yard in Lunenburg. Three years earlier, the shipyard had built a replica of HMS *Bounty* to be used in the film *Mutiny on the Bounty.* The sight of a large wooden sailing ship in the waterfront shipyard generated much excitement and fuelled speculation that a replica of the *Bluenose* could be next. The boom days of the salt fishery and shipbuilding were long gone, but there was enough expertise left in the town to do the job. A local Halifax business, Oland and Son Brewery, understood the enormous potential in advertising and underwrote the building of the replica of the famous Nova Scotian schooner to promote its new label, "Schooner Beer." Both Walters and William Roué were consulted on the construction details. The hull, sail plan and rigging were identical to the original, but the interior was altered to suit her new role as floating ambassador for the province. Walters was thrilled to see his old charge brought back to life in replica, and when he took the wheel on her sea trials in 1963, after studying her lines and the set of her sail, he announced, "She'll do fine."[5] Walters passed away in 1968, secure in the knowledge that his legacy would be passed on for some time to come.

Walters has been seen as hero or villain, depending on the side of the Canada–United States border. Although he was known for his caustic tongue and for playing hard and fast with the rules, even his worst critics could not fault his superior seamanship. The American maritime historian Howard Chapelle later called him "an aggressive, unsportsmanlike, and abusive man," but acknowledged him as "a prime sailor."[6] North of the border, Walters was a champion who contributed greatly to a spirit of nationhood in a young country so often overshadowed by her neighbour to the south. This was especially true during the depths of the Great Depression, when Canada desperately needed larger-than-life heroes who were tough and resourceful. The *Bluenose* became a national icon, her image

‹ THE *BLUENOSE* sails off in the distance with her sails "wing and wing," or, as old sailors like to say, "reading both pages." A following breeze and a fair wind was a joy to sailor and fisherman alike. *Wallace MacAskill Collection, Nova Scotia Archives and Records Management*

appearing on everything from soft drinks to underwear. Today, her likeness remains engraved on the Canadian ten-cent coin.

Although the advance of technology forever changed the fishing industry, until the 1950s the few stalwart souls who clung to tradition continued to work from dories with hook and line. The schooners still at sea seemed to be almost ghosts from the past, come to haunt the trawlers and draggers operating offshore. They were objects of awe and wonder to modern fishermen who, though shaking their heads in disbelief, would make way for their revered elders on the banks. Though their time was long past, the harsh and dangerous life they represented still commanded respect. Today, aside from the expensively restored historic vessels lying alongside museum wharves, there is little left of the traditional fishing schooner.

The irony of the passing of the banks schooners is that they are now seen as symbols of romance. The passage of time has all but eliminated the memory of a working life under sail and, to some extent, the last schooner races served to reinforce the ideal that was also popularized by contemporary writers. Walters, Morrissey, Welsh, Himmelman and Pine have become picturesque folk heroes to a public that admires their skill, resourcefulness and courage and neglects their all-too-human qualities that, at the time, added to the excitement and drama of the races.

The series may have elevated the status of the humble fisherman, but it failed in other respects. Its goal of expanding the fish market proved to be beyond its powers and the anticipated improvements in schooner design did not materialize, as that would have been a pointless exercise for an almost obsolete vessel. Although the International Fishermen's Cup often became mired in controversy and contention and fell victim to pettiness and patriotism, the "race for real sailors" succeeded in giving working boats—and their designers, builders, skippers and crews—an opportunity to prove their worth on a grand scale and the public a last look at those beautiful vessels crewed by a dying breed of fishermen, before both sailed off into the horizon.

NOTES

1 Backman, *Bluenose,* p. 21
2 *Halifax Herald,* n.d.
3 *Maclean's,* June 15, 1950, p. 45
4 *Chronicle Herald,* 1953
5 Backman, *Bluenose,* p. 84
6 Chapelle, *American Fishing Schooners,* p. 296

(1) **PROPOSED RACE RULES**, as published in the *Gloucester Daily Times*, October 13, 1920

1. Vessel must be a *bona-fide* fisherman with at least one year's experience on the banks.

2. Vessels must carry inside ballast only.

3. Sails used in the race to be made of ordinary commercial duck and to be of no greater area than those in ordinary use on the banks and to be limited to mainsail, foresail, jumbo, jib, jib topsail, fore and main working gaff topsails and fisherman's staysail.

4. Crew to be limited to twenty-five men.

5. Skipper to be *bona-fide* fishing captain with at least one year's experience on the banks.

6. Vessels to be not more than 150 feet [45.7 metres] overall length.

7. Race to be sailed boat for boat without any time allowance.

8. Decisions of the sailing committee, on which both sides are to be represented, to be regarded as final in the interpretation of the above conditions.

9. Trophy to be awarded to the winner of the best two out of three races.

(2) **THE RACE RULES 1920**, as published in the *Evening Mail*, October 29, 1920

1. One vessel only to represent Nova Scotia and one only to represent Gloucester.

2. Crew to consist of Twenty-five (25) men including Master; also one representative of the opposing boat. Owners to have the privilege of taking Two (2) invited guests on each boat, one whom may be a Pilot if desired, making the maximum total of Twenty-eight (28) on each boat.

3. The Trophy Cup to be a Perpetual Challenge Trophy. The Cup to remain in possession of the Municipality or some responsible organization. A formal Document to be prepared stating that the Cup is open to yearly challenge. The present series to be the best two out of three Races. Trophy to be raced for this year, 1920, and next year, 1921, off Halifax, and afterwards in accordance with the Deed of Gift.

4. Start to be at 9 a.m. Time Limit nine hours. In case of a later start and the Race not concluded it is to be called off at 6 p.m.

5. Racing Rules: the regular rules of the road.

6. Length of Course: Forty (40) Miles. Weather conditions permitting, one of the first two races shall be a windward or a leeward if possible, the others to be triangle, over course laid down. Sailing Committee to have full jurisdiction over the Race and to notify competitors One Hour before the start what course is selected. Race every day unless postponement for sufficient reasons.

7. Dates, 1920 Race: Saturday, Oct. 30, Monday, Nov. 1, Tues. Nov. 2.

8. Sails: Those only to be used which are a regular part of a fishing vessel outfit, viz: 4 lowers, 2 topsails, 1 jib topsail, 1 staysail.

9. Ballast Rocks or Iron: Owner's option. No shifting of ballast allowed after the firing of the Fifteen Minute preparatory Gun.

10. Guns: One at fifteen minutes before the start, one at five minutes before the start, and the Starting Gun. Competing schooners to be notified of any postponement of the time of starting.

11. All time to be from the foremast of the vessels.

12. Gloucester to appoint a representative to act on the Race Committee.

(3) 1921 DEED OF GIFT

To all Men Greetings

Be it known that William H. Dennis, representing the proprietors of The *Halifax Herald* and The *Evening Mail* newspapers, published in the City of Halifax, in the Province of Nova Scotia, Canada, recognizing the great importance and value of the deep sea fishing industry to the inhabitants of this Province of Nova Scotia, and realizing the necessity of the best possible type of craft being employed in the pursuit of the industry and believing that this can best be obtained by engendering a spirit of friendly competition among the fishermen of this Province and also with the fishermen engaged in similar methods of fishing in the other Maritime Provinces of Canada, the dominion of Newfoundland and the United States of America, has donated and placed under the control of Trustees to be named herein, a TROPHY, of which a photograph and description thereof shall be attached hereto, to be known as:

The Halifax Herald North Atlantic Fishermen's International Trophy

to be sailed for annually under the Rules and Conditions which follow, which may be added to, taken from or modified from time to time to meet changing conditions of the Industry by the Trustees herein appointed or their successors. The said Rules or any modification thereof being always drawn in such manner as to safeguard and continue the intention of the Donors of the Trophy, which is the development of the most practical and serviceable type of fishing schooner combined with the best sailing qualities, without sacrificing utility. For the purpose of maintaining this principle the Trustees are empowered to disqualify from all or any competition any vessel which in their opinion is of such a type or dimensions as would contravert the intention of the Donors and such decisions of the Trustees shall be final; the Trustees shall, however, do nothing which will change the spirit of the intention of the Donors, that the competitors shall be confined to vessels and crews engaged in practical commercial fishing.

The Trustees in whom the control of the Trophy is vested are The Honourable The Premier of Nova Scotia, His Worship The Mayor of Halifax, Messrs. H.R. Silver, H.G. DeWolf, R.A. Corbett, H.G. Lawrence, W.J. Roué, F.W. Baldwin, Capt. V.C. Johnson, being Members of the Original Committee; any vacancies arising to be filled by a majority vote of the remaining Trustees, who, in conference with the representatives of the Gloucester Committee in charge of the races held in the year Nineteen Hundred and Twenty, have drawn the following Rules and Regulations, which shall govern all future races until and unless good and sufficient reason arises for their modifications in such manner as the Trustees may consider advisable.

1. This Trophy is being presented by the proprietors of the The *Halifax Herald* and The *Evening Mail,* as a perpetual International Championship Trophy, to be raced for annually.

2. All Races for this Trophy shall be under the control and management of an International Committee of Five, which shall be elected for each series of races; the Trustees will nominate the two members of the Committee to represent Nova Scotia, and the Governor of the Commonwealth of Massachusetts, in conjunction with the local United States Committee handling the Race, shall name the two members of the Committee to represent the United States. The Chairman of this Committee shall be named by the two members of the Committee representing the country in which the Race is to be held.

3. The Race shall be sailed in the year 1921 off the Harbour of Halifax, Nova Scotia, and alternately thereafter off Gloucester (or a course in Massachusetts Bay to be mutually agreed upon by the International Committee in charge of the Race) and off Halifax, Nova Scotia. The dates on which the Races are to be sailed shall be decided by the International Committee, but shall be fixed so as not to unduly interfere with the business in which the craft are engaged.

4. The only vessels which can compete for the trophy shall be *bona-fide* fishing vessels, which have been engaged in commercial deep sea fishing for at least one season previous to the Race. A fishing season for the purpose of these Rules is considered as extending from the month of April to September, and any vessel competing must have actually sailed from her last port of departure for the Fishing Banks not later than April thirtieth in any year and have remained on the fishing grounds in all weather as customary, until the month of September, excepting necessary returns to port for landing cargo and refitting. Fishing Banks shall mean all off-shore Banks, such as George's, Western, Grand, etc., and vessels engaged in shore fishing and making port in bad weather shall not be eligible.

5. The Captain and Crew of each competing vessel shall be *bona-fide* fishermen, actively engaged in deep sea fishing, and the number of the crew shall be fixed by the International Committee. A list of the crew of each vessel and substitutes therefore shall be forwarded to the International Committee one week before the Series takes place, and each vessel competing shall be furnished with a copy of the Crew List of the opposing vessel or vessels.

6. All competing vessels shall be propelled by sails only and must comply with the following measurements and conditions:
   (a) OVERALL LENGTH, Not to exceed one hundred and forty-five (145) feet [44.2 metres], from outside of stem to outside of taffrail.
   (b) WATER LINE LENGTH, in racing trim, not to exceed one hundred and twelve (112) feet [34.1 metres] from the outside of the stem at point of submersion to the point of submersion at the stern.
   (c) DRAUGHT OF VESSEL, in racing trim shall not exceed sixteen (16) feet [4.9 metres] from the lowest point of the keel to the racing water line, measured vertically.
   (d) NO OUTSIDE BALLAST shall be used.
   (e) INSIDE BALLAST shall consist of any material of a not greater specific gravity than iron.
   (f) COMPETING VESSELS shall race with the same spars, including booms and gaffs (which must all be solid), as are used in fishing.

(g) COMPETING VESSELS must be of the usual type, both in form and construction, sail plan and rigging, as customary in the fishing industry, and any radical departure therefrom may be regarded as a freak and eliminated.

7. (a) The Sails used in racing shall be made of the ordinary commercial duck of the same weight and texture as generally used in the class of vessel and shall have been used at least one season in fishing.

(b) SAILS TO BE USED are Mainsail, Foresail, two Jibs (including Jumbo), Jib Topsail, Fore and Main Gaff Topsails and fisherman's Staysail.

(c) THE TOTAL SAIL AREA, not including fisherman's staysail, to be no greater than Eighty Percent (80%) of the square of the water line length, in racing trim, as expressed in square feet. This stipulation not to apply to vessels built previous to the 1920 Races, but such existing vessels shall not increase their sail area to exceed 80% of the square of the water line if it does not already do so.

(d) THE COMBINED AREA of the Mainsail and the Main Gaff Topsail shall not be more than Fifty percent (50%) of the maximum total sail area, as provided in the preceding subsection "c".

8. The area of the sails shall be calculated as follows:
    › MAINSAIL By the universal rule for mainsails, with the exception that the "B" of the formulae shall be measured from the after-side of the mainmast to the outer clew iron hole.
    › MAIN GAFF TOPSAIL Universal rule
    › FORESAIL AND FORE GAFF TOPSAIL By the universal rule for actual measurement of the sails used and not a percentage of space between the masts.
    › HEAD SAILS Universal rule for Head Sails.
    If more than one Staysail or Jibtopsail are on the vessel they must be of the same area and only one be set at a time.

9. NO BALLAST shall be taken on or put off the competing vessels during the Series and no ballast shall be shifted after the Fifteen Minute Preparatory Gun is fired before each Race.

10. THE INTERNATIONAL COMMITTEE shall have power to arrange all details of the Races in accordance with the Deed of Gift and shall appoint such Sub-Committees as may be necessary to properly carry them out.

11. THE SAILING COMMITTEE shall be a sub-committee, appointed by the International Committee, and shall be an independent body having no financial interest in the competing vessels. They will lay out the courses for each Series, decide the Course to be sailed for each Race, make the necessary sailing regulations and have them carried out.

12. THE COURSES laid down by the sailing committee shall not be less than thirty-five or more than forty nautical miles in length and be so arranged as to provide windward and leeward work. The time limit of each Race shall be nine hours. There shall be no handicap or time allowance, each vessel shall sail on its merits.

13. THE TROPHY shall be awarded to and remain in the possession for one year of the Vessel winning Two of Three Races over Courses as laid down by the sailing committee each year, and a responsible person or corporation representing the Owners of the winning vessel shall give to the Trustees of the Trophy an official receipt therefore, together with a Bond for $500.00 obligating them to return the Trophy to the Trustees previous to the next Race, or to replace the Trophy if it becomes lost or destroyed through accident or otherwise; and to return same to the Trustees if it has not been raced for during a period of five years.

14. THE TOTAL CASH PRIZES awarded in connection with this Race in any one year shall not exceed the sum of five Thousand Dollars ($5,000) for each Series and the distribution of the money shall be decided by the International Committee. The money for these prizes to be provided by the Committee representing the country in which the Race is held.

If for any reason there should be no International Competition for this Trophy for any period of five consecutive years it shall be within the power of the Trustees to make such use of the Trophy as they may consider advisable in connection with the development of the Fishing Industry in the Province of Nova Scotia.

IN WITNESS WHEREOF we have hereunto set our hands and affixed our seals this 23rd day of March in the year of our Lord One Thousand Nine Hundred and Twenty-One AD.

In the presence of

(SND.) W.H. DENNIS
For the Proprietors of The *Halifax Herald* and The *Evening Mail.*

(SND.) H.R. SILVER
For the Trustees.

(4) EXPLANATION of Eighty Per cent Rule for the 1922 Series

The Eighty Per Cent Rule was added to the deed of gift after the 1920 series. The idea was to keep the sail area within an acceptable range of a typical banks schooner and deter "freak" rig and sail development. The measurement was 80 per cent of the square of the waterline as measured before a race. Information concerning the Eighty Per Cent Rule was widely circulated after it was incorporated into the 1921 rules. It certainly would have been a popular topic of discussion among those interested in the series; Thomas McManus would most certainly have known about the rule prior to designing the *Henry Ford.*

The measurements below were those given by the measurer, Evers Burtner, to the *Gloucester Daily Times,* October 21, 1922:

> *Bluenose*
Draft: 15.66 feet [4.77 metres]
Waterline: 111.8 Feet [34.08 metres]
111.8 squared = 12,499 square feet x 0.8 = 9999.39 square feet [928.97 square metres]

Allowed sail area: 9999.39 square feet [928.97 square metres]

Actual sail area: 9771.0 square feet [907.76 square metres]

Difference: 228.39 square feet [21.21 square metres] under the allowed limit

› *Henry Ford*

Draft: 15.12 feet [4.6 metres]

Waterline: 109.47 feet [33.37 metres]

109.47 squared = 11,983.68 square feet x 0.8 = 9586.94 square feet [890.66 square metres]

Allowed sail area: 9586.94 square feet [890.66 square metres]

Actual sail area: 10,077.0 square feet [936.18 square metres]

Difference: 490.06 square feet [45.52 square metres] over the allowed limit

The first cut of the sail of the *Henry Ford* took off 437 square feet [40.6 square metres] and the second cut took away an additional 53 square feet [4.92 square metres]. It should be pointed out in defence of Evers Burtner that he did not make a mistake in his initial measuring, as was implied in the popular press at the time. Rather, the crew had ignored his marks the first time and cut off too little.

(5) ADDITIONAL RULES, 1923

Freeboard and tonnage measurements were added to the 1921 rules before the 1923 series, but so far they are only known from references in other documents; a copy of the actual rules has not been found.

(A) Special Rules, 1923 (also used for the 1931 series)

1. PASSING TO WINDWARD. An overtaken vessel may luff as she pleases to prevent an overtaking vessel passing her to windward, until she is in such a position that the bowsprit end, or stem if she has no bowsprit, would strike the overtaking vessel abaft the main shrouds, when her right to prevent the other having a free passage to windward shall cease.

2. PASSING TO LEEWARD. An overtaken vessel must never bear away to prevent another vessel passing her to leeward—the lee side to be considered that on which the leading vessel of the two carries her main boom. The overtaking vessel must not luff until she has drawn clear ahead of the vessel which she has overtaken.

3. RIGHTS OF NEW COURSE. A vessel shall not become entitled to her rights on a new course until she has filled away.

4. PASSING AND ROUNDING MARKS. If an overlap exists between two vessels when both of them, without tacking, are about to pass a mark on a required side, then the outside vessel must give the inside vessel room to pass clear of the mark. A vessel shall not, however, be justified in attempting to force an overlap and thus force a passage between another vessel and the mark after the latter has altered her helm for the purpose of rounding.

5. OVERLAP. An overlap is established when an overtaking vessel has no longer a free choice on which side she will pass, and continues to exist as long as the leeward vessel by luffing, or the weather vessel by bearing away, is in danger of fouling.

6. OBSTRUCTION TO SEA ROOM. When a vessel is approaching a shore, shoal, rock, vessel or other dangerous obstruction, and cannot go clear by altering her course without fouling another vessel, then the latter shall, on being hailed by the former, at once give sea room; and in case one vessel is forced to tack or to bear away in order to give sea room, the other shall also tack or bear away as the case may be, at as near the same time as is possible without danger of fouling. But if such obstruction is a designated mark of the course, a vessel forcing another to tack under the provisions of this section shall be disqualified.

7. If any competing vessels foul a buoy marking the course or foul another competing vessel during the race, she may be disqualified by the Sailing Committee and in the event of disqualification shall score no points in such race.

8. If a vessel crosses the line before the starting gun is fired, her number will be displayed at the end of the "Breakwater" and she will have to return and recross the starting line, otherwise she shall be disqualified from the race.

9. All protests regarding any race shall be made in writing and delivered to the Chairman of the Sailing Committee on the day of the race. Such protests shall be heard and considered by the Sailing Committee and its decision thereon shall be final.

10. Starting and finishing line to be a line from the end of breakwater at Point Pleasant Park, extending easterly across the harbour, and marked by two poles in line with the breakwater.

Vessels starting and finishing must pass between Ives Knoll and Reid Rock Buoys.

(B) Additional Amended Rules after the First Race, October 31, 1923

By the unanimous vote of the Sailing Committee, at a meeting held this morning, it was decided that the special rules governing the 1923 series of the International Fishing Vessel Championship Race should be amended by adding the following rules thereto, which rules shall be effective this date.

11. Competing vessels shall pass on the seaward side of any buoy indicating shoal water or the approach to shoal water; provided, however that this rule shall not apply to mark buoys of the course being sailed, nor to the following buoys, namely: Middle Ground, Mars Rock, Lichfield, Neverfail, Portuguese Shoal, and Rock Head Shoal buoys.

12. A buoy which must be passed on its seaward side shall be deemed to be an obstruction to sea room under Rule 6.

You will please, therefore, understand that all future races of the present series will be governed by the rules already communicated to you amended above.

(6) SPECIAL RULES, 1930 (also used for the 1938 series)

1. No restriction as to Sails, Crews or Ballast.

2. Passing to Windward. An overtaken vessel may luff as she pleases to prevent an overtaking vessel passing her to windward, until she is in such a position that the bowsprit end, or stem if she has no

bowsprit, would strike the overtaking vessel abaft the main shrouds, when her right to prevent the other having a free passage to windward shall cease.

3. Passing to Leeward. An overtaken vessel must never bear away to prevent another vessel passing her to Leeward—the lee side to be considered that on which the leading vessel of the two carries her main boom. The overtaking vessel must not luff until she has drawn clear ahead of the vessel which she has overtaken.

4. Rights of New Course. A vessel shall not become entitled to her rights on a new course until she has filled away.

5. Passing and Rounding Marks. If an overlap exists between two vessels when both of them, without tacking, are about to pass a mark on the required side, then the outside vessel must give the inside vessel room to pass clear of the mark. A vessel shall not, however, be justified in attempting to force an overlap and thus force a passage between another vessel and the mark after the latter has altered her helm for the purpose of rounding.

6. Overlap. An overlap is established when an overtaking vessel has no longer a free choice on which side she will pass, and continues to exist as long as the leeward vessel by luffing, or the weather vessel by bearing away, is in danger of fouling.

7. Obstruction of Sea Room. When a vessel is approaching a shore, shoal, rock, vessel or other dangerous obstruction, and cannot go clear by altering her course without fouling another vessel, then the latter shall, on being hailed by the former, at once give room; and in case one vessel is forced to tack or to bear away in order to give room, the other shall also tack or bear away as the case may be, at as near the same time as is possible without danger of fouling. But if such obstruction is a designated mark of the course, a vessel forcing another to tack under the provisions of this section shall be disqualified.

8. If Any Competing Vessel Fouls a buoy marking the course or fouls another competing vessel during the race, she may be disqualified by the Sailing Committee.

9. If a Vessel crosses the line before the starting gun is fired, her number will be displayed from the Judges' Boat and attention will be called to it by two blasts of the whistle and she will have to return and recross the starting line, otherwise she shall be disqualified from the race.

10. All Protests regarding any race shall be made in writing and delivered to the Chairman of the Sailing Committee on the same day of the race. In case any damage should occur to any contending sailing vessel during the intervening time between races notice shall be made in writing and delivered to the Chairman of the Sailing Committee prior to 8 a.m. on the day of the race. The decision of the Committee shall be final.

(7) ADDITIONAL SAILING RULES, October 13, 1931

➤ LEAVING HARBOUR: Point Pleasant Buoy and Bell Rock Buoy must be left to starboard; Horse Shoe shoal buoy, Lighthouse Bank buoy and Thrumcap Shoal buoy must be left to port.

➤ ENTERING HARBOUR: Thrumcap Shoal buoy, Lighthouse Bank buoy and Horse Shoe shoal buoy must be left to starboard; Bell Rock buoy and Point Pleasant buoy must be left to port.

COURSES OFF HALIFAX

AS PUBLISHED—ALL COURSES MAGNETIC

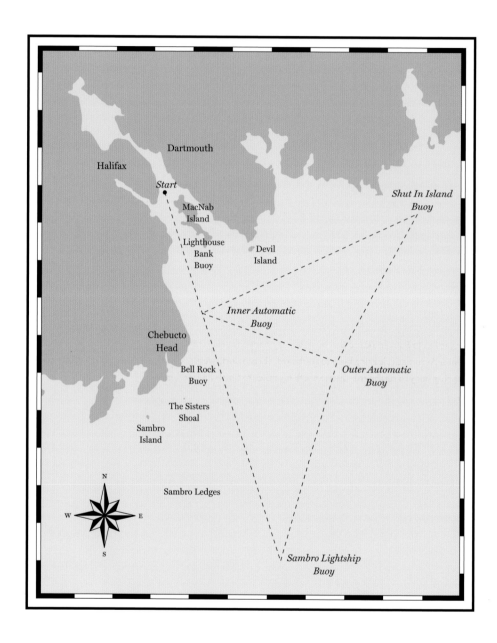

COURSE 1

From starting line south 6.3 miles to the Inner Automatic, leaving buoy to starboard; thence south by west 3/4 west. 11.25 miles to Sambro Lightship, leaving ship to port; thence north east 7/8 east 9.6 miles to Outer Automatic, leaving buoy to port; thence northwest 1/2 north 6.4 miles to Inner Automatic, leaving buoy to starboard; thence north 6.3 miles to finish line. 39.85 miles.

COURSE 2

From starting line south 6.3 miles to the Inner Automatic, leaving buoy to port; thence southeast 1/2 south 6.4 miles to Outer Automatic, leaving buoy to starboard; thence southwest 7/8 west 9.6 miles to Sambro Lightship, leaving ship to starboard; thence north by east 3/4 east 11.25 miles to Inner Automatic, leaving buoy to port; thence north 6.3 miles to finish line. 39.85 miles.

COURSE 3

From starting line south 6.3 miles to the Inner Automatic, leaving buoy to port; thence southeast 1/2 south 6.4 miles to Outer Automatic, leaving buoy to port; thence northeast 3/4 east 9 miles to Shut In Island Bell buoy, leaving the buoy to port; thence west 1/4 south 11.3 miles to Inner Automatic, leaving buoy to starboard; thence north 6.3 miles to finish line. 39.3 miles.

COURSE 4

From starting line south 6.3 miles to Inner Automatic, leaving buoy to port; thence east 1/4 north 11.3 miles to Shut In Island Bell buoy, leaving buoy to starboard; thence southwest 3/4 west 9 miles to Outer Automatic, leaving buoy to starboard; thence northwest 1/2 north 6.4 miles to Inner Automatic, leaving buoy to starboard; thence north 6.3 miles to finish line. 39.3 miles.

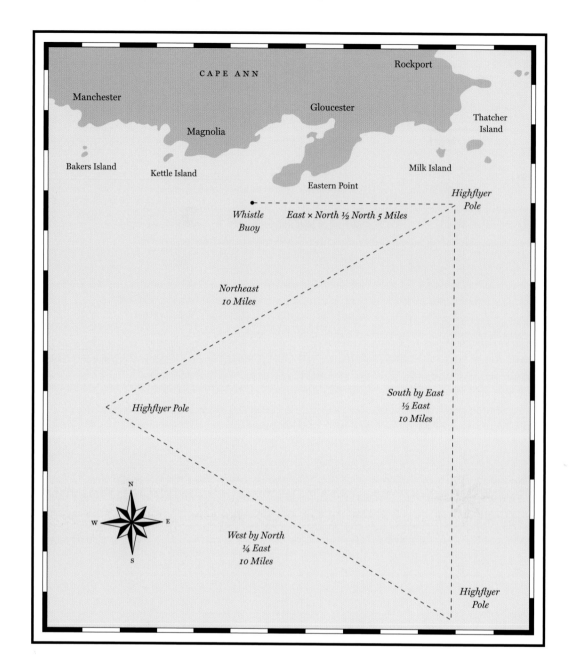

GLOUCESTER LONG COURSE

To and across the starting line between the Mark Buoy and the Judges' Boat; thence east by north ½ north 5 miles to a mark, leaving it to starboard; thence south by east ½ east 10 miles to a mark, leaving it to starboard; thence west by north ¼ north 10 miles to a mark buoy, leaving it to starboard; thence northeast 10 miles to a mark, leaving it to port; thence west by south ½ south 5 miles to the finish line. 40 miles.

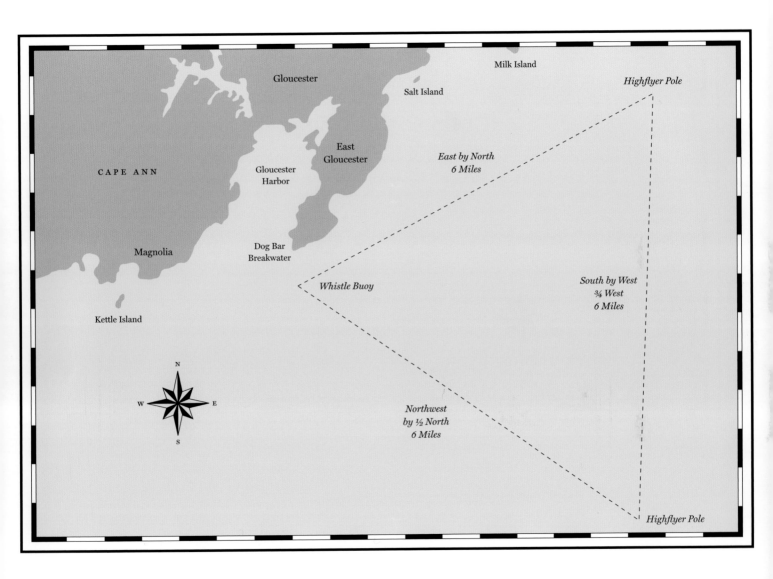

GLOUCESTER SHORT COURSE

To and across the starting line between the Mark Buoy and the Judges' Boat; thence east by north 6 miles to a mark buoy, leaving it to starboard; thence south by west ¾ west 6 miles to a mark buoy, leaving it to starboard; thence northwest ½ north 6 miles to a mark buoy; thence repeating entire triangle to finish line. 36 miles.

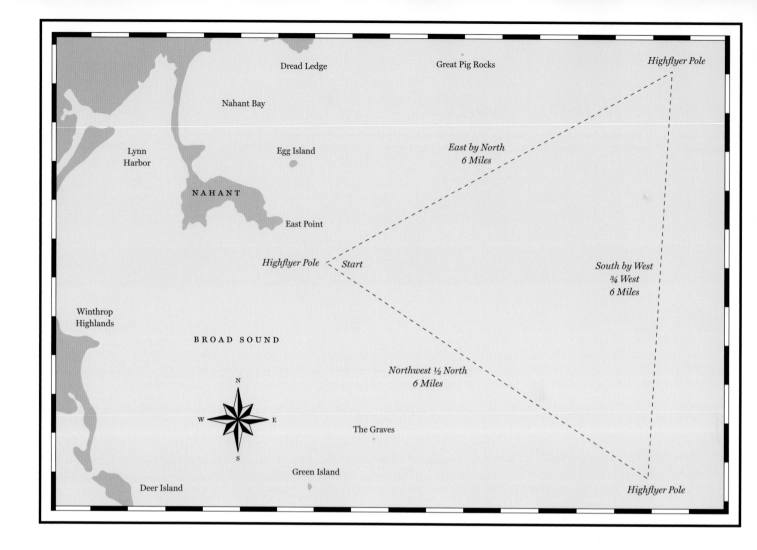

BOSTON SHORT COURSE

To and across the starting line between the Mark Buoy and the Judges' Boat; thence east by north 6 miles to a mark buoy, leaving it to starboard; thence south by west ¾ west 6 miles to a mark buoy, leaving it to starboard; thence northwest ½ north 6 miles to a mark buoy; thence repeating entire triangle to finish line. 36 miles.

BOSTON LONG COURSE

The 1938 series was originally set up with only short courses off Boston and Gloucester. After Captain Walters complained about these "merry-go-round" courses, a compromise of short and long in both locations was agreed upon. The long courses were not published in the race program, as it had been already printed. The long course off Gloucester was mapped out in the local paper, but the only references found to the long course off Boston were in newspapers, which described it as being an irregular 36-mile triangle. The first leg began off the tip of the Nahant Peninsula and led southeast by east, 14 ½ miles to an offshore highliner buoy; the course then ran north-northwest, 12 miles to the New-comb Ledge Whistle Buoy, and the last leg headed west-southwest, 9 ½ miles back to the finish line.

GLOSSARY

AFT: The stern (or "after") part of the vessel, i.e., towards the rear.

BACKSTAYS: Movable or running rigging that supports the upper masts and counteracts the forward pressure of the sails.

BALLOONER: Uppermost of the three headsails on a schooner; also known as jib topsail, balloon jib or flying jib—see illustration on p. 235.

BALLOON JIB: *See ballooner*

BEAM: A direction or bearing at right angles to the fore and aft line of a ship.

BEAR OFF/BORE OFF: To change course farther away from the wind direction.

BEATING IT: Sailing a vessel to windward, i.e., into the wind.

BEND: To attach a sail to a boom or gaff.

BLANKETING: To take the wind from an opponent's sails by blocking the wind with your own sails.

BLOCK: A pulley used to increase the mechanical advantage of ropes when handling sails.

BOLT ROPE: A rope that is sewn around the edge of a sail to keep it from fraying.

BONE IN HER TEETH: The foam or bow wave caused by a ship's motion through the water.

BOOT-TOP: A painted line just above the waterline.

BOWSPRIT: A large spar projecting forward from the bow that carries headsails and provides support to the fore-topmast.

BULWARKS: The wooden planking running along a vessel's sides above the deck, which stops the sea from washing over the deck and prevents crew and equipment from being washed overboard.

CAP RAIL: A flat rail attached to the top of the bulwark.

CAUGHT IN IRONS: A condition that occurs when a vessel's bow is facing into the wind and she is unable to tack in either direction.

CLEW UP: A term used when hauling in the topsails.

CLOSE-HAULED: The vessel is sailing as close to the wind direction as possible.

COMBER: A large wave that rolls and crests.

CROSSTREES: Also known as spreaders or trestles, these are timbers laid across the upper end of a mast to support the topmast and increase the span of the upper shrouds.

DOLPHIN STRIKER: A short, perpendicular spar under the bowsprit to spread the angle of the stay leading to the end of the bowsprit.

DOUBLE-ENDER: A vessel that is pointed at both ends.

DRAWING/DRAFT: The depth of a vessel under the water.

DUDS: A colloquial term for sails.

ENTRY: The shape of the bow under the waterline, which determines how the vessel moves through the water.

FO'C'SLE: *See forecastle*

FOOT: The lower edge of a sail.

FOOTING: A colloquial term for moving quickly through the water.

FORECASTLE: The term used for the crew's living space in the forward end of a ship.

FORESAIL: Gaff-rigged sail between the fore and main mast—see illustration on p. 235.

FORGING UP TO WEATHER: Sailing a vessel towards the wind direction.

FORWARD OF THE BEAM: The wind crossing the hull just ahead of the beam.

GAFF: The spar to which the top or head of a four-sided sail is secured.

GIG: A small open craft often used as a ship's boat for transporting crew ashore.

GLASS DROPS: A drop in atmospheric pressure (the "glass" was a mercury-filled glass barometer).

HAM: Wooden block that supports the crosstrees. Also known as a cheek or hound.

HANK: A small ring or hoop that attaches a sail to a wire stay.

HATCH: A rectangular opening in the deck that provides access from one deck to another.

HAWSE PIPE: A pipe or opening in the upper bow through which the anchor cable is led to the anchor windlass.

HAWSER: A heavy line or rope usually used for mooring or anchoring a vessel.

HEADER: A person employed on board a fishing vessel to remove the head from the caught fish.

HEADSAIL: The collective name for all the sails forward of the foremast, jumbo, jib and jib topsail.

HEAD SEA: A heavy sea coming from the direction of the bow of a ship.

HIGHLINE SKIPPER: A fishing skipper who catches the most fish.

HOGGED: As the result of strain on an aging vessel, the hull droops both fore and aft, leaving the middle arched.

HOVE TO: To move the windward bow of the vessel just off the wind and hold that position while making little or no headway, usually to ride out a storm.

JIB: The middle of the three headsails—see illustration on p. 235.

JIBING: Shifting a sail from one side to another while sailing with the wind aft of the beam.

JIB TOPSAIL: *See ballooner*—see illustration on p. 235.

JUMBO SAIL: The aftermost of the three headsails on a schooner, normally fitted with a boom at the foot—see illustration on p. 235.

KEEL SHOE: A strip of wood fitted along the bottom of a keel to protect it, easily replaced if damaged.

KNOCKABOUT: A schooner that does not carry a bowsprit.

KNOT: A nautical measure of speed. One knot equals one-tenth of a nautical mile (6,080 feet) or 608 feet per hour.

LEECH: The after or outside edge of a sail.

LEE RAIL: The rail on the side of the vessel opposite to the direction of the wind.

LEE SHORE: Shoreline that lies off the lee side of a boat. A lee shore from a sailor's point of view is a windward shore to a person on land.

LIGHT AIRS: A common nautical term for a very light wind of one to three knots.

LIGHT BOXES: Shallow shelves that hold the navigational lights and are located on the port and starboard fore shrouds.

LOO'ARD: A colloquial term for leeward, or the side opposite to the direction of the wind.

LOWERS: The four lower sails on a schooner: mainsail, foresail, jumbo and jib—see illustration on p. 235.

LUFF: The leading edge of a for-and-aft sail; to sail as close to the wind as possible.

MADE FOR WEATHER: Sailing close to the wind.

MIZZEN MAST: A shorter after mast on a small craft.

ON PASSAGE: Sailing to a destination.

PATENT GYBER: A shock absorber on the sheets of the main and foresails, used to ease the strain on the deck when tacking or jibing.

PEAK HALYARD: The block and tackle that hoists the peak or outer end of the gaff on the fore or main sails.

PINCH HIGHER: To sail closer to the wind than another vessel.

PIPES: A colloquial term for an increase in wind.

PLUMB STEM: A bow that is straight up and down.

POINT HIGH: To sail close to the wind.

POINTS OF SAIL: Various headings in relation to the wind. e.g., close-hauled, reaching or running.

PORT: The left-hand side of a vessel, looking forward.

PORT TACK: Sailing with the wind coming from the port side.

QUARTERDECK: A raised portion of deck on the aft part of a ship.

QUARTER RAIL: The railing that surrounds the aft part of the quarterdeck.

QUICK IN STAYS: A description of a vessel that can move quickly from one tack to another.

RATLINES: The footropes on the main and fore shrouds, used for climbing aloft.

REACH: To sail with the wind on or just forward or just aft of the beam.

Beam reach: a point of sailing where the vessel is at right angles to the wind.

Broad reach: a point of sailing where the vessel is sailing away from the wind, but not directly downwind.

Close reach: a point of sailing where the wind is forward of the beam, at a point between a beam reach and close-hauled.

REEF: To reduce the sail area by gathering up the lower portion of the sail and securing it to the boom.

REEVE: A term used when running rope through blocks to form a tackle and more generally used when passing a rope-end through anything.

RUNNING THE LINE: Moving parallel to the start line.

SAIL THROUGH HER LEE: To sail up the leeward side of another vessel.

SALT BANKER: A fishing schooner that works the Grand Banks and salts its catch.

SALT FISHERMAN: A fisherman who works on a salt banker.

SALT FISHERY: The fishing industry that deals with salted fish.

SCUPPERING: Leaning the boat over so far that the sea pours in through the scuppers in the bulwarks.

SCUPPERS: The openings at deck level that allow water to flow off the deck.

SHEER POLE: A metal pole lashed across the shrouds to prevent twisting.

SHEET: A line or purchase used to trim or control the position of a sail.

SHOAL WATER: Shallow water.

SHOE: *See keel shoe*

SHROUDS: The permanent rigging that supports the masts and is rigged from the masthead to the side of the ship.

SPOON BOW: A bow that has a shallow curve similar to the underside of a spoon.

SPREADERS: *See crosstrees*

SPRING: To split or break loose.

SPRIT-SAIL: A four-sided, for-and-aft sail with a long spar stretching diagonally across it and supporting the peak.

STANCHIONS: Wooden pillars that support the bulwarks and rail.

STAND ON: To maintain a course in a particular direction.

STARBOARD: The right-hand side of a vessel, looking forward.

STARBOARD TACK: Sailing with the wind coming from the starboard side.

STICKS: A colloquial term for masts.

STORM TRYSAIL: A small, heavy triangular sail that replaces the mainsail in stormy weather.

SWIBS: A type of wave or comber.

TACK: To work a vessel to windward (sail into the wind) by a zigzag manoeuvre on either side of the windward direction, alternately changing courses from a port tack to a starboard tack.

THROATER: A person employed on board a fishing vessel to remove the stomach from the caught fish.

THWART: Transverse removable wooden seat in a dory.

TOP-HAMPER: A colloquial term for upper, light-air sails.

TRANSOM: The planking that forms the flat stern of a vessel.

TRAWL: A tarred cotton ground line, often over a mile in length, to which are tied, at intervals, shorter and lighter lines with baited hooks at the ends. These are laid over the ocean floor and buoyed at each end.

TRESTLE: *See crosstrees*

TRUCK: A circular wooden cap affixed to the top of a vessel's topmast.

UNDER FOUR LOWERS: Sailing with the mainsail, foresail, jumbo and jib.

UNSHIP THE JAWS: The wooden saddle at the forward end of the boom is pulled back, away from the mast, and comes adrift.

UPPERS: The four upper sails on a schooner: the main gaff topsail, fore gaff topsail, fisherman's staysail and jib topsail—see illustration on p. 235.

WEATHER BILGE: The portion of a vessel's hull adjacent to the keel when exposed due to extreme heeling.

WHALER: A small open boat with fine lines, easy to row. Used originally in the whaling industry to chase whales.

WHERRIE: A small open craft often used to fish inshore or carry small amounts of cargo.

WINDLASS: A mechanical device used for hauling in the anchor.

WINDWARD BERTH: A vessel's position when sailing on the windward side of another vessel.

WING AND WING: Running before the wind (i.e., sailing downwind) with the sails set on both sides, also known as "goose-winged" or "reading both pages."

WORK ONE'S WAY TO WINDWARD: Sail in the direction the wind is coming from, by means of an indirect, zigzagging course (tacking).

ACKNOWLEDGEMENTS

To **BEGIN,** I would like to thank my wife, Judy, for her guidance and wisdom in moving this book towards completion. Her tireless efforts researching and carefully editing, and her endless patience, helped tremendously with the writing of this book. To all my friends in Nova Scotia who assisted me with my quest and made me welcome whenever I visited, especially Ben and Marilyn Verburgh, please accept my gratitude. I am also indebted to many others who have helped along the way, particularly Joe Garland, the master storyteller of Gloucester, who not only gave so much help and insight answering my questions but did so with great humour and warmth. His home at Eastern Point allowed me to daydream of fleets of schooners from a bygone age gracing Gloucester Harbour, which it overlooks. Also, the late Dana Story, of Essex, added so much depth and local insight to the history of schooners and shipbuilding that his loss will be greatly felt by those wishing to keep the history alive. Thanks to Bill Garden for use of his landing grid and his advice on all things nautical. Others, such as Ben Verburgh, Captain Doug Himmelman, Captain Phil Watson, Captain Martyn Clark and Bill Wolferstan, gave freely of their time to read the manuscript and add comments and corrections. I am also grateful to those wonderful people who fill the ranks of museums, libraries and archives, those guardians of our past who give so much time and assistance to the researcher: Andy Price, Gordon Miller, Peggy Tate Smith, Ellen Nelson, Ralph Getson, Gary Shutlak, Aaron Schmidt, Ellen Lampson, Erik Ronnberg, Suzanne Boudet, Debbie Vaughan, Claudia Jew, Michael Lapides, James Craig, Christine Michelini and Stephanie Buck. Without their dedication to the preservation of the past, projects such as this would never be launched. I would also like to acknowledge those great writers and reporters such as George Hudson, Leonard Fowle, Tom Horgan, Jerry Snider, Fred Wallace, Colin McKay, Jimmy Connolly, Frank Sibley, Charlton Smith, William Taylor and Ed Kelly, to name just a few, whose enthusiasm for the subject fills the thousands of pages of print from the 1920s and 1930s. A special thanks to Dusan Kadlec, who allowed me to use his wonderful painting for the cover. Jonathan Dore, Wendy Fitzgibbons and Susan Rana worked so diligently throughout the editing process. Special thanks also to Silver Donald Cameron for writing the introduction. Of course, this book would not be a reality without a publisher, Scott McIntyre, whose faith and support I have enjoyed over the years.

The following museums, libraries and archives provided material for this book:

Boston Public Library, Boston, Massachusetts
The Bostonian Society, Boston, Massachusetts
Canadian Nautical Research Society
Cape Ann Historical Society, Gloucester, Massachusetts
Chicago Historical Society, Chicago, Illinois
Essex Shipbuilding Museum, Essex, Massachusetts
Fisheries Museum of the Atlantic, Lunenburg, Nova Scotia

Fisheries Research Centre, Nanaimo, British Columbia

G.W. Blunt White Library, Mystic Seaport Museum, Mystic, Connecticut

Library and Archives Canada, Ottawa, Ontario

Maritime Museum of the Atlantic, Halifax, Nova Scotia

Maritime Museum of British Columbia, Victoria, British Columbia

Mariners' Museum, Newport News, Virginia

Mystic Seaport Museum Archives, Mystic, Connecticut

National Maritime Museum, Greenwich, United Kingdom

New Bedford Whaling Museum, New Bedford, Massachusetts

Nova Scotia Archives and Record Management, Halifax, Nova Scotia

Peabody Essex Museum, Salem, Massachusetts

Sawyer Free Library, Gloucester, Massachusetts

WEB SITES: The World Wide Web is an invaluable resource to the modern researcher, providing nuggets of information, photographic images and much more, and it would be neglectful not to mention at least some of the sites visited during work on this project.

It is not possible to list them all, so I have included a few of the best. Some, such as Out of Gloucester, occasionally go off-line but are of such superb quality that it is worth waiting for their reappearance.

Nova Scotia Archives and Records Management

Bluenose: A Canadian Icon · www.gov.ns.ca/nsarm/virtual/bluenose

Fishing?—It Was "A Way of Life" and Lost at Sea · www.lostatsea.ca

Out of Gloucester · www.downtosea.com

Fishermen's Own Book · www.mysticseaport.org

The Clayton Morrissey Story · www.ernestina.org/history/index.html

Bluenose II Home Port · www.bluenose2.ns.ca

William J. Roué · www.wjroue.com

Essex Shipbuilding Museum · www.essexshipbuildingmuseum.org

Marty Welsh and the 1920 race · www.hgea.org/~twelsh/

Bluenose · www.cs.ubc.ca/spider/flinn/bluenose/bluenose.html

Brief History of Groundfishing · www.noaa.gov/nmfs/groundfish/grndfsh1.html

SELECTED BIBLIOGRAPHY

BOOKS

Backman, Brian, and Phil Backman, *Bluenose*, Toronto: McClelland and Stewart, 1965

Balcom, B.A., *History of the Lunenburg Fishing Industry*, Lunenburg, NS: Lunenburg Marine Museum Society, 1977

Barss, Peter, *Images of Lunenburg County*, Toronto: McClelland and Stewart, 1978

Cameron, Silver Donald, *Schooner: Bluenose and Bluenose II*, Toronto: McClelland and Stewart, 1984

Campbell, Lyall, *Sable Island Shipwrecks*, Halifax: Nimbus, 1994

Chapelle, Howard I., *The History of American Sailing Ships*, New York: Norton, 1935

——, *American Small Sailing Craft: Their Design, Development, and Construction*, New York: Norton, 1951

——, *The American Fishing Schooners, 1825-1935*, New York: Norton, 1973

Church, Albert C., and James B. Connolly, *American Fishermen*, New York: Norton, 1940

Connolly, James B. *The Book of the Gloucester Fishermen*, New York: John Day, 1927

Darrach, Claude K., *Race to Fame: The Inside Story of the Bluenose*, Hantsport, NS: Lancelot Press, 1985

Dear, Ian, *The America's Cup: An Informal History*, New York: Dodd, Mead, and London: S. Paul, 1980

Dear, Ian, and Peter Kemp, *The Pocket Oxford Guide to Sailing Terms*, Oxford and New York: Oxford University Press, 1987

Dunne, W.M.P., *Thomas F. McManus and the American Fishing Schooners: An Irish-American Success Story*, Mystic, CT: Mystic Seaport Museum, 1994

Garland, Joseph E., *Lone Voyager*, Boston: Little, Brown, 1963; reprinted as *Lone Voyager: The Extraordinary Adventures of Howard Blackburn, Hero Fisherman of Gloucester*, New York: Simon and Shuster, 2000

——, *Eastern Point: A Nautical, Rustical, and Social Chronicle of Gloucester's Outer Shield and Inner Sanctum, 1606-1950*, Peterborough, NH: Noone House, 1971

——, *Down to the Sea: The Fishing Schooners of Gloucester*, Boston: David R. Godine, 1983

——, *Adventure: Queen of the Windjammers*, Camden, ME: Down East Books, 1985; reprinted as *Adventure: Last of the Great Gloucester Dory-Fishing Schooners*, Gloucester: Curious Traveller Press, 2000

——, *Gloucester on the Wind: America's Greatest Fishing Port in the Days of Sail*, Dover, NH: Arcadia, 1995; reprinted, Charleston, SC: Arcadia, 2005

Gillespie, G.J., *Bluenose Skipper*, Fredericton: Brunswick Press, 1955

Goode, G. Brown, *The Fisheries and Fishery Industries of the United States*, 8 vols, Washington: U.S. Commission of Fish and Fisheries, 1884–87

Greenhill, Basil, *Schooners*, Annapolis, MD: Naval Institute Press, 1980

Hale, William, *Memorial of the Celebration of the 250th Anniversary of the Incorporation of the Town of Gloucester, Massachusetts, August 1892*, Boston, 1901

Hayden, Sterling, *Wanderer*, New York: Knopf, 1963

Herreshoff, L. Francis, *The Common Sense of Yacht Design*, 2 vols, New York: Rudder, 1946–48; reprinted, Jamaica, NY: Caravan Maritime, 1973

Innis, Harold A., *The Cod Fisheries: The History of an International Economy*, Toronto: Ryerson, and New Haven: Yale University Press, 1940; revised edition, Toronto: University of Toronto Press, 1954, reprinted 1978

Jenson, L.B., *Bluenose II: Saga of the Great Fishing Schooners*, Halifax: Nimbus, 1994

Kipling, Rudyard, *Captains Courageous: A Story of the Grand Banks*, London: Macmillan, and New York: Century, 1897

Kurlansky, Mark, *Cod: A Biography of the Fish that Changed the World*, Toronto: Knopf, and New York: Walker, 1997

Lipscomb, F.W., *A Hundred Years of the America's Cup*, Greenwich, CT: New York Graphic Society, 1971

McLaren, R. Keith, *Bluenose and Bluenose II*, Willowdale, ON: Hounslow Press, 1981

Merkel, Andrew, *Schooner Bluenose*, Toronto: Ryerson, 1948

Roué, Joan E., *A Spirit Deep Within: Naval Architect W.J. Roué and the Bluenose Story*, Hantsport, NS: Lancelot Press, 1995

Santos, Michael Wayne, *Caught in Irons: North Atlantic Fishermen in the Last Days of Sail*, Selinsgrove, PA: Susquehanna University Press, 2002

Story, Dana A., *Frame Up!: A Story of Essex, Its Shipyards and Its People*, Barre, MA: Barre Press, 1964; reprinted, Charleston, SC: History Press, 2004

——, *Hail Columbia!*, Barre, MA: Barre Press, 1970

Thomas, Gordon W., *Fast and Able: Life Stories of Great Gloucester Fishing Vessels*, Gloucester, MA: Gloucester 350th Anniversary Celebration, 1973

Wallace, Frederick M., *The Roving Fisherman: An Autobiography Recounting Personal Experiences in the Commercial Fishing Fleets and Fish Industry of Canada and the United States, 1911–1924*, Gardenvale, QC: Canadian Fisherman, 1955

Ziner, Feenie, *Bluenose, Queen of the Grand Banks*, Philadelphia: Chilton, 1970; third edition, Halifax: Nimbus, 1986

ARTICLES

Newspaper articles are detailed in the chapter notes and thus omitted here; magazine articles without a byline are listed alphabetically by publication title, chronologically for each publication. If not specified, page numbers are unknown.

Aerenburg, H.R., "The Famous Fishing Fleet of Lunenburg," *Canadian Fisherman*, May 1925, 115–16

Ahlers, H.E., "The Glorious, *Gertrude L. Thebaud*," *Ships & Sailing*, April 1952, 26–30

The American Neptune, "American and Canadian Fishing Schooners," 1966

Atlantic Fisherman, "Preparations for Fisherman's Races," February 1921, 7–8

——, "Contenders Nearing Completion," March 1921, 2

——, "Fishermen's Cup Contenders," April 1921, 3–4, 18–19

——, "The Story of the *Canadia*," August 1921, 6–8

——, "Races Given a Severe Blow," September 1921, 11

——, "How the Big *Bluenose* Beat the Little *Elsie*," November 1921, 5–7

——, "The Story of the *Mayflower*," May 1921, 14–27

——, "Schooner *Henry Ford* Out of Difficulties," May 1922, 6

——, "The Story of the *Puritan*," June 1922, 17–19

——, "*Puritan* and *Henry Ford* Quality Fishermen," June 1922, 20, 28

——, "Schooner *Henry Ford*—A McManus Design," June 1922, 27

——, "The Unhappy Fate of the *Puritan*," June 1922, 5–6

——, "The Case of the Schooner *Mayflower*," September 1922, 7–8

——, "*Bluenose* a True Champion," October 1922, 9, 13, 29

——, "Programs and Regulations Governing 1922 International Fishermen's Races," October 1922, 19–30

——, "Schooner *Columbia*, Salt Banker," April 1923, 7–9

——, "Special Rules Governing the Open Fishermen's Race in Connection with Gloucester Tercentenary," August 1923, 19–21

——, "Talk of the Fishermen's Races," April 1925, 7–8

——, "Nova Scotia Is Always Ready," July 1926, 7

——, "The Fishermen's Races," October 1926, 19, 33–35

——, "Program Open Fishermen's Race," October 1926, 24–32

——, "New Fishing Schooner Built for International Racing," April 1930

——, "Nova Scotia Accepts Gloucester Race Challenge," October 1931, 6–9

Canadian Fisherman, "The Racing Fishermen," April 1920

——, "The Toll of the Sea," August 1920

——, "Schooner Races First Class Publicity," September 1921, 200

——, "Rules and Conditions Covering International Schooner Race," September 1921, 206

——, "The International Fisherman's Race," November 1921, 251–57

——, "Nova Scotia Fishermen's Regatta," November 1921, 247–50

——, "Gossip About Fishermen's Race," March 1922, 50

——, "Rules for Fishermen's Race Amended," September 1922, 191

——, "*Bluenose* Once More the Champion," November 1922, 243–45

——, "Former Bankers Are Now Rum-Running," April 1923, 101

——, "About Those Racing Rules," August 1923, 206

——, "Races Thrill Till Beans Spill," November 1923, 283–85

——, " 'Bank' Fleet Hit Hard," February 1924

——, "Prospect Brightens Lunenburg Fleet," May 1924, 103

——, "In the Wake of the Storm," September 1924, 250

——, "Third Trip for Lunenburgers," July 1925, 311–12

——, "To Race or Not to Race," November 1925, 331–32

——, "The End of International Schooner Races," February 1926, 33–34

——, "*Bluenose* Shows her Quality," June 1926, 197

——, "Capt. Walters Willing to Race," July 1926, 197

——, "Storm Warnings Urgently Needed," September 1926, 263

——, "Tragic Loss Hits Lunenburg," September 1926, 273–74

——, "Next Year's Races," November 1926, 323

——, "*Bluenose* Again Champion Schooner," November 1926, 327–29

——, "Hope Abandoned for Eighty Fishermen and Four Schooners," October 1927, 303–34

——, "Why Should Fishermen Fight the Steam Trawlers?" November 1927, 325

——, "Lunenburg Honours Her Fishermen Lost at Sea," December 1929

——, " '*Bluenose*' Skipper will Not Race in U.S. Waters," June 1930, 27

——, "*Bluenose* will Meet *Gertrude L. Thebaud* in Exhibition Races off Gloucester," October 1930

——, " '*Bluenose*' Tastes Defeat's Dregs in Gloucester Series," November 1930, 24

——, "Lunenburg Fleet had Worst Season in Many Years," November 1930, 21

——, " '*Bluenose*' to Defend Cup at Halifax," October 1931, 23

——, "Make the *Bluenose* a Training Ship," December 1931, 14

——, "*Bluenose* to get New Mainboom for Races," July 1938, 16

——, "*Bluenose* in Peak Condition," September 1938, 13

——, "Fishermen Win Sailing Honours for British Empire," November 1938, 59–67

Church, Albert C., "The Evolution and Development of the American Fishing Schooner," *Yachting*, May–June 1910

——, "The Evolution of the American Fishing Schooner," *The Atlantic Fishermen's Almanac*, n.d., 53–57

——, "The Three New Yankee Flyers," *Atlantic Fisherman*, June 1922, 5–6, 10

——, "The Gloucester Open Fishermen's Race," *Atlantic Fisherman*, September 1923, 5–6, 9, 14

——, "Selecting the Challenger to Meet *Bluenose*," *Atlantic Fisherman*, October 1923, 9–10

——, "The Race at Halifax," *Atlantic Fisherman*, November 1923, 7–10, 15, 18, 30

Conlon, James H., "The Flying Gloucestermen," *Collier's Weekly*, December 25, 1920

——, "Walters' Faux Pas," *Canadian Fisherman*, November 1923

Day, Thomas F., "The Schooner," *Rudder*, March 1906

Dennis, W. Alexander, "The Canadian Races," *Atlantic Fisherman*, November 1926, 16–17, 23

Edson, Merritt A., "The Schooner Rig: A Hypothesis," *The American Neptune*, April 1965

Goodick, E.A., "Schooner Progress Wins North Atlantic Title," *Atlantic Fisherman*, September 1929, 15–18

——, "The '*Thebaud*' Wins the First Race of the Fishermen's Series," *Atlantic Fisherman*, October 1930, 13–16

——, " '*Bluenose*' Retains Title as Queen of the North Atlantic," *Atlantic Fisherman*, November 1931, 6–7

Haliburton, M.A., "The American Fishermen and the Modus Vivendi," *Canadian Fisherman*, June 1925, 187–88

Hudson, George Story, "How the *Esperanto* Won the Fisherman's Races," *Yachting*, December 1920, 296–98

Johnson, Captain V.C., "How the Fishermen's Race Was Sailed," *Yachting*, December 1921, 277–79, 307

Jubien, E.E., "Nova Scotia: Growth and Outlook," *Canadian Fisherman*, June 1925, 167–68, 196

Kelsey, Arthur E., " '*Bluenose*' Still Queen of Atlantic Fishing Fleets," *Canadian Fisherman*, November 1931, 9–11

Kenyon, Paul, "*Bluenose* vs. *Gertrude L. Thebaud*," *Gloucester Magazine*, n.d., 5–8, 16–20

Knowles, A.H., "Ringing the Bell," *Canadian Fisherman*, September 1938, 11

McKay, Colin, "Fishermen's Vessels Race," *Canadian Fisherman*, September 1920, 195–96

——, "The Knockabout Schooner," *Canadian Fisherman*, October 1920, 221–22

——, "Speculation on Fishermen's Races," *Canadian Fisherman*, July 1922, 145

——, "A Substitute for Schooner Races," *Canadian Fisherman*, February 1926, 68

——, "The Machine Age with Its Trawler and Its Relation to Our Off Shore Fishermen," *Canadian Fisherman*, December 1927, 365–66

McManus, Thomas F., "Tom McManus, Designer of the *Henry Ford* Writes His Opinion of Races," *Atlantic Fisherman*, December 1922, 10

McQuire, Agnes G., "The Racing Fishermen," *Canadian Fisherman*, May 1921, 112

Newsweek, "Fishing Schooners' Race," November 7, 1938

Nickerson, Arthur E., "The Sacred Cod," *Canadian Fisherman*, November 1937, 12–13

The Rudder, "*Esperanto* Wins Fishermen's Race," December 1920, 18, 36

——, "Discord Ends Fishermen's Race," December 1923, 1

——, "The Racing Fisherman, *Gertrude L. Thebaud*," December 1930, 60

Sidney, F.H., "Fishermen Race Again," *The Rudder*, November 1923, 35

Smith, Charlton L., "American Fishermen's Elimination Race," *Atlantic Fisherman*, October 1921, 7–8

——, "The First of the New Contenders Launched," *Atlantic Fisherman*, March 1922, 5–6

——, "The Launching of the *Henry Ford*," *Atlantic Fisherman*, April 1922, 5–6

——, "Schooner *Henry Ford* Wins Right to Challenge *Bluenose*," *Atlantic Fisherman*, October 1922, 7–8

——, "The International Fiasco," *Atlantic Fisherman*, November 1922, 5–6, 12

——, "The Open Fishermen's Races," *Atlantic Fisherman*, November 1926, 13–15

——, "The First Fishermen's Race," *Yachting*, January 1939, 64–65, 213–14

Snider, C.H.J., "The Fishermen's Race," *The Rudder*, December 1921, 3–6, 44–45

——, "The International Fishermen's Race," *The Rudder*, December 1922, 3–5

Stone, Herbert L., "How the *Bluenose* Won the Fishermen's Races," *Yachting*, November 1922, 229–33, 258

Time, "Fishermen's Finale," November 7, 1938, 18

Taylor, William H., "Gloucester Once More Holds Fishermen's Championship," *Yachting*, December 1930, 81, 108

Wallace, Frederick M., "A Sailing Race Between American and Canadian Fishermen," *Canadian Fisherman*, August 1920, 169–73

——, "Fishing Schooner Race," *Canadian Fisherman*, November 1920, 240–42

——, "The Yankee *Bluenose* Victory," *Canadian Fisherman*, November 1920, 237

——, "Racing Fishermen Excite Nationwide Interest," *Canadian Fisherman*, June 1921, 130

——, "Life on the Grand Banks," *National Geographic Magazine*, July 1921, 1–28

——, "The International Fishermen's Race," *Yachting*, November 1921, 213–15, 255–56

Walters, Angus J., "The Truth About the *Bluenose*," *Ships and the Sea*, October 1952, 22–26

INDEX

Page numbers in *italics* indicate figures and captions. Subentries that refer to specific dates are in chronological order, after general subentries.

Adams, Charles (skipper, *Resolute*), 46–48

Adams, Ray, 92, 203

A.D. Story Yard, 92, 121, 124, 165

Alachua, loss of, 145

Albertolite, 157

Alcala, 52–53, 77–78

Allen, Lester, on 1938 International Fishermen's Cup, 204, 205, 206

Alsatian, 168, 181

America, 45

American Fishermen's Race (1926), 149–51

America's Cup race, 45–48, 119–20

Annie Healey, loss of, 157

Apt, John (captain), 26

Arethusa, 91–92

Armstrong, E.H., 138

Arras, 166, 169

Arthur D. Story, 160

Arthur James, 75–77, 217

Atlantic Supply Company, 26, 121

"August breezes," 147, 155

banker (boat design), 36

Bartholomew, Freddie, 193

Beard, Commander (captain, HMCS *Patriot*), 78

Bernice Zink, 52–53

Beyer, Elizabeth, 211

Birdseye, Kellogg, 173

Blackburn, Howard, 22–23

Bluenose, 182–83, 206–7, 218–19; construction and launch (1921), 68–69, 70; as celebrity and national icon, 127, 160, 190–93, 219–20; design for fishing vs. racing, 6, 70, 72, 78–79, 89, 92; historic context, 5–9, 215–220; name, origin of, 70; personality of, 8, 212. *See also* Walters, Angus

Bluenose, fishing and racing career: races (1921), 77–86, 80–81, 84–85; races (1922), 88–89, 97–113, 98–99, 114–15, 115, 116; races (1923), 4–5, 66–67, 127, 128–29, 129–32, 134–40, 136–37, 142–43; fishing season mishaps (1926), 145–47; races (1926), 149–54; fishing season mishaps (1927), 157; fishing season mishap (1930), 166; races (1930), 166–67, 168, 169, 171–76, 174–75; races (1931), 180–86; tourist attraction (Chicago and Toronto, 1933–34), 188–89, 190–92; as ambassador to Great Britain (1935), 192–93; engines installed (1936), 193; on ten-cent coin (1937), 193; races (1938), 195–208, 202–3, 210–11, 214–15

Bluenose, post-racing career: signs of age and poor trim, 197, 201–3, 212; bought by Walters (1939), 216; sold to West Indies Trading Company (1942), 216; sinking of (1946), 216–17

Bluenose II (replica), 3, 219

Bohlin, Tommie (captain, *Nannie C. Bohlin*), 41

Boston, *12*; race courses, *234*; Walters' attitudes towards, 171, 209; site of early fishermen's races (1871–1920), 40; vs. Gloucester, concerning *Mayflower* (1921), 71–75; International Fishermen's Cup series (1938), 204–11. *See also* Nahant Bay, MA

Bounty, HMS, replica of, 219

Brittain Cup series, 40

Burgess, Starling (boat designer), 71–72, 91, 96, 120

Burtner, Evers, 101, 102, 226–227

Burton, William (skipper, *Shamrock IV*), 48–50

Bushnell, USS, 126, 127, 129

Butler, Mildred, 211

Cabot, John, 13

Canadia, 70–71, 72, 77–78, 97–100

Cape Ann, MA, 32, 190–92, *232, 233*

Carroll, Mr. (owner, Gorton-Pew Fisheries), 63

Catherine Burke, 56

Century of Progress Exhibition, 190, *190–91*, 192

Champlain, 169

Chapelle, Howard, 36, 39, 219

Chebacco boat, 35

Chebucto Head, 130–31, *230*

Chicago (Century of Progress Exhibition), 190, *190–91*, 192

Clayton Walters, loss of, 157

Collins, Joseph (captain), 23, 36, 37–38

Columbia, 118–19, 122–23; design and characteristics, 8, 26–27, 212; construction and launch (1923), 120–22; mishaps (1923), 124, 125, 126–27; races (1923), 4–5, 125–31, 128–29, 134–40, 136–37; economic difficulties and grounding (1926), 144–45; races (1926),

150, 151, *156–57*; loss of (1927), 158–59, 217; on Pine's headstone (1953), 217, 219. *See also* Pine, Ben

Connolly, James B. (Jimmy), 21–22, 39, 40, 58, 60, 82, 139

Conrad, Joe (captain, *Canadia*), 70–71, 77–78, 97–100, 152

Conrad, Roger, 60

Conrad, W. (captain, *Mary Ruth*), 148–49

Cook, Frederic W., 100

Coolidge, Calvin, 64

Cooney, Marion, 93, 197

Corbett, Mr., 151

Corinthian, 14–15

Cox, Channing, 100

Crouse, Moyle (captain, *Haligonian*), 151, 152–54, 168

Delawana, 52–53, 58–63, *60–61*, 67, 77–78, 217

Democracy, 52–53

Demone, Bert, 116

Denby, Edwin, 100, 104

Dennis, William, 49, 69

Devil Island, 62–63, *230*

Devonshire, Duke of, at *Bluenose* launch, 70

Digby, NS, Brittain Cup series, 40

dogsbody (boat design), 35

Domingoes, Manuel (captain, *Progress*), 160

Donald J. Cook, 77–78

Dorothy M. Smart, 18

Edith Newhall, 155

Effie May, loss of, 157

Effie M. Morrissey, 34–35

Elizabeth Howard: races (1922), 93, 94–96, 99, 105; races (1923), 124–25; loss of, 217

Elsie: design and characteristics, 76–77,

78–79, 212; races (1921), 75–77, 79–86; races (1929), 160; as training vessel for Sea Scouts (1931), 180, 183; races (1931), 183; sinking of (1936), 217

Elsie G. Silva, 75–77, 217

Esperanto, 8, *54–55*, 56–63, 69, 75, 217

Essex, MA, 71, 92, 121, 165–66

Ethel B. Jacobs, 41–42

Fisheries Exhibition regatta, Lunenburg (1930), 168

Flash, 39–40

Fowle, Leonard, 102, 112–13, 201

Freda L. Himmelman, 52–53

Garbo, Greta (spectator, 1938), 200

Geele, Alden (captain, *Columbia*), 122, 125, 132

George V (king of England), and *Bluenose*, 192, *194–95*

Gertrude L. Thebaud, *178–79*, *198–99*, *202–3*; design and characteristics, 6, 163–66, 181, 212; construction and launch (1930), 163–66; as tour boat (1930), *162–63*, 166; races (1930), 169, *170–71*, 171–76, *174–75*; races (1931), 180–86; as emissary for fishing industry (1933), 189–90; at Century of Progress Exposition (1933), *190–91*, 190–92; chartered to Arctic expedition (1937), 193; races (1938), 196–208, *202–3*, *210–11*, *214–15*; sold for anti-submarine duty (war years), 217; sinking of (1948), 217. *See also* Pine, Ben

Gilbert B. Walters, 52–53, 58

Gloucester, MA, as fishing community, 6–7, *12*; Community Fish Pier, 198, *202–3*; fishermen lost at sea, 15–16, 37; fishing fleet, 67–69, 122, 159

Gloucester, MA, schooner racing at: race courses, *232*, *233*; Walters' dislike of, 116, 151, 155, 209; early fishermen's races (1871–1920), 40–42; International Fishermen's Cup (1920), 55–56, 63–64; American eliminations (1921), 75–77; *Mayflower* controversies (1921–22), 71–75, 96; International Fishermen's Cup (1922), 91–116; Lipton Cup (1923), 124–26; American Fishermen's Race (1926), 149–51; reawakening of race fever (1929), 160, 162; Lipton Cup (1930), 166–76; sense of entitlement to International Fishermen's Cup (1931), 181; International Fishermen's Cup (1938), 195–208. *See also* Pine, Ben

Gloucester Community Fish Pier, 198, *202–203*

Gorton-Pew Fisheries, 56, 63

Grace L. Fears, 22–23

Grampus, 37–38

Grand Banks, 11–13

Grant, MacCallum, 100

"Graveyard of the Atlantic." *See* Sable Island and Sable Bank, NS

Grayling, 41

Great Aquatic Festival (1871), 39–40

Great Britain, *Bluenose* as ambassador (1935), 192–93

Griffin, John, 171, 173, 183, 209

Hackett, Jack, 205

Hale, William, on 1892 Gloucester series, 41–42

Halifax: maps, *12*, *230*; *Halifax Herald* as promoter of schooner racing, 49–52, 55, 74–75, 139, 216–17; 1917 explosion, 50; International Fishermen's Cup (1920, 1921, 1923), 56–64, 79–86,

127–40; Provincial Fishing Vessel Contest (1926), 151–54; International Fishermen's Cup (1931), 180–86

Haligonian, 8, 145, 149–54, *152–53,* 168

Hall, Mikey, 62–63

Harrington, G.S, 186

Harry L. Belden, 41–42

Hayden, Sterling, 198, 200, 205

heeltapper, 33

Henry Ford, 94–95, 110–11; characteristics of, 212; design, construction, and launch mishaps (1922), *90–91,* 92, 94; races (1922), *88–89,* 94–96, 99–104, *106–7,* 108–16; races (1923), 124–27; engine added, 144; races (1926), 150, 151, *156–57;* loss of (1928), 159–60, 217

Herreshoff, Nathaneal (designer, *Resolute),* 47

Hilda Gertrude, loss of, 157

Hiltz, Ernie, 110, 115, 116

Himmelman, Albert: in Canadian eliminations (1921), 77–78; on *Bluenose* (1922), 109–10; captain, *Keno* (1923), 122–24; and crowding incident (1923), 131, 132–34; lost at sea (1924), 144

Himmelman, Tommy (captain, *Delawana),* 52–53, 57, 59–63

Hodges, Wetmore, 164

Hogan, Felix (captain, *L.A. Dunton),* 74

Holland, George, on 1920 International Fishermen's Cup, 58

Horgan, Tom, 183, 200

Howard, William, 93

Hudson, George, on Morrissey (1922), 91–92

Ida E., 40

Imo (Halifax explosion, 1917), 50

Imperator, 193

Independence, 52–53, 77–78, 122

International Fishermen's Cup races: assessment of, 1–3, 220; deed of gift, rules, and trustees, 69–70, 222–29; jinx of, 217; public interest in, 119–20, 180–81, 183, 195, 215; resumption, support for (1926), 149–50, 151–52, 154–55

International Fishermen's Cup series (1920), 56–63

International Fishermen's Cup series (1921), 75–77, 79–86

International Fishermen's Cup series (1922): preparations, contenders, and eliminations, 91–101; races and protests, 101–13; post-race controversies, 113–16

International Fishermen's Cup series (1923), *4–5, 132–33;* preparations, contenders, and eliminations, 122–28; races and protests, 129–37; post-race controversies and reaction, 137–40

International Fishermen's Cup series (1931), 176, 180–86

International Fishermen's Cup series (1938): preparations, contenders, and eliminations, 195–96; races and protests, 196–208; post-race controversies, 208–11

James S. Steele, 41

J. Duffy, 77–78

J.F. James and Son shipyard, 71, 92

Joffre, 56

John C. Lochlan, loss of, 157

John H. McManus, 40

Johnson, Charles (captain, *Thebaud),* 172–76

Johnson, Christopher, 93

Jones, Bassett, 164

Joyce M. Smith, loss of, 157

Kelly, Ed, on aging *Bluenose,* 212

Keno, 122–24, 144, 217

Killarney, 24–25

Kinsella, James T., on 1920 International Fishermen's Cup, 58

Knickle, Captain, on 1930 Lipton Cup, 174

La Champlain, 124, 125

L.A. Dunton, 74, 94–96, 99–100

Lady Laurier, 80, 83, 130, 134, 183

Langsford, Joe, 121

Larkin, Henry (captain, *Mayflower),* 74, 75, 100–101, 120

Lawlor, Dennison J. (boat designer), 37–38

Lipton, Thomas, 40, 46, 119–20, 124, 166

Lipton Cup race (1923), 124–26

Lipton Cup race (1930), 166–76

Locke, George, 148

Lodge, Henry Cabot, 100

Lohnes, Calvin (captain, *Ruby Pentz),* 55

Lufkin, W.W., 139

Lunenburg, NS, *1, 12;* fishermen lost at sea, 15–16; *Bluenose* construction and launch (1921), *68–69,* 70; support for *Bluenose,* 144; Fisheries Exhibition regatta (1930), 168; victory celebration (1931), 185–86; *Bounty* replica (1960), 219. See also Walters, Angus

Lyons, Captain, 195–96, 197, 203, 205, 208, 211

MacAskill, Wallace, 201

McCoy, Bill (captain), 92

McCurdy, Robert H., 164

Mack, Captain (*Mahaska),* 97–100

McKay, Colin, 48–49

McKay, Donald (boat designer), 48

McManus, Thomas: "Father of the Fishermen's Races" (1886), 40; designer, *Elsie* (1910), 78; and *Henry Ford* (1922), 92, *94–95*, 101; designer, *Elizabeth Howard* (1922), 93; and American eliminations (1922), 100

MacMillan, Donald, 193

Mahala, loss of, 157

Mahaska, 97–100, 217

Mahone Bay, NS, 122–24

Malloch, Al (captain), 112

Manta Club, 91, 120

Marblehead, MA, 33–35

Marblehead schooner, 33

Marechal Foche, 56

Margaret K. Smith, 97–100, 168

Marion McLoon, loss of, 157–58

market fisherman (boat design), 36

Mary Ruth, 148–49

Mary Sears, 158

Master Mariners Association, 126, 163

Matheson, John (captain, *Thebaud*), 183, 185

Mayflower, 8, *72–73*; disqualified, 1921 and 1922 racing seasons, 71–75, 85, 94–97, 100–101, 116; end of racing attempts, 120, 124; as freighter in West Indies (1930), 164

Mayotte, 149–50, 217

Mellow, Joseph, 163–65

Millet, Arthur, on 1892 Gloucester series, 41

Millet, Ed, on American eliminations (1922), 99–100

Mona Marie, 52–53

Montague, H.L., 150

Mont Blanc (Halifax explosion, 1917), 50

Morrissey, Bessie, 92, 108

Morrissey, Clayton (captain): and *Henry Ford* (1922), 91–92, 94, *94–95*, 98–115, 124–27; attempts to race (1926), 149, 151, 154–55

Morrissey, Winnie, 94

Mosher, Gordon (captain, *Newhall*), 155

Moulton, Cecil (captain), 201–11

Murray, G.H., 100

Nahant Bay, MA, 1, 40, 196–97, *234*

Nannie C. Bohlin, 41

Nova Scotia Fishing Schooner Regatta (1921), 77–78

O'Hara brothers, 124

Oretha F. Spinney, 193

Owens, George, 101

Paine, Frank (designer, *Gertrude L. Thebaud*), 165, 181

Patriot, HMCS, 78, 100, 108, 112, 134

Paulding, USS, 101, 104

Pearce, Frank C., 92

Peeples, George (captain), 115–16

Pentz, Amos (designer, *Canadia*), 70–71

Philip P. Manta, 75–77

Pigeon, Fred, 71, 100–101

Pine, Ben (captain), *122–23, 146–47*; character and background, 121, 132–34, 137–40, 198; enthusiasm for racing, 149–50, 151, 154–55, 168, 186, 211; captain, *Philip P. Manta* (1921), 75–77; races (1922), 91, 93, 99–100, 105–7; *Columbia* and races (1923), 120–22, 124–27, 129–40; and *Columbia* in declining schooner fleet (1923–6), 144–45; efforts to resume international racing (1926–27), 149–51, 154–55;

loss of *Columbia* and other boats (1927), 157–60; *A.D. Story* and races (1929), 160; *Thebaud*, construction and launch (1930), 163–65; as tour boat operator (1930), 166; *Thebaud* and races (1930), 168, 169, 171–72; *Thebaud* and races (1931), 180, 183–85; and *Thebaud* in Depression years, 193; *Thebaud* and races (1938), 195–201, 208, 211; sells *Thebaud* (1944), 217; continued friendship with Walters, 217; death (1953) and memorial, 217–19

Pinky (boat design), 35, 38

Pollard, F. Wilder, 92

Post, Steve, 135

Powers, Carlin, 173

Proctor, Ed (captain), 196, 201–3, 208

Progress, 160

Provincial Fishing Vessel Contest (1926), 151, 152–54

Puritan, 8, 91, 92–93, 217

Quadros, Alvaro (captain), lost at sea, 158

Ralph Brown, 75–77

Raymond, Jonathan (Jack), 92, 107, 115

Raymond, Mrs. Jack, 104

Reed, Wilmot, 72, 150

Resolute, 45–48, *50–51*

Rhodenhiser, Fred, *110–11*, 198, 200, 204, 208

Robinson, Andrew (captain and boat designer), 32–33

Roosevelt, Eleanor, and *Thebaud*, 190

Roosevelt, Franklin D., and *Thebaud*, 190

Roosevelt, John, 201

Ross, Harry (captain, *Dorothy M. Smart*), 18, *34–35*

Roué, William: designer, *Bluenose* (1921), 69; and *Mayflower* controversy (1921), 72; prepares *Bluenose* for International Fishermen's Cup (1923), 127; designer, *Haligonian*, 145; on Nova Scotian response to American Fishermen's Race (1926), 150; and *Bluenose* ballast problems, 152, 203–4; and *Bluenose* replica (1963), 219

Royal Yacht Squadron, 192

Ruby Pentz, 52–53, 55

Russell, William, 41

Sable Island and Sable Bank, NS, *12*; *Bluenose* accident, 145–47; *Columbia* accident, 124; *Esperanto* sinking, 75; as "Graveyard of the Atlantic," 75, 93, 147–48, 157–58, 217; *Puritan* sinking, 93

Sadie Knickle, loss of, 148

schooner design, 32–39

shallop, 33

Shamrock (fishing schooner), 124–26

Shamrock IV (racing yacht), 45–48, *50–51*

sharpshooter, 36

Shaw, Sam, on race delays (1938), 204

Shelburne, NS, 71, 145

Sibley, Frank Palmer, on 1920 International Fishermen's Cup, 58

Silva, Manuel, 203

Silver, H.R., 132, 137

Smith, Audrey, 70

Smith, Richard, 70

Smith, Russell, 63, 83, 115

Smith and Rhuland shipyard, 70, 219

Snider, Jerry: on Canadian eliminations (1922), 97–100; on challenges between Morrissey and Walters (1922), 108; on International Fishermen's Cup (1922), 109–10, 113; on *Keno*'s speed

(1923), 124; controversy, International Fishermen's Cup (1923), 132–34; and Walters in Toronto, 192

Sparrow, Jack, *110–11*

Stevens, David, 8, 38–39

Stevens, Randolph, 116

Stiletto, 56

Story, Arthur D., 92, 121, 145

Story, Dana, 72, 125

Sylvia Mosher, loss of, 148

Tampa, 158

Tancook whaler, 38

Taylor, Bill, on 1930 Lipton Cup, 176

Thebaud, Louis A., 163–64, 180

Thetis, 203

Thomas, Bill, 91

Thomas, Jeff (captain, *Puritan*), 91, 92–93

Thomas S. Gorton, 160

Tomaka, previously *Arethusa*, 92

Toronto, *Bluenose* on display (1933–4), *188–89*, 192

Tracy, Spencer, 193

Tyrian, 53

Uda R. Corkum, 77–78, 157, 217

United Sail Loft, 101

United States Fish Commission, 23, 37–38

Venosta, 159

Vienna, loss of, 157

Wallace, Fred, 18, 25–26, *34–35*, 40, 82, 116

Walters, Angus (captain), *102–3*, *146–47*, *206–7*; Boston, attitudes towards, 171, 209; as celebrity, 127, 190–93, *194–95*, 211; character and reputation, 78, 138, 219–20; controversies and challenges, 75, 96, 120, 127, 143–44, 149, 166, 168,

195–96, 200–203, 209; Gloucester, dislike of, 116, 151, 155, 209; in retirement, 216, 217, 219; sportsmanship, 105, 140, 176, 180, 211; death (1968), 219. *See also Bluenose*

Walters, Angus (captain), fishing and racing career: captain, *Gilbert B. Walters*, 52–53; design, construction, and launch of *Bluenose* (1921), 69, 70; races (1921), 75, 77–86, *80–81*; races (1922), 97–105, 108–13, *114–15*; races (1923), *66–67*, 120, 127, 129–40, 143–44; damage to *Bluenose* (1926), 147; races (1926), 149–50, 152–54; damage to *Bluenose* (1927), 157; refusal to race (1929), 166; races (1930), 168, 171–76; races (1931), 180–86; touring with *Bluenose* (1933–35), 190–93, *194–95*; installs engines on *Bluenose*, 193; races (1938), 195–212. *See also Bluenose*

Walters, John, 166

Washington, DC, 190

Welch, Tom, 22–23

Welsh, Marty (captain), 56–64, 75–77, 78–86, 124–26, 160

We're Here (fictional boat), 193

West Indies Trading Company, 216

Westward, 192

Whalen, Maurice (captain, *Harry L. Belden*), 41–42

Wharton, Lewis (captain, *Columbia*), 158

Whynacht, Captain (*Margaret K. Smith*), 97–100

Yankee, 94–96, 99–100, 124, 166

Yarmouth, NS, *12*, 26

Zinck, Ammon, 116

Zwicker, A.H., 138